CHALLENGES FOR
RUSSIAN ECONOMIC
REFORM

Russian and CIS Programme |  THE ROYAL INSTITUTE OF INTERNATIONAL AFFAIRS

Alan Smith, *editor*

CHALLENGES FOR RUSSIAN ECONOMIC REFORM

Published by The Brookings Institution, *Washington, D.C.*
for The Royal Institute of International Affairs, *London*

Published by
THE BROOKINGS INSTITUTION
1775 Massachusetts Ave., N.W., Washington, D.C.

for the

ROYAL INSTITUTE OF INTERNATIONAL AFFAIRS
Chatham House, 10 St. James's Square, London SW1Y 4LE
(Charity Registration No. 208 223)

Library of Congress Cataloging-in-Publication Data

Challenges for Russian Economic Reform / Alan Smith [editor].
p.   cm.
Revised versions of four papers published originally in the Post-Soviet business forum
Includes bibliographical references and index.
ISBN 0-8157-8025-7 (pbk.: alk. paper)
1. Russia (Federation)—Economic Conditions—1991– 2. Russia (Federation)—
Economic policy—1991–   3. Privatization—Former Soviet republics.
4. Former Soviet republics—Commerce.   I. Smith, Alan, 1944–
II. Brookings Institution.   III. Series.
HC340. 12.C42   1995b
330.947'086--dc20   95-20354
                                                                            CIP

9 8 7 6 5 4 3 2 1

The paper used in this publication meets the minimum requirements of the American National Standard for Information Sciences—Permanence of Paper for Printed Library Materials, ANSI Z39.48-1984.

Typeset in Times Roman

Composition by Blue Heron, Inc.
Lawrence, Kansas

Printed by R. R. Donnelley & Sons, Co.
Harrisonburg, Virginia

Contents

Introduction

THE ECONOMIC CHALLENGE FACING RUSSIA

Alan Smith

Introduction: Three-quarters empty or one-quarter full?

The evaluation of the progress made towards the introduction of a market economy in Russia's inner empire and of the prospects for economic recovery depends to a considerable degree on the initial perspectives and expectations of the individual observer. Few analysts of the Soviet economy expected that the transition from a highly regulated and centralized planned economy, with an exceptionally high concentration of resources in the military sector, to a series of separate independent capitalist market economies would be achieved without great hardship and difficulty. Students of Russian history also pointed to the historical precedents of centrally imposed attempts to modernize Tsarist and Soviet society from Ivan the Terrible through to Gorbachev which demanded sacrifices from the population but which failed to achieve a social and economic structure that would be capable of adapting to changing circumstances. However, many observers underestimated the severity of the problems that overwhelmed the Soviet economy in 1990-91 and the difficulties that this would create for the former Soviet republics in creating economies that were more responsive to the demands of domestic consumers and world markets, while simultaneously attempting to reverse one of the largest-ever

1

declines in output in a peacetime economy, to eliminate the threat of hyperinflation and to introduce a more democratic system of government.

Three years into the transition, none of the former Soviet republics (with
the exception of the Baltic states) are showing the signs of macroeconomic
stability (measured in terms of substantially reduced levels of inflation, the
bottoming out of the fall in output and a significant increase in exports to the
West) that had been achieved in central and eastern Europe at a roughly similar stage of the transition process (the beginning of 1993). Even there, two of
the economies that made successful progress towards the introduction of a
market economy (Poland and Hungary) subsequently elected governments
dominated by former communists, as popular disaffection at the lack of material progress was reflected in the ballot-box.

Those who take a pessimistic view of Russia's economic prospects can find
ample support for their arguments from official statistics relating to Russian
macroeconomic performance in the first three years since the formal dissolution of the Soviet Union in December 1991. These indicate that industrial output and GDP have fallen by more than 10 per cent in each year since 1991,
that inflation rates remained at dangerously high levels at the end of 1994 and
the beginning of 1995, that the exchange rate of the ruble had not been stabilized by the end of 1994 and that there has been decline in real incomes combined with a substantial increase in poverty. The fall in output has not been accompanied by an equivalent fall in employment; this indicates a deterioration
in labor productivity and the possibility of a deeper social crisis when hidden
unemployment will be translated into open unemployment.

This need not mean that the transition to a market economy in Russia
should be dismissed as a failure. Three years is too short a time to be able to
pass judgment on the success or failure of the transition process that may take
a generation to accomplish.

Strategies for the transition to a market economy in Russia

THE COMMUNIST LEGACY AND THE FAILURE OF REFORMS UNDER
GORBACHEV.   Many of the problems confronting the Soviet economy when
Gorbachev came to power in 1985 were economic-systemic in nature and
were being experienced in the other centrally planned economies in Eastern
Europe. These problems included:

— an overemphasis on the development of heavy industry and defense
    sectors at the expense of consumer production;

— an undeveloped and overregulated private sector which lacked access to sources of capital;

— a highly distorted structure of retail and wholesale prices which did not reflect scarcity or utility;

— the widespread phenomenon of shortage and the development of legal and illegal secondary markets;

— a passive monetary system in which money balances could not be exchanged into goods, service or factors of production on demand;

— a high degree of product monopoly with a single enterprise often responsible for the production of a specific good, sometimes located in single-company towns;

— the prevalence of soft budget constraints, whereby enterprises knew that losses would be subsidized by the state budget or by soft credits and they faced no threat of bankruptcy, resulting in little, or no, incentive to satisfy market demand or to use resources efficiently;

— the isolation of domestic enterprises from world market prices and international competition, as a result of which the quality and performance standards of manufactured and processed products fell below those required in world markets;

— most critically, the system of bonuses which rewarded managers and the workforce for fulfilling (or overfulfilling) centrally determined output targets not only deprived them of an incentive to innovate and introduce new products, but actually provided them with a perverse incentive to produce outmoded goods; the absence of competition from existing producers was reinforced by the absence of the *threat* of competition, which was reflected in the inability of new enterprises to enter the market.

By the end of 1991 these problems had become more severe in the Soviet Union than they had been in the majority of East European economies when the communist economic system collapsed. Furthermore they had been aggravated by Gorbachev's economic policies. The decentralization of wage controls, combined with the initial reluctance to free prices, contributed to the growth of involuntary savings (inflationary overhang) and the appearance of severe shortages of even basic goods in major cities. The reluctance of the Soviet government to curtail pressures for increased public spending, or to raise the taxation required to finance them, led to growing budget deficits, which were exacerbated by the decentralization of budgetary powers to republics which refused to supply revenues to the central budget. Budget deficits were financed by the printing press, contributing to an explosion of the money sup-

ply. Repressed and open inflationary pressures contributed to growing external
debt as shortages in the domestic market resulted in domestic supply bottlenecks. This, in turn, contributed to the collapse of output which was first officially recorded at the end of 1990 and which accelerated in 1991.

One of the principal weaknesses of Gorbachev's economic reforms was
that although he was aware that the performance of the Soviet economy was
unsatisfactory, he appeared to have no clear conception of how far-reaching
economic reforms would have to be at the outset of the process which he
called 'perestroika'. Indeed, he appears to have started with the idea that accelerated investment in technical modernization, and an increased emphasis
on discipline in the workplace, would be sufficient to bring a lasting improvement in economic performance. As this view was shown to be wrong, Gorbachev was forced to adopt progressively more radical reform proposals
which eventually brought him into conflict with conservative elements in the
Communist Party and the Soviet government, and he encountered increasing
resistance from the military and enterprise directors. Although central planners had lost the ability to control production and distribution by the spring of
1990, the institutional and legal foundations of a market economy had not
been established. The invisible hand of the market had not replaced the de-
funct, visible fist of central planning. Gorbachev's attempts to win back the
support of conservatives and his reluctance to embrace wholeheartedly the
transition to a market economy now brought him into fresh conflict with the
Russian president and the Russian government, who supported a faster and
more radical transition to a market economy. His loss of authority after the
failed coup of August 1991 culminated in the dissolution of the Soviet Union
the following December. Gorbachev's attempts to reform the Soviet economy
failed because they lacked consistency and credibility, because they did not
replace plan discipline by market and financial discipline, and because they
encountered major opposition not just from conservative elements in the party
and the new parliament, but from the population as a whole.

Strategies for the transition in post-communist economies: Shock therapy and gradualism

The collapse of communism in Eastern Europe at the end of 1989 provided
the Russian reformers with one significant advantage: they could benefit from
the experience of the former centrally planned economies in Eastern Europe
which had encountered similar economic problems and which had already

embarked on the transition to a market economy. The most influential strategy was that of Poland. This strategy was strongly influenced by IMF and World Bank analyses of successful and unsuccessful stabilization and liberalization programs which had been adopted in Latin America in the 1980s. The ideal strategy incorporated a number of interdependent measures including macro-economic stabilization; the liberalization of retail and wholesale prices; the removal of constraints to the development of a grassroots private sector and the privatization of state-owned enterprises; the elimination of subsidies and the imposition of hard budget constraints; and the creation of an export-oriented economy that is open to foreign trade and investment. The creation of a social welfare system, targeted on the individual to compensate for the removal of job security, and the abolition of subsidies on basic staple goods which were the major method of alleviating poverty under communism, were also seen as essential parts of the program by many economists with a special interest in communist affairs.

While many economists agree that macroeconomic stabilization, price liberalization, trade liberalization and the development of a thriving private sector are necessary features for the transition to a functioning market economy, disagreements remain over a number of basic issues. The most critical questions concern the optimal sequencing of the components of the transition and the speed of their implementation. More specific debates center on the severity with which deflationary fiscal and monetary policies should be pursued in the early stages of reform before a social welfare net has been created; the need for tariffs to protect newly emerging and restructuring industries from foreign competition so that they can establish a foothold in the domestic market before they can compete in international markets; the degree of reliance that should be placed on privatization as a means to achieve the essential restructuring of industry and whether privatization should be achieved by 'give-away' schemes or by seeking out genuine purchasers; the need for specific policies to break up and regulate monopolies; and the limits to be placed on the role of the state in the process of transition.

The two competing schools of thought are known in popular terminology as 'shock therapists' and 'gradualists'. The majority of those who could be described as shock therapists accept that structural changes will take time both to implement and to bear fruit. However they argue that it is necessary to move with the greatest possible speed to achieve the goal of a consistently functioning market economy in the shortest possible time. This need not preclude the possibility that specific aspects of the transition program will have to be modified in the light of prevailing events, as and when they occur, as long as the emphasis is on progression rather than retrogression in order for the transition to be pursued with credibility and consistency.

Gradualists, on the other hand, support an evolutionary approach which attempts to fine-tune and sequence the components of the transition in accordance with the specific features and institutional structure of the individual countries. They hope that this will reduce the loss of output and employment that the transition inevitably entails. Shock therapists counter that the future cannot be predicted with any certainty and that deliberate diversions from the long-term equilibrium risks creating new problems whose solution may incur even greater social costs. For example, attempts to alleviate unemployment by encouraging early retirement with generous pension provisions in Romania have placed an enormous burden on the state budget. This has limited the financial resources available for other social programs and for employment-creating investment in essential infrastructure.

A strong economic argument in favor of a rapid transition is that this will minimize the time during which remnants of the planned economy will be required to coexist with elements of a market economy within a single economic system. A rapid transition reduces the possibility of economic distortions arising from contradictory or inaccurate price signals (e.g. the subsidization of energy) that could result in a wasteful choice of inputs and in sub-optimal investment decisions which will have lasting consequences. Shock therapists argue that a rapid transition to market clearing prices will weaken the power of the *nomenklatura*; they will no longer be able to exercise discriminatory allocation of resources, licenses and permits, which will be allocated instead by price criteria. They claim that this will also reduce organized economic crime, which thrives on the economic shortages resulting from quantitative restrictions and price controls.

Shock therapists with neoclassical views tend to be optimistic about the ability of unregulated, free markets to generate economic recovery, while those who draw their economic ideas from the 'Austrian School' argue that private entrepreneurs will react more quickly and efficiently to the changing demands of a consumer-driven economy than former Soviet managers, who have become accustomed to meeting a central plan. Consequently they advocate the rapid development of a private sector. This will require immediate measures to remove existing barriers to the development of a small-scale private sector from below, and the rapid privatization of state-owned enterprises.

There are some technical economic arguments that support a more gradual transition which places more emphasis on a gradual reduction of inflationary pressures, combined with attempts to preserve output and employment in the short run. Firstly,

— An over-rapid attempt to bring about macroeconomic stabilization will result in large falls in output, employment and income in the short run which in turn will make it harder to reduce budget deficits as tax revenues fall and welfare expenditures are increased.

— A restrictive monetary policy will drive up real interest rates and choke off essential private-sector investment.

— Excessive reliance on market-led investment, combined with the need to reduce budget deficits, will prevent investment in infrastructure which is also essential for economic recovery.

— Short-run reductions in employment and incomes and the uncertainty caused by structural adjustment will result in a fall in demand for consumer goods and affect the viability of industries with long-run potential, while over-rapid exposure to foreign competition will also kill off firms with long-term potential that are incapable of competing in the short term.

— Over-rapid privatization may result in 'insider privatization', which is unjustified on grounds of both equity and efficiency.

Russia and the Polish experience

A strategy for the transition to a market economy modeled on the transition strategy adopted in Poland in January 1990 was proposed by the Russian government under the direction of Yegor Gaidar in October 1991 (before the dissolution of the Soviet Union). Several of the foreign advisers who came to assist the Russian government in 1992 had worked on the Polish program (Åslund, 1994, p. 157). The three determining features of the Polish transition were rapid price liberalization and the abolition of retail subsidies, the pursuit of a strict deflationary policy which incorporated a balanced budget in 1990, and the introduction of current-account convertibility for domestic residents at a fixed but highly depreciated exchange rate (in relation to purchasing power parity) at the very outset of the reforms. The latter allowed commercial undertakings, enterprises and citizens to exchange zlotys into foreign currency in order to conduct commercial transactions that fell within the current account of the balance of payments. This, combined with trade liberalization (which devolved the right to trade to all enterprises in the state and private sectors) and the removal of quantitative restrictions on trade, exposed domestic enterprises to foreign competition and broke up their monopoly power. This also facilitated the introduction of world market prices into the domestic economy as the domestic price of imported goods and those goods that could be exported (tradables) would be expected to approximate world market levels at the prevailing exchange rate. Consequently the choice of a highly depreciated exchange rate offered a degree of price protection to domestic producers and a considerable stimulus for producers to seek external markets. On the negative side, a relatively depreciated rate contributed to greater inflationary pressures and a greater fall in domestic incomes than a higher rate and drove up the domestic price of internationally traded goods (including food and energy); this led to genuine poverty, as welfare payments had to be kept below wage rates which were already close to subsistence levels. Finally, the choice of a fixed rate forced the financial authorities to adopt strict fiscal and monetary policies to prevent over-emission of the domestic currency which could lead to a run on foreign-exchange reserves.

During the first year of the reform, Poland achieved a substantial reduction in the monthly rate of inflation and a substantial increase in exports to the OECD region (32 per cent by volume), which resulted in a surplus in the convertible currency balance of payments. Nevertheless domestic inflation undermined the competitiveness resulting from the initial depreciation of the exchange rate, leading to balance-of-payments pressures in 1991. The zloty was devalued in May 1991 and was subsequently allowed to depreciate by 1.8 per cent a month to accommodate inflationary pressures. GDP fell by 11.6 per cent in 1990 and by 7 per cent in 1991 before an upturn in the second half of 1992 when unemployment had reached 15 per cent. Initial proposals to introduce the rapid privatization of state-owned industry by means of a voucher scheme were abandoned in favor of attempts to expand the private sector from below and to restructure industry prior to privatization. This has contributed to a relatively slow pace of privatization of state-owned enterprises *per se*, although the productive assets of state-owned firms have been sold off to the private sector. There is also the possibility that the return of a communist-dominated government will slow or reverse proposals for privatization. In summary, the Polish strategy involved a rapid transition in the areas of macroeconomic stabilization, price liberalization, trade liberalization and the development of a private sector from below, combined with a relatively slower pace of privatization of state-owned industry.

Anders Åslund, who has acted as a senior adviser to both the Polish and the Russian governments, argues (1994 *passim*) that despite a serious attempt by the Gaidar government to implement a strategy modeled on that of Poland during the first eight months of 1992, the results of the transition in Russia have been virtually the opposite of those in Poland. Like Poland, Russia has experienced substantial falls in industrial output and GDP since the collapse of central planning. Unlike Poland, however, there has been no sign to date of a resumption of stable growth under conditions of macroeconomic equilibrium. Attempts to control the money supply in the first half of 1992 were undermined by massive credit expansion by the Central Bank of Russia (CBR) in the third quarter, primarily intended to ease the build-up of inter-enterprise debt. Subsequent attempts to implement tighter macroeconomic policies in 1993 and 1994 have also been undermined by credit expansion and difficulties in reducing the budget deficit.

Although the majority of retail and wholesale prices were liberalized on January 2, 1992, administrative controls were retained over a number of critical consumer goods and industrial inputs (Dabrowski 1994, p. 26). Furthermore, the deregulation of prices was devolved to regional authorities, which frequently imposed additional restrictions and controls. Consequently price liberalization has been partial, particularly with respect to energy prices, creating widespread opportunities for arbitraging and corruption. Although direct price regulation applied only to a small number of goods by the end of 1994, many industries remained subject to profit controls. There are also signs that ministries responsible for energy and heavy industry are colluding in setting prices. The liberalization of foreign trade has also been inconsistent and partial with the retention of import and export quotas, while domestic inflation has prevented the stabilization of the nominal value of the ruble exchange rate or the implementation of a formal peg for the ruble. At the same time, the failure to establish positive real interest rates on ruble balances has provided no incentive to repatriate hard currency earnings from export activities and other operations in hard currencies. Consequently balance-of-trade surpluses have resulted in capital flight.

Even Russia's policy towards privatization has been the opposite of that of Poland, with far faster privatization of state-owned enterprises; this has been achieved through implementing a mass privatization scheme prior to restructuring which has emphasized management and employee buy-outs (see Michael Kaser's contribution to this volume).

The Russian economy at the beginning of 1995 [1]

THE FALL IN OUTPUT.   Data published by the Russian State Committee for Statistics (Goskomstat) indicate that the fall in Russian GDP and industrial

1. Data in this section are taken from EBRD (1994), OECD and *Russian Economic Trends* (various issues).

output, first recorded in official statistics in the last quarter of 1990, has accelerated since 1991. GDP fell in real terms by 13 per cent in 1991, by 19.4 per cent in 1992, by 12 per cent in 1993 and by 15 per cent in the first three quarters of 1994. As a result GDP in 1994 was only just over half the level recorded in 1990. Similarly industrial output in 1994 was less than half the 1990 level, while industrial output in December 1994 was only 56 per cent of the level officially recorded in December 1991. However, these figures overstate the real fall in production since the collapse of communism as they fail to capture a considerable proportion of the growth of small-scale private sector output, while existing medium- and large-scale enterprises which had an incentive to over-report industrial output under communism (in order to achieve bonuses linked to the fulfillment of output targets) now have an incentive to under-report production to evade taxes. Similarly, the fall in production overstates the impact on economic welfare as it partly reflects the decline in output of intermediate goods and materials resulting from the elimination of inefficient production techniques. Another part of the reduction in output reflects falls in investment and production of heavy industrial goods that provided little or no utility to the Soviet consumer. On the positive side there are indications that the decline in industrial output started to bottom out in the second half of 1994, with a small growth in industrial output in the last quarter of 1994, even after allowing for seasonal factors.

INFLATION AND THE EXCHANGE RATE. The failure to bring inflation under control remains the biggest threat to stable development. Consumer prices in December 1994 were 750 times their level in December 1991 and just under 2,000 times their level in December 1990. The year-on-year rate of consumer price inflation was reduced to 203 per cent in 1994 compared with 843 per cent in 1993 and 2,322 per cent in 1992. However the apparent success reflected in the consistent annual reduction in the growth of the retail price index conceals a build-up of inflationary pressures in the third quarter of 1994 which resulted in consumer price inflation reaching a monthly rate of 16.4 per cent in December 1994 (this is equivalent to an annual rate of over 500 per cent). This followed a steady fall in the monthly rate of consumer price inflation from August 1993 to August 1994 when the CBR managed to pursue a more restrictive monetary policy, including the imposition of positive real interest rates. The re-emergence of inflationary pressures largely reflected the relaxation of monetary and credit policy earlier in the year and the granting of credits to agriculture and to enterprises in financial difficulties (particularly in the defense sector) in August 1994 in response to parliamentary pressure. In many cases credits were used to pay off the accumulated backlog of unpaid wages.

The exchange rate of the ruble has not fallen as fast as the growth of domestic consumer prices, resulting in a tenfold real appreciation of the ruble between January 1992 (when the nominal rate was established at 213 rubles to the US dollar) and the end of December 1994, when it had fallen to 3,550 rubles to the US dollar. The real appreciation of the ruble has contributed to an increase in the average wage expressed in US dollars, from approximately $7 a month in January 1992 to $98 a month in December 1994, and this has reduced the competitiveness of Russian manufacturing industry. Critically, the ruble continues to show considerable fragility: on October 11, 1994, it fell by 27.4 per cent in a single day, following a persistent real depreciation during the preceding weeks. This fragility reflects a lack of confidence by the general public and investors in the ability of the CBR to restrict the money supply in the face of political pressures and to maintain positive real interest rates over the long term. This has contributed to a reluctance to increase ruble savings, and to substantial capital flight even when interest rates have been positive and the rate of return on ruble holdings has exceeded that on dollar holdings.

REAL INCOMES AND THE STANDARD OF LIVING. As a result of the partial liberalization of prices and wages in January 1992, real incomes fell by 55 per cent in the first quarter of 1992 and real wages fell by roughly 42 per cent (compared with the first quarter of 1991). However, it must be remembered that the retail sector in the Soviet economy was unable to meet demand at the prevailing wage and income levels in 1991; this led to a widening gap between incomes and expenditure, resulting in repressed inflation and growing shortages. Consequently Soviet wages and prices were not in equilibrium and cannot be regarded as an accurate basis for comparison. Despite the consistent fall in GDP and industrial output since January 1992, nominal incomes and wages have grown faster than the rate of inflation; the result has been an increase in real wages and incomes in the aggregate. In November 1994 (December wages and incomes have traditionally been inflated by additional annual payments and are not valid for purposes of comparison) real incomes (aggregate incomes deflated by the consumer price index) were estimated to be 60 per cent higher than in January 1992. The average real wage in November 1994, however, was only 4 per cent higher than in January 1992 and was 6.4 per cent below the level of November 1993 and 14 per cent below the level of November 1992. This largely reflects the fact that incomes in the emerging private sector have grown far faster than wages in state-owned (or former state-owned) enterprises. Similarly workers who have remained in the traditional budget-financed sectors, including health and education, where the average wage is now less than three-quarters of the national average, have experienced a fall in real incomes.

The figures for the growth of total incomes of the population as a whole conceal major differences between the growth (or decline) of incomes for different individuals at different periods of time, between different sectors of the population, and in different regions. Lags in the adjustment of welfare payments to inflation and uncertainty about what proportion of the population (if any) is actually dependent on specified minimum wages and pensions as the sole or main means of support make the interpretation of quoted wage and pension rates a hazardous guide to changes in income distribution and the growth of poverty over time. Furthermore the interpretation of wage rates is complicated, if not invalidated, by the non-payment of wages for significant periods, while many employees do not actually receive the specified minimum wage. However there is considerable evidence to support the popular view that there has been a major growth in income inequality since the collapse of communism and that a far larger proportion of the population lives in poverty than was the case under communism.

Widening gaps in income distribution in part reflect the fact that the rich have got much richer, leading to the phenomenon of conspicuous consumption—including the purchase of assets overseas by those who benefit from capital flight (which is not reflected in income statistics)—and that the very poor have become poorer in relation to average incomes, which in turn have not kept up with the growth of incomes as a whole (although there is some indication of a slight reversal of the latter trend in 1994). Goskomstat data (*Russian Economic Trends* 1994/3) indicate that while the income (from all sources) of the lower decile income recipient (the person whose income was at the top of the lowest 10 per cent of income earners) was 32 per cent of that of the upper decile (the person whose income was at the bottom of the top 10 per cent of income recipients) in January 1992, this proportion had dropped to 18 per cent by the third quarter of 1994. While the income of the upper decile income earner was 74 per cent higher than that of the median income earner in January 1992, it had grown to 149 per cent greater in the third quarter of 1994. However, the lower decile income recipient got only 43 per cent of the median income in the third quarter of 1994, compared with 56 per cent in January 1992. Furthermore wage arrears, which affect the lowest paid most acutely, reached 4.2 trillion rubles in September 1994, equivalent to 45 per cent of monthly wages.

A detailed analysis of income distribution in Russia has been conducted by

Illarionov et al. (1994, pp. 127-56). They defined poverty as the minimum income required to purchase sufficient food to maintain body weight, plus an element for non-food expenditure. They concluded that family size was a major factor contributing to income inequality and that the incidence of poverty was greatest in families with three or more children, while half the children in Russia lived in poverty. Pensioners were no more likely to live in poverty than the rest of the population. More recent data (*Russian Economic Trends* 1994, no. 3, p. 53) indicate that the incidence of poverty (defined in terms of a minimum subsistence income) has fallen from 34 per cent of the population in the third quarter of 1993 to 20 per cent in the third quarter of 1994. This was largely the result of the increase in child benefits from 3 to 10 per cent of the average wage in January 1994.

The widening of income differentials and the growth of poverty highlight the difficulties inherent in the transition to a market economy in Russia. Under communism workers in state enterprises and work collectives received stable incomes, guaranteed employment and a range of welfare benefits and other facilities (such as housing and health facilities) administered by the workplace, which were extended to their dependents. Prices of basic staple goods (including housing) were also highly subsidized, and this helped compensate those with low incomes and large families. This was seen by many as a form of unwritten social contract between the workers and the Party. Consequently poverty largely resulted from the inability to secure employment for personal reasons (e.g. disability). In theory at least the worst incidence of poverty could be alleviated by welfare payments.

The question of low incomes and poverty has become far more complex in the transition to a market economy. The widening of wage differentials means that employment alone is insufficient to guarantee freedom from poverty, and workers in employment on low wages may not earn the minimum for basic subsistence. Although this is a global phenomenon and is not confined to Russia, it is a new experience for Russian workers and one which can be exploited by populist politicians. The problem is exacerbated in the Russian case (in comparison with Central-Eastern Europe) by the fact that low relative wages are occurring at lower absolute levels than in Central-Eastern Europe. The average dollar wage in Russia at the end of 1994 was $98, compared with $200 in Poland and $250 in the Czech Republic. As price and trade liberalization drive domestic prices of basic staple goods up to world market prices at the prevailing exchange rate, those on below-average incomes fall into real poverty more quickly than their counterparts in Central-Eastern Europe. Poverty arising from low wages also complicates the problem of the level at which welfare payments can be provided. If welfare payments (including pensions for early retirement, unemployment benefits and so on) are pitched too high in relation to minimum and average wages, workers will be provided with an incentive to leave the labor force. This will also stimulate pressures for budgetary expenditure while tax revenues will decline.

THE ECONOMIC IMPLICATIONS OF THE WAR IN CHECHENIA. The fundamental problems confronting the Russian economy in early 1995 will be further aggravated by the economic and political costs of the war in Chechenia. The direct economic costs include those involved in maintaining the war (including arms, wages and costs of treatment of the injured), which will be followed by the costs of reconstruction in Chechenia itself after a settlement of the conflict. These costs will have to be met from an already constrained state budget (and had not been adequately accounted for in the original budget expenditure forecast for 1995, which was approved by the parliament and submitted to the IMF) and will severely complicate the problem of restricting the fiscal deficit and controlling inflation. There are also indirect economic costs: the pressures imposed on the budget may cause the IMF and government bodies to withdraw external finance intended to help stabilize the economy. The political repercussions of the war may be far more serious. The internal effects include a possible strengthening of the lobby for military expenditure, which will complicate budgetary stability in the long term, and the strong possibility that international reaction to the war will deter foreign investment and will make Western governments far more reluctant to provide financial assistance. At its very worst, a prolonged and bloody military campaign conducted against an essentially civilian population, which could spill over into terrorist actions in other Russian cities, might lead to a significant withdrawal of Western support and even the possibility of sanctions.

Why has the economic transition been so difficult in Russia?

THE NEED FOR MICROSTABILIZATION. Despite the monetarist leanings of the majority of the advisers to the Yeltsin government, the failure to bring about a lasting macroeconomic stabilization has been one of the most critical failings of the Russian transition program. Macroeconomic stabilization is probably the most essential component of a successful transition, but one which poses acute social and political problems. A market economy simply cannot function effectively without at least the minimum degree of price stability that allows citizens and enterprises to make sensible judgments about relative prices through time. Changes in relative prices tend to be obscured by rapid changes in the absolute price level. Furthermore price criteria themselves become meaningless if enterprises are not exposed to hard budget constraints and know that any losses they incur will be written off by the central authorities.

However, macroeconomic stabilization in the former Soviet republics required the immediate implementation of policies to eliminate inflationary overhang which had accumulated in the form of involuntary savings during the communist era. This was largely achieved by inflation (which reduced the real value of money balances) followed by the implementation of tight fiscal and monetary policies to prevent the emergence of renewed inflationary pressures. Under Russian conditions, where capital markets were undeveloped and the government did not have the financial instruments available to borrow significant amounts from the public to finance budget deficits, strict monetary control required that the budget deficit had to be reduced to a level that could be financed from foreign borrowing. Budget revenues were adversely affected by the transition to a tax system based on predetermined rules of assessment in place of the traditional *ex post* confiscatory systems of taxation, whereby enterprises were forced to relinquish profits to the state budget. This required a drastic reduction in government expenditure which considerably limited the scope for welfare payments at a time of increasing hardship. Tight fiscal and monetary policies also had a deflationary impact on the economy which aggravated the loss of output to be expected from essential structural changes.

Why did these problems prove so much harder to solve in Russia than in Poland or Czechoslovakia? Åslund (1994, p. 161) proposes three principal causes. The first was the failure to make a clean political break from the past. The most damaging failure here was the inability to bring the Central Bank under the control of the reformers, which effectively meant that monetary policy was determined by an unreconstructed parliament that had been elected in the communist period. The second cause was the continued burden of credits to the other former Soviet republics; and, finally, these were difficulties in balancing the budget. These and other difficulties are analyzed in greater detail by the contributors to this volume.

THE FAILURE TO MAKE A CLEAN POLITICAL BREAK FROM THE PAST. Many Sovietologists anticipated that the transition to a market economy in Russia and the other newly independent states of the former Soviet Union would encounter strong political resistance from the former Soviet elite (the *nomenklatura*), who stood to lose the privileges they had derived from their roles as administrators of the centrally planned economy and as allocators of goods in shortage; there would be resistance, too, from industrial and agricultural workers, who stood to lose their principal means of support. Serious opposition was also anticipated to the introduction of a capitalist market economy, not just from party ideologists (whose authority had waned considerably in the late 1980s) but from those who retained a genuine belief in the principles of full employment and an equitable distribution of incomes. Resistance to change was also anticipated from workers and employees who had become accustomed to job security, stable prices (which incorporated substantial subsidies for basic staple goods) and, at least until the late 1970s, a gradual increase in real incomes. A further critical source of opposition to the transition to a consumer-dominated economy with a reduced emphasis on military expenditure has come from Russian nationalists who are unable to come to terms with the passing of the Russian empire and the diminution of Russian power in world affairs, as well as from Slavophiles who opposed the introduction of Western ideas and market concepts, and who favored a path of economic development which excluded foreign investment. The latter sources of opposition were not present in Poland, where the transition to a market economy was combined with the achievement of greater national independence. Taken together, then, these disparate sources posed a far stronger opposition to genuine marketization than in Central Europe.

THE REGIONAL DIMENSION. In his contribution to this volume Philip Hanson demonstrates how the sheer size of Russia and the relative strength of regional interests compared with a relatively weak center have created a powerful resistance to the implementation of reform measures. Regional opposition to reform has been strengthened by the absence of a nationwide consensus on the nature and desirability of macroeconomic stabilization and liberalization. First, regional leaderships were largely composed of the old *nomenklatura* and of representatives of the old communist system of industrial management in particular. Secondly, the regional opposition to reform has been institutionalized at the central level by the large number of regional administrators elected to the upper chamber of the Russian parliament in December 1993. In the absence of properly functioning political parties capable of commanding obedience from parliamentary representatives to central party policies when these may conflict with the short-run interests of constituents, regional representatives are motivated by specific regional interests. This gives rise to the phenomenon that Hanson calls 'NIMBY stabilization'. Macroeconomic stabilization and a sound currency are collective goods from which all members of the public benefit in the long term, but to which no single individual or region has an incentive to contribute. Furthermore, there is a critical problem of public perceptions: while there is some analytical and empirical support for the idea that the poorest sections of the community are less able to protect themselves from the impact of inflation and will benefit in the long-term from macroeconomic stabilization, they are also the most vulnerable to attempts to bring about macroeconomic stabilization which include lower welfare spending. Consequently they are more likely to support levels of welfare spending that cannot be met from taxation. Studies of popular attitudes to the transition in Poland also show that the greatest opposition came from workers and their families who were extremely worried by the fear of unemployment in a society with a poorly developed welfare system in which prices of basic staples are growing faster than incomes (Bresser Pereira et al. 1993). Consequently local administrators and representatives in the parliament have a greater incentive than usual to oppose policies that create the threat of unemployment, to support controls on prices for basic staple goods and to vote for budget deficits and support loose credit and monetary policies at the national level, if these help to sustain employment in the short term and to support increased expenditure on welfare payments as well as lobbying for increased assistance for their specific region.

MONOPOLY AND COMPETITION POLICY. David Dyker and Michael Barrow also argue that local politicians who come from the former Soviet *nomenklatura* have played a critical role in resisting freedom of entry into markets in order to protect enterprises in their regions from competition. The principal sources of monopoly in Russian industry remain inherently different from those in most market economies. Although there were fewer dominant corporations and conglomerates in Soviet industry, there was a far higher degree of product monopoly (i.e. a single enterprise producing a significant proportion of Soviet output of a specific product). This was reinforced by the absence of freedom of entry into the domestic market and by protection from foreign competition (enshrined in the state monopoly of foreign trade), which meant that Soviet enterprises did not have to worry about even the threat of potential competition as their markets were not contestable. Significant falls in imports of the majority of manufactured goods mean that, unlike Poland, Russian enterprises have not been exposed to major foreign competition and to the need to raise product quality for manufactured goods to world market standards. Again, the failure to macrostabilize and to liberalize foreign-exchange regulations is important in this respect. Importers (and Western exporters) have little incentive to compete in the domestic market on a large scale, or to invest in production facilities for the domestic market while they remain uncertain about the value of ruble earnings and their ability to repatriate profits.

Furthermore Dyker and Barrow indicate that, even after the collapse of communism, enterprise directors remained reluctant to break into new markets, or to turn to nontraditional sources of supply. This reflected a noncompetitive 'mindset' inherited from communism, which could also be interpreted as a form of networking, in which the former *nomenklatura* preserved their old connections. This is particularly disturbing as privatization in Russia has predominantly taken the form of *nomenklatura* buyouts which may impede rather than improve competitiveness and the growth of efficiency.

PRIVATIZATION. Michael Kaser's contribution to this book takes the issue of privatization in Russia and then other former Soviet republics even further. Only three former Soviet republics, Russia, Kyrgyzstan and Uzbekistan, had privatized more than half of state-owned enterprises by the autumn of 1994, while a further five had privatized approximately one-quarter of state-owned enterprises. Privatization in the Commonwealth of Independent States has differed from that in Eastern Europe and the Baltic republics (all of which were independent states with widespread private ownership in their market economies in the interwar period) in that the issue of compensation to previous owners did not have to be contemplated; this facilitated a more rapid privatization. However, the absence of such a private sector in industry and agriculture in that period has deprived the former Soviet republics of a private-sector ethos and a body of legislation which could be adapted to current circumstances and which could have incorporated the principles of the rule of law.

The Russian government embarked on a strategy of rapid privatization of Russian industry under the direction of Anatoly Chubais. The choice of a strategy of rapid mass privatization by means of a voucher system, which would be implemented before industrial restructuring could take place, was intended to reduce the power of the state to intervene in the day-to-day management of industry, and to create a new class of property owners and entrepreneurs who would provide the social basis for a market economy. In practice 'insider privatization' involving majority manager and employee ownership of the enterprise has proved to be the norm in Russia. This has further increased the power of the regional industrial *nomenklatura* which, as Michael Kaser shows, had been strengthened in the Gorbachev era by the deliberate weakening of the powers of the local party and devolution of power to the regions.

Will this form of privatization lead to a more competitive, profit-oriented and innovative climate that will contribute to gains in efficiency and the production of higher-quality goods demanded in domestic and foreign markets? The problems associated with employee ownership, including the tendency to vote for increased wages and reduced investment, are well-documented. There is some evidence that the predominant reason for enterprises' choosing the manager/worker option was defensive—that is, to prevent rather than to stimulate change. On the positive side, it can be argued that as shares can be traded, worker control will be progressively reduced and that this was the only feasible method of privatization available. Even 'insider privatization' has created vested interests in local industry which will prevent any possibility of a return to state management and control.

THE REPLACEMENT OF DOMESTIC TRADE BY FOREIGN TRADE. Finally, in my own contribution I examine the impact of the break-up of traditional trade links between the former Soviet republics and the faltering attempts to institute new currencies and new monetary relations. The initial decision to preserve a ruble zone provided the governments of the newly independent states with a perverse incentive to pursue loose credit and price policies in order to attract an inflow of resources from other republics. Russia continued to make substantial resource transfers to the non-Russian republics during 1992 as Russian enterprises continued to supply non-Russian enterprises, despite their lack of financial viability. This undermined the initial attempts by the Russian government to introduce tighter monetary and fiscal policies. However, efforts to prevent an outflow of resources from the Russian republic have been undermined by loose domestic credit policies. The break-up of the ruble zone has both required the non-Russian republics to introduce separate currencies and contributed to the collapse of trade links, while Russia has succeeded in diverting the export of oil in particular from the CIS to world markets. The collapse of inter-republican trade has been especially damaging for the non-Russian republics which were highly dependent on both exports to and imports from Russia and which had benefited from significant resource transfers from Russia during the communist period. The low level of integration of the former Soviet republics with the world markets means that (with the exception of the Baltic states and the energy-exporting republics) they have little immediate prospect of replacing their trade links. Consequently methods to overcome the technical problems of payments with other republics and the problem of financing structural trade deficits are an urgent requirement for the non-Russian republics of the CIS. These will be impossible, however, if macroeconomic stability is not restored to the region.

References for the Introduction

Åslund, Anders (1993), *Systemic Change and Stabilization in Russia*, Royal Institute of International Affairs, London.

Åslund, Anders (ed.) (1994), *Economic Transformation in Russia*, Pinter, London.

Bresser Pereira, Luiz Carlos, Maravall, Jose Maria and Przeworski, Adam (1993), *Economic Reforms in New Democracies: A Social-Democratic Approach*, Cambridge University Press, Cambridge.

Dabrowkski, Marek (1994), 'Two Years of Economic Reform in Russia: Main Results', *Most: Economic Policy in Transitional Economies.*

EBRD (1994), *Transition Report*, European Bank for Reconstruction and Development, London.

Illarionov, Andrei, Layard, Richard and Orszag, Peter (1994), *The Conditions of Life*, in Åslund (ed.), 1994.

Koves, Andras (1992), *Central and East European Economies in Transition: The International Dimension*, Westview Press, Boulder, San Francisco and Oxford.

OECD, *Short-Term Economic Indicators: Transition Economies* (various issues), Paris.

Portes, Richard (ed.) 1994, *Economic Transformation in Central Europe: A Progress Report*, Center for Economic Policy Research, London/Office for Official Publications of the European Communities, Luxembourg.

Russian Economic Trends, Government of the Russian Federation and Center for Economic Performance, LSE, Whurr Publishers, London.

Winiecki, Jan (1993), *Post-Soviet-Type Economies in Transition*, Avebury, Aldershot.

Part 1

REGIONS, LOCAL POWER AND ECONOMIC CHANGE IN RUSSIA

Philip Hanson

Much of the current reporting and analysis of Russia's attempt at economic transformation is about national-level politics and nationwide macroeconomic aggregates. This paper is a review of the influence of the economic changes on the regions, and their influence on the process of change.

Is Russia in danger of fragmenting? How wide are the variations in economic conditions across the regions? How much variation is there across regions in the implementation of policies aimed at changing the economic system? How do regional elites influence national policy? All these questions are addressed.

The focus is on the 89 so-called 'federal subjects' of Russia—the main administrative territories. These are the 21 republics (associated, at least in principle, with non-Russian ethnic enclaves), 55 ordinary provinces, two

The author is indebted for comments to David Dyker, John Mitchell, Elizabeth Teague and participants in a Chatham House Study Group meeting in July 1994; also to Michael Bradshaw and Julian Cooper for sharing with him information from their own research in progress, and to the work of Ann Sheehy, Elizabeth Teague, Vera Tolz and Julia Wishnevsky on Russian domestic politics. Michael Bradshaw produced the two maps. This paper draws on work supported by the Economic and Social Research Council (project L309.25.3001).

cities with province status (Moscow and St Petersburg) and the eleven smaller autonomous districts.

The institutional structure of these regions is partly inherited from the Soviet era. The ethnic-enclave approach to delineating administrative territories goes back to Stalin. It is now a source of conflict over regional powers and budgets.

The most fundamental difficulty with the institutional structure in 1992–4, however, has been the lack of clarity about the distribution of powers and responsibilities between regions and center. This has not been resolved in the new constitution adopted in December 1993. Nor has it been helped by the blurred distinctions between the functions of representative and executive bodies at regional level. During the past three years the attempts to govern from above have been extremely patchy, and often ineffective.

Regional elections in March 1990 and again in 1994 have put representatives of the old, Soviet-era *nomenklatura* elite into the majority of elected offices at regional level, with Moscow and St Petersburg the chief exceptions. One result has been a tug-of-war over both political and economic change between a mainly reformist central leadership and a mainly traditionalist local leadership.

This tug-of-war, and its results across regions, are analyzed for each of the main blocks of economic reform measures: liberalization, stabilization, privatization and internationalization.

Initial differences in income levels between regions were very large, and have become larger, though the general shake-out that would clarify the regional pattern of winners and losers due to transformation has yet to come. Regional price controls have been kept in place in many regions; regional elites have resisted spending cuts and exerted inflationary pressures on the budget; privatization has proceeded at very different speeds in different regions. A small number of generally reformist regions are identified and the reasons for their reforms analyzed.

Politically, Russia is not about to fragment. Economic differences across regions are, however, likely to increase. The paper concludes with alternative scenarios for Russian regional development.

CHAPTER ONE

Issues and Institutes

Introduction

Why should anyone interested in economic change in Russia be concerned with particular questions about particular Russian provinces? The creation of a functioning market economy might be expected, in time, to present us with Russian firms and the Russian national government as the chief actors in the economy. The location of particular activities would be important for all the usual reasons of economic geography; but would we expect regional policy-makers to play a large part in economic outcomes? No doubt, especially in what is supposed to be a federal system, they would be of some importance, as they can be in Canadian provinces, German *Länder* or the states of the USA. Still, one would not expect them to loom large in the determination of national economic policies or in setting the rules of the game for firms that operate on their particular territories.

In writing this paper, I have taken as a starting-point the view that the Russian provinces do matter for economic change in Russia—at least for the present and for the near future (say, up to three years), and that they may continue to matter a great deal for longer than that. It is quite true that in a country with a reasonably well-functioning market economy and a constitution like the new Russian constitution, the economic role of provincial governments would be modest. It is precisely the present turmoil of Russian political and economic change that gives the provinces their present position: center-stage. It will be argued that provincial elites are themselves a source of much of Russia's turbulence. On any reckoning, this turbulence, and the center-stage position of regional politics, are not about to disappear overnight.

The role of regional politics in Russian economic change can be considered under various headings. I shall emphasize the following three:

— centrifugal tendencies and the de facto devolution of decision-making;
— the wide regional variation not only in economic circumstances but in provinces' economic policies;
— the influence of regional elites on national policies.

De Facto Devolution

Since the attempt at economic transformation got under way at the beginning of 1992, the Russian central government has in practice been weak in its dealings with the regions, despite its evident efforts to make economic reform a top-down process, and the limited formal powers of regional governments. During 1992, and again from late 1993, President Boris Yeltsin has been able, officially, to appoint and dismiss provincial heads of administration ('governors') in most of the 89 so-called 'subjects of the federation'. The powers of those governors to appoint lower-level officials and to veto decisions of elected regional councils are, on paper, quite strong. The reality, at both levels of administration, is very different.

A semi-official Ministry of Finance review (*MinFin VE* 1994)—anonymous but mostly written by Boris Fedorov—observes that all the 89 provinces had managed to get their budgets rejigged in the course of 1993. In addition, the extent of price decontrol varies very widely by region (see Chapter 4, section 3 below). One corollary of this is that barriers to trade across provincial boundaries have been set up in a number of regions. Talk of secession or, more commonly, of the establishment of greater regional autonomy is still common. In 1994 the Russian central government embarked on the signing of a series of treaties with some of the more assertive provinces, beginning with Tatarstan. In short, the distribution of powers and functions between center and provinces is, like most of the rules of the economic game in Russia, shifting and uncertain and subject to negotiation. There is no stable balance of power between the two. Regional leaders, in their contest for control with the center, keep testing Moscow, and as often as not they get what they want.

Regional Policy Differences

One result of the center's weakness is that individual regions have gone a fair way towards creating distinct economic environments. To some extent, this is to be expected in a country of such size and regional variation. Not only do natural resource endowments vary enormously, from oil-rich Tyumen' to poor north-westerly provinces like Pskov, on the Estonian border, but development and income levels vary enormously: on one assessment real per capita household income varies over the range 1:2.5 across just the 11 major geographical regions (Nemova, 1993, and see Chapters 2 and 3 below). On top of these 'inherited' differences, provincial governments pursue a wide range of economic policies, from the Brezhnevian conservatism of Ul'yanovsk to the strong liberalization and privatization approach of St Petersburg or Nizhnii Novgorod.

The Provinces and Central Government Policy

The central government has found it necessary, variously, to cajole, threaten and succumb to regional leaders over matters that might be taken to be the preserve of national policy-makers. On 6 August 1993, for instance, the program that was intended to keep inflation within targets that had been agreed with the IMF was approved, not by the regular cabinet, but by an expanded cabinet meeting, with representatives of the 89 administrative territories present (*Financial Times* 7.viii.1993: 2).

A fundamental ingredient in the situation is that elected leaderships in almost all the provinces are dominated by representatives of the old *nomenklatura*, and particularly by members of the old management *nomenklatura*. (This point will be discussed more fully in Chapter 3 below.) Of four elite groups surveyed in summer 1993 (members of parliament, military leaders, new entrepreneurs and directors of state enterprises), the last group was by a wide margin the most critical of government financial policy (*Nezavisimaya gazeta* 2.vii.1993: 1).

The overlap between enterprise managers as a pressure group and local governments as a pressure group is therefore considerable. It has been semi-formalized in links between such groups as Yurii Skokov's Federation of Consumer Goods Producers and the New Regional Policy group (headed by an oil industry man) in the Duma (RFE/RL *Daily Report*, henceforth RFE/RL *DR*, 31.i.1994). This linkage was illustrated in summer 1994 by the stand taken by the upper house of parliament, the Federation Council, over defense spending. The Federation Council is dominated by regional administrators and other local officials (Tolz 1994a); in a statement on 7 June 1994, the Federation

Council stressed, not security concerns, but the dependence (they said) of eight million jobs on defense spending (RFE/RL *DR* 8.vi.1994).[1]

In general, the fluid state of play—if that is not too much of an understatement—between the center and the regions means that the latter have both considerable latitude to pursue their own policies and considerable leverage on the policies of the national government.

So much by way of justification for a study of this topic. The remaining chapters of this paper contain a description of the institutions involved in Russian regional government in 1992–4; a review of the pressures, interests and institutional linkages affecting center-provincial relations; an account of the features of provinces' policies on the key issues of economic change; and some conclusions.

The main emphasis is on trying to grasp what is going on between Moscow and the provinces with respect to economic policy. But I have also tried to devise criteria for judging the economic prospects of particular regions. Consequently, some of what follows might be read as an exercise in picking winners amongst the regions of Russia. But picking winners in Russia is an even chancier business than it is in countries with a more settled life-style. Western business people tend to look for winners in over a hundred other countries ahead of Russia. Where they do put money into Russia, they mostly keep their exposure low. The really important question is about the medium-term prospects (two to five years) for the whole of Russia. I think the most interesting element in what is going on in the Russian provinces is the way in which their elites influence the process of economic change in Russia as a whole. Equally interesting are the prospects for change in the composition of those elites themselves. All of these points will be addressed below.

1. The level of defense industry employment is the subject of some controversy. Total Russian military-industry (VPK) employment, including in R&D, 'recently', was put at 4.5 million by the Chair of the Duma Sub-Committee on the VPK, Stepan Sulakshin (*Krasnaya Zvezda* 28.v.94: 3). My Birmingham colleague, Julian Cooper, working from data on numbers of enterprises and average enterprise employment size, arrives at a total for industrial employment only (excluding employees in VPK R&D institutions) of about 6.5 million in the early 1990s. Brenda Horrigan, using Goskomstat employment data for 1985, and extracting from them a residual that was close to, but not identical with, VPK industrial employment, arrived at a 1985 total of 5.4 million for Russia (Horrigan 1992). In the 1994 budget dispute the Federation Council eventually backed down, and military spending was only very slightly increased. One explanation offered for this failure is that the military and military-industry lobbies are not united; regional leaders side with those who want to see military personnel cut further, to accommodate more spending on military hardware procurement (*Segodnya* 7.vii.1994, cited in RFE/RL *DR* 13.vii.1994). Another explanation that has been put forward is that the farm lobby, which did win budgetary concessions on

What Bits of Russia?

This paper is chiefly about the 89 'federal subjects' the first subnational tier of government. They will be referred to variously as territories, provinces or regions, and adjectivally as regional or provincial. They are not the only possible units for an examination of center-periphery relations.

One alternative way of dividing the country up would be to consider the eleven geographical—formerly planning—regions of Russia. The names of these eleven appear in several of the tables in this paper. There is a good deal that is common to the administrative territories within a geographical region that can distinguish them economically from provinces in other geographical regions. However, the political and economic distinctions between administrative territories within a region can also be enormous—for example, between the relatively businesslike and open 'Russian' provinces of Rostov, Krasnodar and Stavropol' in the North Caucasus and their strife-ridden cohabitants of that region that are 'ethnic' republics, including Chechenia and North Ossetia.

Moreover, the 89 territories are political and administrative entities, and the eleven former planning regions are not. The eleven regions are therefore not political actors or domains within which similar policies are likely to be developed. There has been a tendency, in some parts of Russia, for regional economic associations to take shape amongst neighboring provinces. This is a potentially important development, of which more will be said later on. But such associations so far have no formal status.

An analyst of Russian provincial developments could also sharpen the focus of the inquiry, and consider the lower tier of sub-national units: towns and rural districts—and indeed urban districts within towns. These are administratively real enough, but there are two reasons for not focusing on them. One is the unsatisfactory but compelling reason that detailed published information about most of them is lacking. The second, and intellectually more satisfactory, reason is that their administration is subject to appointment from the province level, so that their autonomy, formally at least, is much less than that of the tier above them. Nonetheless, there are certain center-periphery issues *within* Russian provinces, and some attention will be paid to them.

agricultural subsidies, had stronger backing in the Federation Council than either of the military spending lobbies, and was in competition with them.

Why Eighty-Nine Provinces?

The present structure of Russian provinces, insofar as it is established at all, was established in the Federation Treaties of 31 March 1992 (texts and lists of signatories in *Etnopolis* no. 1 [1992]). These were treaties between the Russian state, on the one hand, and three categories of federal subjects, on the other. The three categories were the republics within Russia (known in Soviet times as autonomous republics, to distinguish them from the union republics that made up the USSR); what might be called the standard, or ordinary Russian provinces (*oblasts* and *kraia*, singular *oblast'* and *krai*, in Russian); and the autonomies—eleven smaller units, each located within one of the first two kinds of provinces but having traditionally been accorded a special status as the homelands of various ethnic minorities.

Eighty-six entities signed the original Federation Treaties. Two republics, Chechen-Ingushetia and Tatarstan, refused at that stage to sign. In December 1992 the separation of Chechenia from Ingushetia was accepted by the Russian parliament, bringing the total of republics from 20 to 21. Chechenia asserted its independence from the outset; Tatarstan has consistently held out for a special formal status. It finally achieved this in a treaty signed by the Russian and Tatarstan presidents on 15 February 1994 (*Financial Times* 17.ii.94: 2). The line-up in early 1995 is therefore 21 republics (one of which claims not to be part of Russia at all), 57 standard provinces (55 *oblasts* and *kraia*, plus the cities of Moscow and St Petersburg, which have the status of *oblasts* in their own right and are distinct from Moscow and Leningrad oblasts), and eleven autonomies.

The formal federal arrangements perpetuate those created by Stalin. By 'arrangements' is meant, not just the list of components of the Russian Federation, but also two damaging characteristics of the rules of the game that accompany that list. The first of these is that some federal subjects are more equal than others. The second is that the division of powers and responsibilities is as clear as an old-fashioned London fog. In each of the treaties, there are lists of powers to be exercised by the federal authorities, powers to be exercised jointly, and powers devolved entirely to the federal subjects. The last of the lists is short. It is also short of the meaty substance that ambitious provincial politicos would like to chew on. Most of the potential for contention is in the list of joint powers, and there is no guidance on how the relevant joint decisions might be made.

In the Soviet Union of the 1960s-1980s such opacity presented no problems. The Party ran things anyway. And however much latitude Brezhnev may have given to his satraps in, say, Uzbekistan or Georgia, there was a clear chain of command up to Moscow. Both political authority and the control of resource allocation clearly resided there. There might be effective lobbying from the union republics and regions (Bahry 1987). The intervention of Party officials in the running of the economy may not have been conspicuously successful (Rutland 1993, for the 1960s–1980s). But there was no doubt about where the lobbyists had to go to lobby, or where the Party's *apparatchiks* were appointed. Once constitutional arrangements began to take on at least some practical importance, the traditional fogginess became a problem.

The component elements of the Federation are as near to being entrenched as any political institution is in Russia. The Federation Treaty was incorporated in the patched-up, Soviet-era Russian constitution. It was then referred to (though not in the final draft incorporated) in the new constitution submitted to a referendum in December 1993. Under that constitution the composition of the upper house of the federal parliament, the Federation Council, directly reflects the administrative structure of the provinces. It is supposed to contain two representatives of each of the 89 territories, regardless of their considerable variation in size. In this and other ways, the administrative territorial structure inherited from the Soviet regime has been reinforced. It is true that province-level elections proceeded patchily and with delays in the first half of 1994, with turnouts quite often below the 25 per cent required to validate the result (early details and analysis in Teague 1994; see also Wishnevsky 1994). The election of the Federation Council in December 1993, however, together with the adoption of the new constitution, consolidates the administrative-territorial divisions enshrined in the 1992 Federation Treaty.

This structure is widely believed to be unsatisfactory. It could have been different. Before the Federation Treaty there was active discussion amongst politicians and policy advisers of other possible components of a Russian federation. One idea favored by many specialists was to make a fresh start with a new and smaller list of territories—perhaps making the eleven former planning regions into administrative territories, but in any case creating territorial units that would be closer in their weight in the whole federation to the *Länder* of Germany. In the judgment of some of the specialists involved in this debate, the Russian leadership balked at the notion of a federation of fewer, larger units primarily because such units seemed likely to acquire more power in their dealings with the center, and perhaps to be better able even to go so far as to secede (interview with the Russian economic geographer Andrei Treyvish, 4.v.94).

Another explanation of the decision to stick with the inherited 80-plus federal subjects may be that the established administrative territories had acquired a new democratic legitimacy. The regions in existence in early 1992 had councils that had been elected in March 1990. Those elections had, it is true, been held under the old order. Nonetheless they appear to have been reasonably open and competitive. Gerrymandering seems to have been limited. A case-study of Yaroslavl' *oblast'* found little evidence of electoral fraud (Helf and Hahn 1992). It later became clear, however, that there were but weak grounds for extrapolating from the Yaroslavl' case-study. There was certainly strong evidence for electoral fraud in the 1993 national elections, and there was also evidence of gerrymandering in the early 1994 local elections (Teague 1994). Thus this explanation can only complement, rather than compete with, the explanation along the lines of a fear of large and powerful federal subjects.

The unsatisfactory features of the federal structure

Even if one leaves aside the fog surrounding powers and responsibilities (a characteristic of a great many Russian arrangements), the 89-strong roster of federal subjects has several drawbacks.

First, it perpetuates the Stalinist ethnoterritorial principle. This is embodied in the distinction between republics and autonomies, on the one hand, and ordinary Russian provinces, on the other. Both republics and autonomies are identified on the basis of an association between the territory in question and a non-Russian ethnic group. This distinction was originally a divide-and-rule device facilitating dictatorial control. It is now a source of trouble in what is meant to be an open society. (On the logic of the old nationalities policies see Zaslavsky 1992.)

To begin with, the Federation Treaties give certain advantages to the republics over the ordinary provinces. Some of these advantages may be more apparent than real, because what looks like a privilege for republics in some parts of the treaties is undermined by wording elsewhere that makes the privilege retractable by the center. For instance, republics, unlike the other provinces, are said to have control over the natural resources on their territories. But elsewhere the treaty says that the use made of those natural resources must be compatible with federal legislation. However, there has been one clear advantage associated with republican status: the republics have not been subject to the imposition from Moscow of centrally appointed heads of administration and presidential representatives (see below). Significantly, when

Yeltsin, on 22 October 1993, ordered the dissolution of elected councils in the regular Russian provinces, he only *recommended* to republics that they dissolve their parliaments (Teague 1993).

The special status of republics facilitates the development of three kinds of conflict. The regular Russian provinces claim they are being discriminated against, blame the net budgetary reallocations on the special status of republics, and demand equal treatment. Members of the old local elite in the republics have a temptation to play the ethnic card in much the way that the old elites in Ukraine, Kazakhstan and elsewhere succeeded in doing, in order to cling to power. And leaders in the lesser autonomies are tempted to seek to raise their status to get similar advantages.

The republics in Russia are in fact an odd bunch. The anomalies that characterize their size distribution and ethnic composition make the tensions arising from their constitutional status seem to have been willfully contrived. They are small, housing on 1 January 1991 23.54 million people, or 15.9 per cent of the Russian population. Their average population size is about half of that of the regular Russian provinces (if the lesser autonomies are counted in with the latter): 1.1 against 2.2 million. As far as their ethnic composition is concerned, nine of the original 20 had a majority Russian population at the 1989 census, and only in four was the titular nationality (in two of these cases, the sum of two titular nationalities) a majority of the population (see Table 1).

This arrangement for the territorial government of the country, considered as an amplifier of possible ethnic rivalries, might best be described as daft. In Russia as a whole, at the 1989 census, ethnic Russians made up 81.5 per cent of the population. This is close to the share of ethnic Lithuanians in the population of Lithuania. That particular historical inheritance is generally believed to have saved Lithuania a great deal of trouble in comparison with Latvia and Estonia. Towns and districts in Lithuania that have a large Polish or Belorussian population were the focus of some ethnic tension in 1990–91; but nothing much seems to have come of this, partly because of the modest role of local government in Lithuania (Gazaryan 1993). In contrast, the structure of these often dubiously 'ethnic' republics in Russia has exaggerated any problem of this sort.

Only about half of the non-Russians in Russia (some 13.6 million people in 1991, about 9 per cent of the population) are located in the 'ethnic' republics, where they constitute only about 58 per cent of the population.[2] In the overwhelming majority of these republics the titular nationality does not itself

2. 'About' because I have taken the 1989 census data on nationality shares of the populations and applied them to republic population data for the beginning of 1991. More up-to-date informa-

form a majority of the population. Yet the whole notion of national identity (in the old Soviet passport sense) has been elevated into an organizing principle for the delineation of administrative territories.

There are, however, several mitigating circumstances. In most of these republics, ethnic identity has not, so far, been a strong political issue. Where it has (Chechenia, North Ossetia), the consequences have not been all that damaging for the rest of the country. The very fact that the titular nationality is so seldom the majority limits the opportunities for local elites to play the nationality card. The location of many of the republics deep inside Russia, i.e., without borders with other states and without much control over transport links that matter to them, reduces the temptation to seek too much 'sovereignty'. And many of the republics are too poor to be pushy.

So far, therefore, the problems particularly associated with the republics are a chaotic and conflict-ridden situation in much of the North Caucasus; assertive behavior towards Moscow over the control of resources on the part of some resource-rich republics (notably Bashkortostan, Sakha, Tatarstan), and the inducement to the regular Russian provinces to try to catch up with the perceived privileges of the republics.

Table 1 shows the ethnic composition of the original 20 republics, according to 1989 census data.

The lesser autonomies are a lesser problem. In some cases they are a joke. In the Jewish Autonomous Region in the Far East, 4 per cent of the population were Jewish at the 1989 census, and 83 per cent were Russian. In some cases an ethnic homeland for a small aboriginal population is based on history that does not correspond to the present facts of the case. For instance, the Khanty-Mansi Autonomous Region in West Siberia has a population that in 1989 was 66 per cent Russian, 0.9 per cent Khants and 0.4 per cent Mansi. The practical complications arising from these arrangements, however, can be considerable. The Khanty-Mansi Autonomous District happens to contain a great deal of oil and gas. In the Soviet era it was just a name for a part of the Tyumen' *oblast'*. The temptation for local (Russian) elites to make the most of the status of a federal subject, and of the revenues involved, is not a great help to the management of the industry, and of the region as a whole.

In general, the line-up of federal subjects is one that is not helpful to good government. It is also one that is now not easy to change.

tion on ethnic composition by region is poor. By and large, the shares of non-Russians are likely to have increased. The population growth rates of the non-Russians have generally exceeded those of the Russians, and in some cases (e.g. Chechenia) there has been substantial emigration of ethnic Russians.

Table 1. *Russia's Republics: Ethnic Composition in 1989*
(Percent of population at January 1989 census)

Republic	Non-Russian	Ttular
Adygeya	32	22
Altai	40	31
Bashkortostan	61	22
Buryatia	30	24
Chechen-Ingushetia	77	72*
Chuvashia	73	68
Dagestan	91	80**
Kabardino-Balkaria	97	57*
Kalmykia	62	45
Karachai-Cherkessia	58	41*
Karelia	26	10
Khakassia	21	11
Komi	42	23
Marii-Eil	53	43
Mordovia	39	32
North Ossetia	70	53
Sakha (Yakutia)	50	33
Tatarstan	57	49
Tuva	68	64
Udmurtia	41	31

* Sum of two titular nationalities.
** Sum of several indigenous nationalities.
Source: 1989 census, from USSR Goskomstat, *Natsional'nyi sostav naseleniya SSSR*, Moscow: *Finansy i Statistika*, 1991.

Elected Local Government or Management from Moscow?

In a country of Russia's size and regional diversity there would in most circumstances be an overwhelming case for devolution to regional elected government of a substantial array of powers and responsibilities, and particularly of a substantial degree of budgetary autonomy. In the special circumstances of Russia now, the case for regional autonomy is less clear.

Take political and public-administration issues first. Federal systems are generally considered to work effectively where there is a broad consensus across regions on what are and are not desirable policy aims and what is and is not acceptable political behavior. Russians—or at any rate the sum of their regional elites—possibly do not share such a minimum necessary consensus. If this is so, it must in part be the result of the bewildering speed of recent change and the extreme uncertainty of the future.

At all events, there has been a strong regional pattern of support for and op-

position to political reform. The opposition, insofar as referendum and election votes and opinion surveys are concerned, has tended to concentrate in the
more southerly regions. A case can be made for the 55th parallel's being the
dividing line (Teague 1993). Whether these apparent regional political differences are deep and durable enough to undermine a genuinely federal system is
not clear. But they certainly give rise to fears in the center of an arc of anti-
reform regions. This affects policy in Moscow.

As regards budgetary devolution, the case for it in Western societies, on
grounds of economic efficiency, is quite a strong one. The preferences of the
populations of different regions with respect to the mix of tax burdens and
local provision of public services are likely to vary. Information about those
preferences is more cost-effectively obtained at the regional level than at the
national level, particularly in a large and diverse country. Elected local policy-
makers will have more incentive (through local competitive elections) to cater
to local preferences than policy-makers elected to national office. Provided
that local tax collection and the provision of 'local public goods' can be managed with reasonable efficiency, an autonomous local tax base, with spending
determined by locally elected politicians, will tend to be more efficient in
meeting local preferences than financing and provision of public services determined at national level (see, e.g., Oates 1992).

In Russia, clean and efficient government is in short supply, both locally
and nationally. The very large differences in real incomes across regions
would justify a substantial reallocation of budgetary finance amongst regions
from the center. That would not necessarily be incompatible with a high degree of fiscal devolution, but it complicates it by reducing local incentives to
cost-effective tax collection and spending in both poorer and richer regions.

Assertions that Russia remains in reality closer to a unitary than a federal
state are well-founded, as later sections will show. What is less clear is
whether that is at present a weakness in terms of the process of economic
change. A more worrying, but equally plausible, assertion about the present
arrangements would be that Russia is a centralized state with a weak center.

President Yeltsin has periodically tried to strengthen presidential control
over the regions. Part of the package of special presidential powers that he got
from the Russian parliament in late 1991 was the power to postpone local
elections for at least a year, and the power to confirm the appointment of regional heads of administration (except in the republics) and to dismiss them.
(Relevant legislation in *Vedomosti Verkhovnogo Soveta RSFSR 1991* no. 41,
pp. 1718-66, and no. 51, pp. 2045-6; for an excellent review of the subsequent
development of center-regional politics, see Wishnevsky 1994.)

During 1992, as a result, the ordinary Russian provinces, in which some 84 per cent of the Russian population live, operated under a tripartite regional leadership: an elected council, dating from the March 1990 USSR-wide regional elections which also produced the Russian parliament of that time; a head of administration ('governor') with extensive powers, removable by the President; and a regional presidential representative, whose function was (and still is) to monitor developments in the region and report back to the president—particularly about deviations from nationally determined policies. As usual in Russia, it was not clear exactly who had what powers, and turf battles were endemic. Perhaps the only common ground amongst most of the participants was a belief that the presidential representative was a pest (author's interviews in a regional administration, May 1994).

The regional governors, despite their formal ties to the president, often went native and sided with the local elites against the center (examples in Hanson 1993a). Nonetheless, when parliament reasserted the regions' rights to appoint their own heads of administration, elections were held in Chelyabinsk, Orel, Smolensk, Lipetsk, Penza and Bryansk provinces, in which representatives of the local *nomenklatura* won against Yeltsin appointees (Wishnevsky 1994). A little later (May 1993), the council of Primorskii Krai also managed to replace a Yeltsinite reform governor with a member of the old local elite (*Utro Rossii* 19.v.93: 2).

In September–October 1993, when Yeltsin dissolved the Russian parliament, the pattern shifted again. Several regional governors who had come out on the side of the parliament against Yeltsin were dismissed by the President. In Bryansk it took OMON (special purpose militia detachments) troops to clear the administration building of supporters of the sacked governor, Yurii Lodkin (BBC *Summary of World Broadcasts*, henceforth *SWB*, SU/1805 C/5 of 28. ix. 93). Many regional councils, predictably, sided with the parliament, facilitating Yeltsin's subsequent move to disband *krai* and *oblast'* councils generally, and to reassert presidential control over the regions.

A rash of presidential edicts in late 1993 gave concrete formulation to this control. In an edict of 7 October, Yeltsin laid down that regional governors must once again be appointed by the President, and subject to dismissal by him. In an edict of 22 October he stipulated that elections to new, smaller regional councils should be held by the end of March 1994. And in an edict of 22 December he allowed regional administration staff to be eligible for election to regional councils (Teague 1994). As *Izvestiya* pointed out (on 2. ii. 94, cited in Tolz 1994b), under this dispensation a regional head of administration could be drafting legislation for approval by a council of which he was a member; later, as a legislator, he could be monitoring his own implementation of that legislation.

The subsequent delays in the holding of valid elections in a number of Russia's regions have left presidentially appointed governors and presidential representatives, in those regions, with a free hand. But even where new councils have been elected, the presidential prefects are, at least on paper, relatively strong. They report to the Control Commission of the Presidential Administration (Wishnevsky 1994). This is presumably in addition to reporting to the government proper, in the form of Goskomfederatsii, the government body overseeing federal links. A third central body, the Security Council, may have considerable powers to decide certain issues relating to the regions, such as the role of Cossack units in keeping order and guarding borders (author's conversation with a member of the Security Council secretariat, April 1994).

To anyone familiar with the old Soviet order, the most appropriate adjective to describe these top-down, prefectural arrangements, with the dual or triple subordination and the opacity of powers and responsibilities involved, is— Soviet. However, in practice, there are two large differences from the old Soviet order: the center's means of getting its own way are, in the absence of the old Party hierarchy, much weaker; and there is a widespread expectation that locally elected councils have (or, when elected, will have) a serious role.

The republics

The description just given covers the federal subjects other than the 21 republics. These, under the new constitution and the various presidential edicts of late 1993, have discretion to determine their own governmental arrangements, subject to the primacy of Russian federal legislation, including the Russian constitution.

The indeterminacy of all the rules of the game, however, is illustrated by the treaty concluded on 15 February 1994 between Russia and Tatarstan, referred to earlier. This treaty, which came into effect on 24 February (RFE/RL DR 25. ii. 94), allows Tatarstan to keep its existing constitution, which asserts Tatarstan's right to veto Russian federal legislation. The fact that the treaty does not give Tatarstan the right unilaterally to determine the share of tax revenues raised on its territory that goes to Moscow may be some consolation to those who worry about the possible break-up of Russia. The fact that the then head of Goskomfederatsii, Sergei Shakrai, described the treaty as a model for deals with other problem republics is less encouraging.

The Republic of Tuva, for example, has adopted a constitution that conflicts with the Russian constitution in at least two respects: it does not allow private agriculture; nor does it allow for judges, once appointed, to be immune from removal from office by the state. These differences, according to the Tuvin President, Sherig-ool Oorzhak, have nothing to do with any intention of seeking independence.[3] The constitutional differences arise from differences in local circumstances (RFE/RL *DR* 14. vi. 94). Whether these local circumstances amount to anything more than authoritarian and *étatiste* tendencies on the part of the local elite is not clear; in any case, the preservation of such basic constitutional discrepancies is not helpful to the development of a single economic and social space.

Representative links between center and provinces

Finally, in respect of the institutional structure, the constitutional arrangements since December 1993 formalize a regional-center legislative link in the form of the upper house of the Russian parliament. It is still possible in Russia to hold office at two levels of government at once. As has already been mentioned, the Federation Council is made up of two representatives from each federal subject. Of those elected in December 1993, about half seem to be from the regional administration, including many heads of administration. In addition, it can be deduced from the published list of deputies elected to the lower house, or Duma (*Rossiiskaya gazeta* 28. xii. 93: 1-5) that 50 out of 444 deputies came from regional or lower-level local government posts—38 from executive and only twelve from representative positions in local government. Moreover, 40 of those 50 entered the Duma through the so-called single-mandate elections, rather than through the party-list process, under which half the deputies were elected by proportional representation from party lists.

Thus regional administrations are strongly represented in the national parliament. Relatively few of the deputies who also hold local office are beholden to national, Moscow-based parties. The general intermingling of executive and legislature and of regional and national government, together with the independence from parties of many of the 'regional' parliamentarians, produces an odd picture. It is a picture that is characteristic of the muddle and improvisation surrounding Russia's political institutions. An optimist would call it transitional.

3. Which is just as well, since the population of Tuva is only 306,000. The fact that Tuva was an independent state between 1921 and 1944 may, nevertheless, help to explain the specificities of the Tuvan stance.

CHAPTER TWO

The Forces at Work

The social pressures and resistances influencing the different rates and directions of economic change in different provinces can be put under three main headings: local elites, regional diversity, and the uncertainty surrounding both the institutions and economic prospects of different regions. I have written on these subjects elsewhere (Hanson 1993a, 1993b; Kirkow and Hanson 1994; Bradshaw and Hanson 1994), and will only summarize them here.

Local elites

The March 1990 elections at regional level produced councils dominated by members of the Soviet *nomenklatura*—not necessarily members of the Party apparatus, but people who were on the Party's lists of appointable officials and managers, and who occupied posts such as factory directors and chairmen of collective farms. The evidence is that this electoral success of the old elite had more to do with the weakness of the organized 'democratic' opposition outside Moscow and Leningrad (as it then was) than with electoral skullduggery (Helf and Hahn 1992; McAuley 1992). The old elites are once again doing well in the regional elections taking place in 1994. To what extent, if any, this is attributable to the unorganized character of campaigning by 'new people', the explanation suggested by McAuley and Helf and Hahn for the 1990 elections, is not clear. It may well be partly or wholly the outcome of gerrymandering and electoral fraud (Teague 1994).

The number of people on regional and local Party committee *nomenklatura* lists in the late Soviet period has been estimated at 1.8 million, with All-Union and Union-Republic lists to be added to that (Rutland 1993). That is for the

USSR as a whole. A very rough estimate, therefore, of the *nomenklatura* inherited by Russia alone would be about one million, or 0.7 per cent of the population. That total would provide more than enough *nomenklaturshchiki* to dominate local politics in the 89 regions, if that is what they chose to do. It appears that a sufficiently large number of them did.

The following generalization about provincial elections in Russia is crude, but not too crude to be helpful: they have left local representative bodies dominated by the old local elites, who as a result have a previously unheard-of legitimacy. At the same time the old chains of command tying them to a national *nomenklatura* elite in Moscow have been destroyed. The cohesion of local management and Party elites within a region was well described in the 1970s (Andrle 1976). It may quite possibly have endured.

These people still have useful contacts and know-how but they are not subject to commands from Moscow as they were before 1991, and they find themselves at odds with much of the policy emanating from the capital. The Yeltsin-appointed regional administrators were meant to provide a chain of command from Moscow, but have tended either to find themselves at odds with provincial councils or, being disinclined or unable to beat the local elite, to join it.

The overlap between executive and representative bodies at provincial level has already been mentioned. It extends to overlaps of personnel and responsibilities between the secretariats of committees of councils and the departments of the administration (Campbell 1993).

There is also a great deal of overlap with local business interests. Local gatekeeping, in the form of power to issue licenses, to register companies and to put public-sector contracts in the way of this or that concern, is believed to be an important source of income to local officials and elected representatives. If Russia is indeed best classified as a 'high-corruption' country, along with Nigeria, Venezuela and the Philippines (*Economist* 28. iv. 94: 96), the large extent of corruption is not only a feature of the federal level of government. One of the reasons why it is widely believed by business people that corruption is worse now than it was in the Soviet era is precisely that it is not controlled by a single national hierarchy (ibid.).[4]

Some developments are more favorable to an orderly process of economic reform. Democrats and reformers have been elected in substantial numbers in the councils of Moscow and St Petersburg, and in some other cities (though

4. This is not meant as a sweeping indictment of all provincial deputies and officials. My personal observation is that many seem honest, competent men or women of good will. But the environment does not foster these characteristics.

Table 2. *Russia: Real household income per capita, 1993 I-II, by major economic region*

Region	Income	Region	Income
North	126.9	North Caucasus	86.6
North-West	60.4	Urals	109.8
Central	74.0	West Siberia	154.1
Volga-Vyatka	83.3	East Siberia	113.4
Central Black Earth	100.4	Far East	112.5
Volga	126.4		

Source: L. Nemova, 'Rynok truda', *Eko*, 1993:10:39.
Note: Russian Federation average = 100; local price differences reportedly allowed for.

apparently not in other provinces). The local elites are by no means hostile to all economic reforms (see Chapter 3). But they have been confronted with Yeltsin's attempts to enforce market reforms from above, through his governors and presidential representatives. Their responses to those attempts are described in Chapter 3. In general, local elites and the national government have tended to pull economic policy in opposite directions since 1991.

Regional diversity

REAL INCOMES   The 89 Russian provinces probably differ more widely in development level than the member states of the European Union. Certainly, differences in per capita real income, in urbanization and in the extent of industrial development are very large. In many respects, moreover, Russia is not yet a single economic space. One illustration of this is the fact that levels of prices and real wages differ widely. The differences in money wages and per capita money incomes are quite misleading, because the price differences are so huge (see Chapter 3).

One estimate, the reliability of which cannot be accurately assessed, purports to show levels of per capita real personal income amongst the eleven former planning regions, with adjustments for price differences. It is presented in Table 2.

If comparable estimates could be made for the 89 federal subjects, the range from poorest to least poor would presumably be even greater than the 1:2.5 range between the North-West and West Siberia shown in Table 2. So long as most housing is socially owned, geographical labor mobility is inhibited, so that any lessening of these inequalities through labor movement is improbable. Meanwhile the actions of provincial authorities in maintaining local price controls and therefore barring some cross-provincial-border deliveries of goods further impedes the creation of a single market (see Chapter 3).

URBINIZATION Differences in the extent of urbanization are also striking. In the 1989 census, the average share of urban in total population for Russia as a whole was 73.7 per cent. Amongst the 89 federal subjects (excluding the cities of Moscow and St Petersburg, and the region of Murmansk, where anything but urban habitation is perilous), the urban population ranged from 37.4 per cent of the total in the republic of Kalmykia to 87.3 per cent in Kemerovo. Of 77 main regions (not counting the autonomies separately, and with Chechenia and Ingushetia taken together), six were less than 50 per cent urban (five of them republics). Of 74 regions (again omitting Moscow, St Petersburg and Murmansk), 12 had urban shares of population of 80 per cent or more (Brad-shaw and Hanson 1994).

NATURAL-RESOURCE ENDOWMENTS AND INDUSTRIAL PROFILES These likewise vary widely. Tyumen' *oblast'* is the obvious example of a region rich in oil and gas. Areas with at least potential strengths in agriculture include the Central Black Earth (former planning) region, containing Belgorod, Voronezh, Kursk, Lipetsk and Tambov, and also parts of the North Caucasus—Rostov, Krasnodar and Stavropol'.

Some industries are highly concentrated regionally. Horrigan's calculations of regional dependence on military-industry (VPK) employment in 1985 can serve as an example (Horrigan 1992). There are some acknowledged deficiencies in the Goskomstat data Horrigan used: they do not cover all VPK employment (in particular, they exclude military R&D institutions), and they probably include some non-VPK employment (e.g., in gold-mining); but for our present purposes they can be treated as a proxy. Her estimated percentages of 1985 population that represent members of households containing at least one VPK employee range from zero in Tuva to 36.4 per cent in the republic of Udmurtia, against a Russian average of 12.1 per cent.

FOREIGN ECONOMIC RELATIONS One other aspect of Russia's economic geography should be mentioned. There are border, or gateway, regions and hinterland regions. The former include St Petersburg and, on the Pacific coast, Primorskii Krai. The pull of foreign trade already has strong regional effects. In the case of the Russian Far East, the combination of its Pacific Rim location and its relatively weak input-output links with the rest of Russia has prompted speculation that it is drifting away from the rest of the country economically. The Russian government was sufficiently worried about its own Far East becoming a speck on Moscow's horizon to arrange a meeting of the Commission for Operational Problems on the subject on 25 May 1994 (*Kommersant daily* 26.v.94: 3).[5]

In the measure that Russia's economy adapts towards a functioning market system, this pull of trade with established capitalist countries will strengthen. Gravity-model projections of the future patterns of trade of the former Soviet republics predict a massive reorientation towards Western partners, as and when the post-Soviet economies come to behave like normal market economies (Williamson 1992). That is not surprising, because the logic of these projections is that the trade-partner composition of trade flows between market economies is strongly determined by the economic size of each country and the distance between each pair of trade partners. The relatively large economic size of not-too-distant Western countries, compared with that of East European and Soviet-successor states, will tend to produce predictions of just such a reorientation. Other circumstances may affect the outcome, but the predicted tendency is in general terms plausible.

What existing gravity models have not done is to break Russia up into regional segments. The distances used in the projections are those between capital cities. In practice, the gravitational pull on trading links for the Russian Far East will be different from that on Moscow. There is in general nothing particularly problematic about differences in the geography of trade amongst different regions of a large country—consider the east and west coasts of the USA—but in a political system as fragmented as Russia's, and subject to so much uncertainty about future developments, it is not surprising that such differences in regional trade orientations can make politicians nervous.

Uncertain center-periphery relations

The flux of regional institutions has already been described. The constant alteration of the composition and powers of regional government would cause less trouble if other institutional links bound regional and national policy-

5. The concerns were not only to do with Pacific trade and regional economic autonomy tending towards secession. Reportedly, 'demographic pressure' from China was also discussed. The *Kommersant daily* report claims that 150,000 Chinese citizens are already resident in the Primorskii Krai, many of them illegally.

makers together. But neither political parties nor the courts nor a shared view of the likely future perform this function.

POLITICAL PARTIES AS UNIFYING INFLUENCES   The parliamentary elections of December 1993 showed that political parties were still primarily creatures of Moscow and St Petersburg. At best they have only shallow roots in the provinces—the Communist Party of Russia being a partial exception (see Chapter 2 above, Tolz 1994b and Wishnevsky 1994). The provincial elections of 1994 have mostly strengthened this impression. For example, the main blocs contesting the mid-June Buryat parliamentary elections were Education and the Future, Social Justice (containing communists and agrarians), and a bloc called For a Worthy Life (RFE/RL DR 14. vi. 94). None of these seems to be closely tied to any national party. Moreover, when local politicos have pro-claimed affiliation to a national party, they often switch that affiliation later, or simply disown any national-party ties.

One consequence is that party discipline seldom ties regional politicians, through their career ambitions, to any nationally proclaimed party platform. It is therefore likely that, where their perceived local political interests clash with a policy emanating from the center, they will be less likely to sacrifice the former for the latter than would be the case in countries with established polit-ical parties.

THE JUDICIARY   The judicial system is also too weak, so far, to be used systematically to ensure that failures to implement national policies, where il-legal actions are involved, can be corrected through the courts. Often the courts in a particular region are under the thumb of the local elite. In 1994, ac-cording to Argumenty i Fakty (1994: 16: 5), a backlash against private farming got under way in the Kuban' (Krasnodar), initiated by the local state-farm di-rectors and collective-farm chairmen. Investigating alleged breaches of law in the repossession of privatized land, the author of the article was told by a local judge that he and his colleagues were under instructions 'to save the collective farms'. This may be an extreme case, and the backlash may be halted as a re-sult of national publicity; but we cannot be sure that it is untypical; nor can we be sure that it will be necessarily halted by publicity.

FUTURE PROSPECTS AS GUIDES TO LOCAL POLICIES   It is tempting, but un-profitable, to seek guidance to local economic policies in the economic prospects of particular regions. It might be thought that the prospect of a par-ticular region's being a loser or a winner from economic change would tend to influence regional leaders' policies towards market reforms. One attempt to find such a link with 1992 data, with the rate of small-scale privatization in 77 regions as the variable to be explained, did not produce a statistically significant result (Bradshaw and Hanson 1994).[6] More generally, it is hard to detect a systematic variation in approach to economic change that corresponds to variations in what might be thought to be the prospects of different regions.

One plausible reason for this has been suggested by Andrei Treyvish (interview, 4.v.94). It is that there is so little confidence about the nature and direction of future economic developments in Russia that local political leaders, in general, have no clear idea about the prospects for their particular regions.

Treyvish and his associates at the Institute of Geography in Moscow consider that different scenarios of Russian development could find any one of four kinds of region leading the way: gateway regions, natural-resource regions, farming regions or (in their view, least likely) manufacturing regions. These prospects will be considered in the next chapter. The point to be made here is that the chances of each region seem to be too uncertain to be a guide to a region's policies.

One qualification should, however, be made to this judgment. It is that leaders of resource-rich regions at present show a disinclination to reform, since they are making plenty of hard currency without changing their ways. That is how, for example, the Russian politician and economist Grigorii Yavlinsky justifies his concentration on Nizhnii Novgorod as a pilot region for attempting his own bottom-up reform policies. When asked why he did not start in Tyumen', with a strong hard-currency base, he points to the complacency of local elites there; in contrast, Nizhnii Novgorod, with its heavy defense-industry dependence, had leaders who saw no way ahead except through radical reform (discussion with Yavlinsky at Ebenhausen, 13. iv. 94). It should be added, though, that by no means all regions dependent on military industry have local leaders who share the Nizhnii Novgorod governor's enthusiasm for reform.

It seems safest to argue that certain features of the economic geography of a region may be a deterrent to reform policies at the local level. For example, confidence in a region's ability to generate hard currency may tend to deter local leaders from reform. And experience of a particularly steep fall in eco-

6. Multiple regression (ordinary least squares) was the method used. Amongst other potential explanatory variables, dependence on VPK employment (Horrigan's estimates) and level of urbanization did not emerge as significant at the 5 per cent level. The reform reputation of local leaders did. So, less strongly (15 per cent level) did the proportion of non-Russians in the population. The latter was inversely related to the rate of small-scale privatization.

nomic activity in a given region may tend to intensify, in that region, the antipathy that all local leaders have to macroeconomic stabilization. On the other hand, the reasons why a few local leaderships have been more reformist than most have less to do with economic geography, and more to do with the social circumstances that allow a reformist counter-culture to be formed, and perhaps also with the role of a few individuals.

The Provinces in Transition
Center Stage

General

THE CURRENT ECONOMIC STATE OF THE REGIONS Running an economic health-check on the Russian regions is tricky. Information on production declines by region is confined to official measures of industrial-sector output. That is neither sufficiently reliable nor sufficiently wide in its coverage of the economy to be much help. A better indicator has been devised by Michael Bradshaw: official unemployment plus recorded short-time working as a proportion of the employed population. His compilation of figures for end-1993, taken from Goskomstat data, is given in Appendix Table A1, and mapped in Map 1.

No doubt these numbers have their deficiencies. But in principle, at least, they should reflect the situation in all sectors of the economy, and not just in industry. And adding reported short-time working to officially registered unemployment avoids undue reliance on the official unemployment figures. The latter are still quaintly low for a country whose officially recorded GDP has fallen by almost a half since 1989.[7] Spokesmen of the Russian Ministry of Labor have in the past used a combined measure of unemployment and short-time working to portray the 'real' employment situation in the country at large, so this measure should be more or less applicable region-by-region. At the same time, it must be assumed that effective stabilization would produce a much larger shake-out of labor than even this combined figure shows. Whether

---

7. The 'true' fall is certainly less than this, for reasons that have been sufficiently rehearsed elsewhere. What a better measure might be, however, is impossible to say.

that shake-out would follow the regional pattern of Map 1 and Table A1 is something that can only be guessed at.

At least this indicator shows a plausible regional pattern. There is relatively high unemployment plus short-time working in three regional clusters—Volga-Vyatka, the ethnic republics of the North Caucasus, and the southern Urals—and in two regions of the Central area, Ivanovo and Vladimir. In the case of Ivanovo, a region with a heavy concentration of textile production, the break in cotton supplies from former Soviet Central Asia may be part of the story. More generally, Ivanovo has less of the research-intensive defense industry than is characteristic of the Central area. The Volga-Vyatka and Urals areas could both be seen as rust-belts. They have a high concentration of heavy engineering and the less research-intensive parts of the VPK (Horrigan 1992, and communication from Julian Cooper). The North Caucasus republics are relatively backward in general, had a record of labor surpluses even in the Soviet era, and have been convulsed by conflicts in the recent past. It is also noticeable that the poorer republics generally—not only those in the North Caucasus—have relatively high measures of unemployment plus short-time working.

It will be shown later, however, that not all areas that seem, on this measure, to be particularly battered are dragging their heels when it comes to reform.

THE INTERESTS OF PROVINCIAL ELITES IN GENERAL. The background and circumstances of most regional elites suggest a certain common logic in their attitudes towards economic transformation. This logic provides a plausible account of typical attitudes, but need not apply strongly to all local leaderships. It can be summarized in terms of the following features: NIMBY ('not in my backyard') stabilization, populist anti-liberalization, insider privatization, and localism in the pursuit of foreign-trade privileges.

Stabilization

NIMBY STABILIZATION. Macroeconomic stabilization is an effort to provide a national public good—a stable currency; but no elected regional government within a single currency area has an interest in the observance of financial discipline in its own backyard. The benefit that is hoped for is a national one, in which, with luck, all will eventually share. The regional political leaders, however, will not gain any credit from that. Meanwhile, the pain is felt locally in restricted public services, bankrupt enterprises and redundant

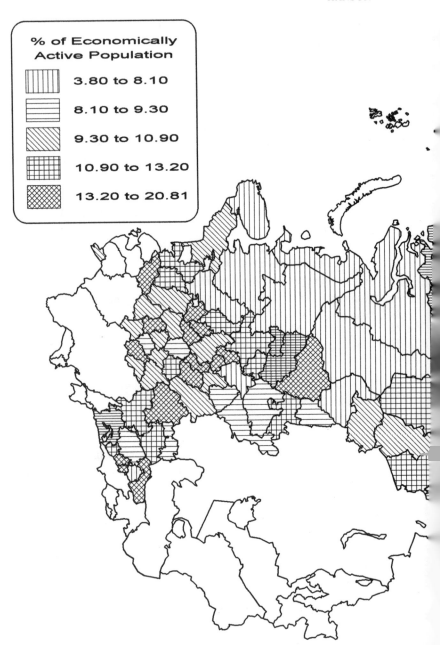

% of Economically
Active Population

3.80 to 8.10

8.10 to 9.30

9.30 to 10.90

10.90 to 13.20

13.20 to 20.81

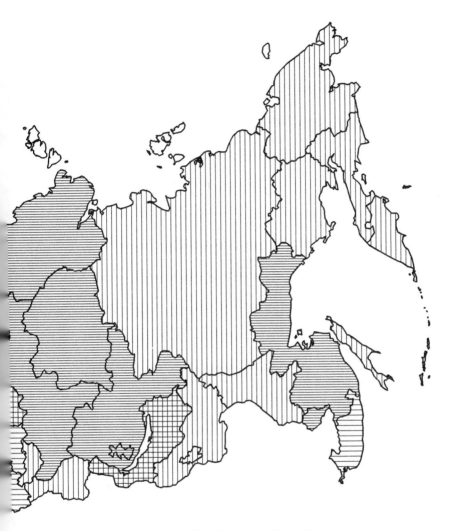

Sources: All data are from Goskomstat Rossii

Map 1 Unemployment, plus short-time working, end of 1993.

workers. If one region can avoid the pain, its elected political leaders, or any local political elite that feels vulnerable to local public discontent, will seek to do so. It is only the reformers at the national level who will regard stabilization as their responsibility.

The options for local politicians faced with a national regime of financial stringency are to seek special favors for producers in trouble in their region or to attempt an exit from the single currency area by developing a local surrogate currency. Numerous local ration coupon schemes in Russian territories exemplify the latter; the former is endemic, though the mechanics of favor-seeking depend on the structure of political institutions.

One variant might be an attempt to establish a regional central bank of one's own that could determine local money supply. That would amount to setting up a separate currency. Boris Fedorov, the former Russian Finance Minister and the most consistent and determined exponent, when in office, of monetary control, says that some of the republics have tried to move in this direction by seeking greater autonomy for the regional branches of the Russian Central Bank located on their territory. For that reason he advocates a smaller network of regional branches of the central bank, with each branch spanning several administrative territories (*Izvestiya* 26. iv. 94: 2).

THE NATIONAL CONTEXT OF REGIONAL BUDGETS. The national policy issues surrounding the Russian state budget are well known. There is a pressing need to curtail the overall government financial deficit. Only if this is done will the rate of growth of the money supply be brought down and inflation thereby brought under control. There is little alternative to this approach. Noninflationary financing of the deficit through foreign credits is tempting. But it reduces the pressure to exercise budgetary discipline, and carries with it balance-of-payments burdens for the future. Funding of the budget deficit by the issue of bonds can also help; but it requires procedures and markets that are only just being created, and cannot make a large contribution to policy in the short term.

Reducing the budget deficit is difficult. The machinery for raising government revenue from taxation is primitive and faulty, and the pressures on the government to spend are high. Much of the spending consists of subsidies or subsidy-equivalents in the form of soft credits initiated by the government. To complicate matters, controversy over the meaning and reliability of official budget numbers is intense (Hanson 1994).

THE ROLE OF REGIONAL BUDGETS: REDISTRIBUTION AMONG REGIONS. The inherited system of tax collection involves the initial collection of most tax revenue by regional organizations, and the 'sharing upwards' of the revenues according to supposedly standardized region/center percentage divisions of revenues from particular taxes. This is then followed by various kinds of redistribution of funds from the center 'back' to the regions. The redistribution has not been based so far on a standardized formula that would compensate for differences in requirements for local public services, relative to the local tax revenue base.

One fundamental characteristic of Russia's subnational budgets is the lack of local autonomy. Local budget outcomes stem from games of tug-of-war between regions and the center, without the regions' having much formal autonomy in the determination of their own tax bases and tax rates. They do have some autonomy, however, in the manipulation of so-called extra-budgetary funds. These have by tradition been outside the control of elected councils, and have been built up in some secrecy by local administrations in collusion with their local allies in the management *nomenklatura*. In Moscow in early 1994 the city Duma's new budget and finance committee was in the process of trying to find out what was in these funds, and who controlled them (Moscow edition of *Ekonomika i zhizn'. Vash partner*, 1994 no. 9).

The size of these off-budget funds, and therefore the scale of any real local budgetary autonomy, is typically unknown to outsiders. Unusually, St Petersburg published figures for its 1993 out-turn: own off-budget funds revenue was put at 15 per cent of total St Petersburg revenue from all sources (including an element of redistribution from the center, some of which was from the center's own off-budget funds; *Gorod Sankt P* 1994). If the scale of off-budget funds were similar across the country, the true state of local finances would be very different from that which is published. But probably St Petersburg is in this respect unusually well-off, as well as unusually honest.

The center has developed the habit of striking *ad hoc* budget deals with regions. This generates a leap-frogging of claims by various regions against the center. According to the Ministry of Finance, in 1993 every federal subject had by the end of the year secured a budget deal that differed from the allocation originally set by the center (*MinFin VE 94*). A common complaint is that regions that make the most fuss or have the most political leverage get the most, to the detriment of equitable treatment across regions.

In particular, it was argued in early 1993 that the republics within the Russian Federation were using their special status to obtain unduly large net redistributions to themselves, at the expense of a core of net contributors to the federal budget: Moscow, St Petersburg, Moscow and Leningrad oblasts, the Urals region, Nizhnii Novgorod, Samara, Krasnodar, Tyumen' and Krasnoyarsk (Leonid Smirnyagin in *Segodnya* 25. vi. 93). This cutting of deals with republics remains a target for criticism in 1994. Boris Fedorov cited the special tax deals for Bashkortostan, Tatarstan and Chechenia as a sign of weakness at the center that could bring about the break-up of the federation (*Izvestiya* 12. iv. 94: 2).

Some of the recent redistribution amongst regions is defensible: most of the republics are probably poorer than most of the regular, 'Russian' provinces. But this is not true of some who do well out of these arrangements, such as Tatarstan and Sakha. The most convincing explanation of the pattern of redistribution in 1993 is that it was determined by a weak central government and president seeking to appease the more assertive federal subjects.

A World Bank study has provided a detailed description and analysis of the relations between national and territory budgets through autumn 1992 (Wallich 1992). The main points are summarized below.

Under the old Soviet system, the allocation of government functions and expenditure to republican and local levels corresponded broadly with the principle of national provision of national public goods (goods such as defense whose benefits are enjoyed by all members of a national community, and cannot be pre-empted by or restricted to some members and not others) and local provision of local public goods (goods like the provision of public parks, about which the same could be said of members of the local community only). Below national level, there was very little discretionary power over taxing and spending, but the assignment of tax revenues by central-government discretion to local levels bore some general relationship to the expenditures assigned to these levels.

Both legislation and practice in Russia in 1992 tended to depart from these principles in the course of 1992. A good deal of the responsibility for social protection, and some infrastructure investment spending, was devolved to subnational levels, beyond what the local public goods principle would entail. New guidelines for assigning shares of tax revenue to territories were developed. But no mechanism was constructed for ensuring that revenue devolved to particular territories matches the expenditure required by the spending responsibilities assigned to them. The general rules for tax-sharing that operated in 1992-3 left each territory's budget revenue, prior to *ad hoc* negotiation with Moscow, determined by its tax base. This is because they took the general form: 'x per cent of value-added tax collected in the region stays in that region, and 100 minus x per cent goes to the federal budget'. Officially, there is still very little devolved authority under which territories can independently set tax bases and tax rates. Nor is there a general and transparent equalization formula for determining grants from the center to territories. (This is not because the Russian government's own advisers had failed to understand the need for such a formula, or to advocate one, at any rate in general terms.)

The World Bank report cited above makes recommendations for administrative reform within and for a framework in which equalization grants could be determined in a fair and transparent manner. It also addresses the question of how natural-resources taxes might be better designed, and the revenue from them shared between resource-rich regions and the center.

Under Boris Fedorov, the Ministry of Finance was trying to move in this direction in 1993. The aim as of late 1993 was to set aside a block of revenue (22 per cent of VAT proceeds) to deploy as a fund for regional redistribution according to an appropriate grant equalization formula (*MinFin VE 94*). The size of the sum involved is reasonable. In 1993 it would have amounted to about 1.5 per cent of GDP. The development and use of such a fund is still the aim in 1994, but it is not clear that the aim is being implemented.

REGIONAL BUDGETS AND STABILIZATION. From the point of view of macroeconomic stabilization, the attractive feature of local budgets is that local government cannot print money. As we saw, Boris Fedorov has warned of pressures from the republics to have their regional branches of the Russian Central Bank turned into 'national banks', but this is an attempt that can probably be thwarted. It follows that the republics and provinces can only run deficits to the extent that they can issue bonds or raise foreign credits. So far, even within a generally underdeveloped bond market, the development of municipal and regional bonds is barely visible (R100 million in 1993, about a tenth of the size of a bond issue by the VAZ (Lada) car works; *MinFin VE 94*).

It is perhaps in part for this reason that the center has tended to push down to subnational levels many of the responsibilities for spending on social protection, and to some extent for spending on subsidies. In 1993 the bulk of most local budget spending was either for 'social-cultural measures' or 'on the economy' (*RazvReg 93*: 103-4). It was apparently hoped that passing the buck would slow the printing of additional bucks.

If so, the results have been at best a partial success. The regions, facing a weak center, have pressed for more revenue, and have tended to get it. As a result, although deficits cannot generally be created at subnational level, pressures from that level contribute to the federal budget's deficit, while the regions' overall share of public revenue, and of public spending, has tended to rise.

The available data on regional budgets are unclear, and often contradictory. Appendix Table A2 (from *GKStat Jan 94*) indicates a total 1993 deficit in

Russian regions' budgets of R1.29 tr., or 0.8 per cent of GDP. Other sources have generally shown the regions in modest aggregate surplus. Table A2 probably shows the picture before redistribution from the center back to the regions. (Characteristically, the Goskomstat source gives no definitions.) If this is so, the identity of the regions with positive balances is of interest. They include St Petersburg, Moscow city and *oblast'*, Nizhnii Novgorod, Krasnodar and Ul'yanovsk, but also the republics of Tatarstan, Bashkortostan and Sakha. In the case of the republics in question, the positive balances probably reflect the outcome of special deals in the initial split of tax revenues.

Liberalization

POPULIST ANTI-LIBERALIZATION. The initial Russian price liberalization of 2 January 1992 was in several respects less thoroughgoing than that in Poland two years earlier. One difference was that the Russian central government left open to lower-level authorities in the regions the option of maintaining some price controls at their own discretion. The variation in the exercise of this power across the administrative territories has been enormous and persistent. Ul'yanovsk, for example, has the reputation of maintaining as much of the old order as possible. That includes price controls and (therefore) rationing of price-controlled goods and border controls on shipments from the region. Nizhnii Novgorod, St Petersburg and some others have been at the other end of the spectrum.

The resulting price differences (at least for rationed goods) show up in the regular Goskomstat price surveys in 132 cities. On 1 September 1993, bread prices were controlled in 40 per cent of those cities, sugar in 11 per cent and milk in 26 per cent (*Delovoi mir* 18. ix. 93: 7). Correspondingly, the total ruble cost of a consumer basket of 19 basic food items varies greatly among cities. For this as well as other reasons, regional differences in money incomes can be misleading.

REGIONAL PRICE CONTROL AND REGIONAL INCOMES. Table 3 illustrates the extent of this distortion in the case of the two familiar suspects for high and low food prices—Magadan and Ul'yanovsk, respectively.

Are food prices a good guide to the overall cost of living in different regions? They probably are, since traditionalist local leaders who have kept extensive food-price controls are likely also to have maintained low levels of controlled rents, and other basic items. If that assumption is correct, real in-

Table 3. *Money incomes, food prices and food purchasing power of average incomes, Magadan and Ul'yanovsk, 1993–94*

	Food basket mid-Sept. '93 % of Russian Federation average	Food basket Jan. '94 % of Russian Federation average	Average money income Jan. '94 rubles/ month	Average real income Jan. '94/5 rubles/month at average RF prices
Magadan	268.8	241.3	165,364	68,530
Ul'yanovsk	52.3	51.9	54,584	105,170

Sources: *Izvestiya* 22. ix. 93: 4; *GKStat Jan 94*: 107, 217; last column derived.

comes in Ul'yanovsk were on average higher than in Magadan, despite the fact that average money incomes were three times higher in the latter than in the former. In general, the money income data by themselves tell us nothing about welfare. They are, however, of relevance to investors, including foreign investors, provided that hidden social protection costs for employers (subsidized workplace food supplies, subsidized enterprise housing, and the like) are not systematically higher where money wages are lower.

The only published estimates of regional real incomes that supposedly take regional price differences into account are those of Nemova (1993), already shown in Table 2.

Local price controls impede the development of a single economic space across Russia. Their deployment in particular regions is a traditionalist gambit on the part of the local leadership. The gambit may at first help to maintain local support for the region's political leaders, but it will tend to be undermined by the growth of the private retail sector, which is less amenable to control. So long as the private sector is relatively small, the price-controlled official distribution system may keep all prices relatively low; but once the price-controlled sector begins to contract in relative terms, the political dividends from maintaining controls tend to fall (Berkowitz 1993). Meanwhile, however, price controls tend to be supported by local controls on deliveries across the region's border, and by rationing.

Regional leaders practicing this sort of control are probably buying short-term local support at the expense of longer-term structural change and the development of local private enterprise.

Identifying the regions which have maintained local price controls is not easy. Some cases, such as Ul'yanovsk, are extreme, and well known. Many less extreme cases cannot readily be detected from the available data. It would be plausible to argue that regions with both relatively low money wages and low shares of private retailing in total turnover would be likely examples, but data for the second of these indicators are lacking.

The evidence for the period 1992-early 1994 suggests that the extent of regional price control has tended to fall. One likely reason for this is that regional budget limitations (to fund subsidies and price monitoring) have tended to become more severe.

Privatization

In 1991–2 the Russian government divided responsibilities for privatization between small-scale (trade, catering, small-scale building and transport, etc.) and large-scale, with the former being devolved to municipal level. Larger-scale units were divided into four categories: those subject to mandatory privatization; those for which privatization was forbidden; and, between them, two intermediate categories: enterprises whose privatization required the approval of the State Property Committee (GKI), and those whose privatization required the approval of the government as such.

During 1992-4 a number of government decisions and legislative acts reduced the scope of the no-privatization category, in part by extending privatization to a large segment of the designated military-production (VPK) sector. In the revised version of the 1993 privatization plan, local governments were given a free hand to privatize enterprises with a 1992 book value of assets below one million rubles, and the breakdown of privatization routes by 1992 book values was: excluded from privatization 30 per cent; requiring government approval 31 per cent; requiring GKI approval 20 per cent; at discretion of regional authorities 17 per cent (Dmitrii Vasil'ev of GKI in *Izvestiya* 20.v.93: 4; the missing 2 per cent may or may not be due to rounding).

The role of regional initiative has in practice been substantial in all forms and channels of privatization. Local committees of the GKI have been closely linked with the local administration and council, and the latter, particularly the elected councils, have in turn been closely linked with the local state-management elite. Well-informed analysts say that in practice the privatization process has largely been pursued 'from below'—in the sense that the initiative to move ahead with corporatizing and then privatizing an enterprise tends to come from its management, which is not always tightly constrained in practice by the framework of rules and procedures set by the government and the GKI (Boycko et al. 1994).

It should follow from this that variations in the rate of privatization across

Table 4. *Industrial and farm privatization in selected regions, early 1994*

Region	No. of industrial enterprises actually privatized/mandatory no. (ratio) Feb. 1994	Private population Jan. 1994
Stavropol	4.6	16.2
Altai krai	3.72	5.2
Ryazan'	2.72	4.4
Voronezh	2.6	3.2
Vologda	2.58	4.3
Tambov	2.32	8.3
Krasnodar	1.62	8.2
Rostov	1.52	8.8
Arkhangel'sk	1.51	2.7
Lipetsk	1.32	3.7
Nizhnii Novgorod	1.14	4.2
Kemerovo	0.97	7.9
Omsk	0.95	10.5
Saratov	0.5	18.3
Moscow oblast'	0.48	4.1
Perm'	0.46	7.2
Sverdlovsk	0.46	5.2
Kaliningrad	0.38	12.7
Irkutsk	0.32	5.9
St Petersburg	1.05	...
Moscow city	0.33	...
RF average	0.79	6.9

Sources: *CEER* 1994, 2:2:13, *RazvReg 93*: 90–92.

regions will be a good guide to the general orientation of the local elite within a region.

However, there are difficulties in applying this criterion.

— Data on cumulative numbers of enterprises or initial book value of assets privatized are not published for end-1993 or end-March 1994 by region (though regional data for privatization *during* first-quarter 1994 are available).

— The development of small-scale and large-scale privatization is not necessarily positively correlated across regions (see Table 4 and Figure 1 for evidence that they are not). This leaves the observer in a quandary as to how to characterize particular regions.

— The role of environmental influences, as against that of local policy orientation, can be hard to disentangle. The best information available in a number of regions will no doubt indicate that the scope for any particu-

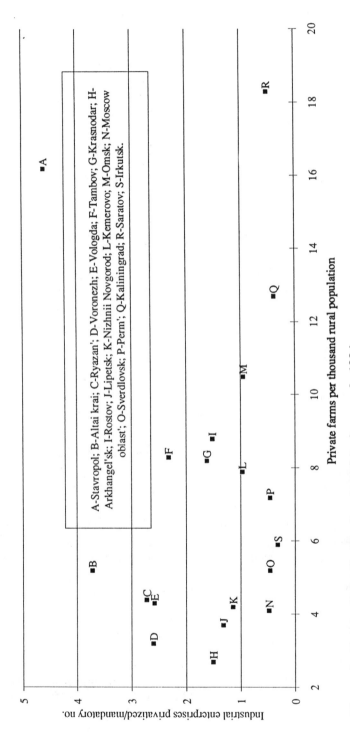

Figure 1 Russia: Privatization in selected regions, early 1994

A-Stavropol; B-Altai krai; C-Ryazan'; D-Voronezh; E-Vologda; F-Tambov; G-Krasnodar; H-Arkhangel'sk; I-Rostov; J-Lipetsk; K-Nizhnii Novgorod; L-Kemerovo; M-Omsk; N-Moscow oblast'; O-Sverdlovsk; P-Perm'; Q-Kaliningrad; R-Saratov; S-Irkutsk.

Industrial enterprises privatized/mandatory no.

Private farms per thousand rural population

lar kind of privatization is in varying degrees limited by legal prohibitions and poor economic prospects for the privatized concerns. Ideally,
policy orientation should be judged against the limits of the possible and
the attractive. Those limits, however, are hard to judge without more information than is available to observers from outside a given region.

Table 4 gives some information for 21 regions. These are the 20 regions
that had the highest absolute numbers of privatized (medium and large) enterprises by 1 February 1994, plus Kaliningrad. The 'performance' of each region in industrial privatization has been assessed (column 1) by the ratio of
that number to the reported target number of required privatizations (mandatory privatization targets) for the region. Thus Moscow city, for example, had
a high absolute number of privatized enterprises at this date, but a level of performance, in this sense, that is below the national average.

The second column of figures is a measure of performance, for these 21 regions, in the creation of private farms. The measure used here is the number of
private farms per thousand rural population at 1 January 1994. This might
sometimes give a different picture from a measure of performance by the
share of farmland privatized. (e.g., the Altai Krai, with very large average-size
private farms, might look more impressive on a hectare basis).

Figure 1 indicates that the relationship between the two performance indicators is weak (more correctly a correlation between the two variables of
+0.02). This could be because farm privatization is controlled by rural district
elites, and not by the leadership of the region as a whole or the leaderships of
the main towns in the region—which will largely determine the rate of industrial privatization. Alternatively, the explanation may have more to do with the
prospects facing the two sectors in each region. Thus, farm privatization has
apparently gone faster in the more fertile, southerly regions within this group
of territories, than in the poorer, more northerly, ones. The full set of data on
farm privatization is shown in Table A2.

Even without the evidence of the simple correlation coefficient, it is apparent from Figure 1 that there is no systematic relationship between performance in farm and in industrial privatization amongst these regions. (And
these include the 20 regions with the largest absolute numbers of privatized
industrial enterprises.) There may be good reasons for this that have nothing to
do with the policy orientation of regional-level leaderships (see above). On
the other hand, it seems fair to say that those regions within this group that
score well on both performance measures are in general terms reform-oriented
regions. They are Stavropol', Tambov, Krasnodar, Rostov, Kemerovo, and

Omsk. These six regions all have scores that are above average-Russian scores on both indicators.

St Petersburg is excluded from the reckoning because it has no farm land to begin with. On any general assessment it would need to be added. Moscow city, excluded from the reckoning for the same reason, should still not be added to the list of fast privatizers. Its low score on privatization reflects, amongst other things, a long-running battle over the issue between the mayor of Moscow, Yurii Luzhkov, and the GKI chairman, Anatolii Chubais.

The Moscow city administration has, in effect, been seeking to exclude itself from the national privatization program. The conflict came to a head in May 1994. At the beginning of April Luzhkov suspended the privatization process in Moscow. Chubais fought this behind the scenes for some time. According to *Kommersant daily* (1994 no. 20, 7 June: 28-32) he argued that the mayor of Moscow was breaking the law by refusing to implement national legislation. On 25 May Prime Minister Chernomyrdin, probably at Chubais's insistence, issued an order to Luzhkov, giving him three days to resume the registration of joint-stock companies in Moscow. At this time, GKI information was that there were 8 million Moscow-issued vouchers that had not yet been used to purchase assets, though the period of validity of vouchers was due to end on 30 June, and across the country as a whole the overwhelming majority of vouchers had been used.[8]

Luzhkov told journalists on 30 May that he was not obeying the Prime Minister's order. Chubais stated publicly on 2 June that he would seek to have Luzhkov removed from office. Luzhkov persisted, saying that he wanted the usage of vouchers in privatization to be specially extended in Moscow beyond mid-1994. In the event—and with little regard for the damage to the government's authority—President Yeltsin intervened to allow a special extension of voucher use in Moscow.

The reasons for this conflict in the capital city are unlikely to bear much resemblance to those in Udmurtia (with its exceptionally high VPK dependence) and Ul'yanovsk (with its notoriously unreconstructed Brezhnevite leadership). The Russian press has said little directly about the rationale of the Moscow city administration's behavior. By implication, however—and this is

---

8. While voucher usage was approaching 100 per cent in many regions (though by no means all vouchers were used to purchase assets located in the region where the vouchers were issued), it is noteworthy that Chubais referred on 30 May to Moscow city, Kalmykia (only 3 per cent of vouchers used), Udmurtiya (10 per cent) and Ulyanovsk (39 per cent) as lagging particularly far behind. These are all regions where the local leadership has particularly resisted change, albeit for somewhat different reasons. *Kommersant daily,* loc. cit.

supported by the views of knowledgeable people in Moscow with whom I have discussed the issue—the press coverage links the Moscow mayor's resistance to privatization with the benefits gained by the city administration's personnel from their control over state property in the city. In other words, privatization would reduce their income from corrupt practices as gatekeepers.

That, in turn, only raises a further question: why should this problem be so acute in the open, sophisticated capital city? My guess is that this has to do with Western capital. Until 1991 almost all Western joint ventures were in Moscow (see below, especially Table 5). The city administration probably developed a coy relationship with Western investors or with their Russian state-enterprise partners, or both. Privatization of assets in Moscow would tend to exclude them from the making of such deals and the collection of kick-backs. Nowhere else in Russia had this kind of relationship loomed large when privatization was launched.

Nizhnii Novgorod is another special case. Its farm privatization performance measure may be misleading. The region scores low on farm privatization in Table 4, yet its particular approach to farm privatization was endorsed by the government as a model for other regions, in a decree of 16 April 1994 (Russian TV 18. iv. 94). These two observations could be reconciled in various ways. For example, there may in fact be little enthusiasm for farm privatization in the rural areas of the province, and a locally devised scheme that looks impressive but has not in fact been applied may have been endorsed for the sake of appearance rather than in reality.

A less cynical interpretation, however, is also possible. Special attention, and Western technical assistance, have been focused on privatization in this province, and that applies to farm as well as non-farm privatization. The particular approach adopted in Nizhnii Novgorod has been to link the privatization of farm land with opportunities for the new private farmers to purchase lorries and to acquire a stake in the wholesale and retail distribution of farm produce in the region—in other words, to develop vertically integrated private firms that extend forward to transport, processing and distribution (Grigory Yavlinsky in discussion at Ebenhausen, 13. iv. 94). This approach presumably takes longer to put into practice than the usual selling-off of land as an isolated operation. Insofar as it is carried through, however, it should put the new farmers into a stronger position than the 'vertically disintegrated farm privatization' approach, in the sense that they will be less at the mercy of transport and distribution networks with monopoly power.

With these ad hoc amendments, then, the short list of regions with particularly promising starts in privatization across sectors of the economy becomes the following: Stavropol', Tambov, Krasnodar, Rostov, Kemerovo, Omsk, St Petersburg and Nizhnii Novgorod.

THE 55TH PARALLEL AND ALL THAT. At first sight, the southerly location of most of these regions might seem surprising. Isn't the South anti-reform? That would be an over-simplification, in two respects.

First, the observation of particularly weak support for Yeltsin during 1991-3 covers 29 regions. Of these, 23 are indeed below the 55th parallel. Not all southerly regions, however, come into this category (Teague 1993).

Second, the measures by which the 29 regions were identified were measures of political support. There is no necessary connection between the popularity of democratic politicians in a region and the alacrity with which people in that region embrace private enterprise. Two of the eight regions to whom we have given good marks for privatization, Tambov and Nizhnii Novgorod (yes, Nizhnii Novgorod, so often described as the front-runner in economic change), are amongst the 29 regions showing relatively traditionalist voting behavior. In the December 1993 parliamentary elections (not included in Teague's account of regional political patterns earlier in 1993), voting in the city of Nizhnii Novgorod favored the democratic groups (particularly Yavlinsky's Yabloko), but voting in the rest of the region favored the communists (Yavlinsky at Ebenhausen, 13. iv. 94).

There is, after all, no reason why a Russian citizen should not be unhappy about the rise of crime and insecurity and continue to feel more trust in the old *nomenklatura* of a region than in the smart young democrats, while simultaneously making the most of the new opportunities for enrichment. Many of the *nomenklaturshchiki* themselves are doing precisely that. At the same time, regions with relatively strong farm sectors may exhibit the political traditionalism that seems to go with tilling the soil anywhere; yet they may come to flourish in the future, while more urbanized regions with larger contingents of democratic voters may find that modernization is, for them, the route to the rust-belt.

Foreign trade and investment

PROBLEMS WITH REGIONAL TRADE NUMBERS. The available published data on foreign trade by region, from Goskomstat (*Vneshne-ekonomicheskie 1993*) are subject to crippling limitations.

First, they appear to report exports by place of shipment and imports by location of importer. The importance of foreign trade to regions, and of particular regions to foreign trade, does, of course, depend on where the value is added to the export (perhaps successively in different regions at different stages of processing), and where the final user of an imported consumer or investment good is located. Only access to detailed and reliable regional input-output tables could enable us to establish this information.

Two examples will illustrate the difficulty. Samara looms large as an exporting region, chiefly because it houses the VAZ car plant. But part of the value of the cars exported from the city of Samara derives from coal, steel, rubber, and plastic inputs into the final product, a substantial part of the value of which was added by labor, capital and natural resources in regions other than Samara. On the import side, Moscow and St Petersburg appear as dominant 'importing' regions for consumer goods, though of course much of the inflow of consumer goods into those cities is subsequently redistributed to retail outlets in other regions.

It is true that in the case of raw material exports like timber and crude oil, the region of shipment generally is the region where all or almost all the value of the export will have been created. However, this is not too much help, because of the next problem with the numbers.

The regional trade data are in domestic ruble prices. These, unfortunately, still bear little relationship to world market prices. In particular, the ruble trade data by region cannot tell us about the weight of regions in the dollar value of Russia's trade, even if the first problem with the numbers could be disregarded. If the ruble totals for 1992 are compared with the dollar totals for Russia's non-CIS trade (the latter from *Russian Economic Trends* 2:4), they imply exchange rates of R38 to the dollar for exports and R26 to the dollar for imports. The actual exchange rate, determined on the Moscow Inter-Bank Currency Exchange (MICEX), rose from R180 = $1 at the start of the year to R418 at the end of the year. This might not matter too much if the dollar values by region could be derived just by scaling up the conversion rate. They cannot, however, because the structure of Russian domestic prices of tradable goods, though adapting towards the structure of world market prices, was still a long way away from it in 1992, the last year for which the regional trade data are available. In particular, domestic pricing grossly understated the relative dollar value of oil and gas, and therefore understated the importance in exports of regions like Tyumen'. The Goskomstat numbers which purport to show, for instance, that Samara was the leading export region in 1992 are extremely misleading, both because of the value-added problem and especially because of the domestic price problem.

It is true that the regional trade values in domestic prices could be of interest as a measure of the perceived importance of foreign trade within a region, provided that we had GDP or net material product (NMP) data by administrative region. Unfortunately, we do not.

The third and last problem with the regional trade data is a mundane one. It applies to all Russian trade data, whether in dollars or rubles, regional or national. It is not therefore necessarily trivial, however. It is that there is, quite simply, a great deal of unreported trade—perhaps particularly in consumer imports. As far as regional patterns are concerned, allowance for unrecorded trade, if it could be made, would very probably show border regions looming larger than they otherwise would.

In mid-1994 the publication for the first time of customs-based trade data (for first-quarter 1994) indicated the extent of the problem. The import total for the quarter was 65 per cent higher than the Goskomstat total. The export totals were close, but the two sources gave widely different figures for individual products. And these do not represent differences between figures for goods deliveries and figures for payments, where one would expect divergence. Both series are for deliveries. The Goskomstat data are based on enterprise—reporting to the statistical authorities; the customs data are based on customs forms from ports and other transit locations (*Finansovye Izvestiya* 23. vi. 1994: II).

For all these reasons, the regional pattern of foreign trade will be discussed here only in a broad and qualitative way.

NATURAL-RESOURCE V. OTHER REGIONS. In 1992 and 1993 taken together, when total Russian non-CIS merchandise exports were running at about $42 billion a year, oil, natural gas and petroleum products accounted for 45.8 per cent of the total. Machinery, equipment and vehicles, presumably including the Ladas, were 5.5 per cent (derived from *Russian Economic Trends* 2:4). As the major oil and gas producer region, Tyumen' looms large as a source of exports. Notoriously, the gains to the region itself from this circumstance have been restricted. One reason is that the internal price of energy has remained under control, and relatively low. Also, partly to offset this and impede diversion to exports, the center has continued to control quantities exported and to impose an export tax. In 1993 the rates were (per cent): crude oil 30, natural gas 18, petrol 40, diesel fuel 30, residual fuel oil 8 (*Russian Economic Trends* 2:4).

In the past, the grievances of major exporting regions like Tyumen' were exacerbated by the central control of all trade, under which export earnings were used to buy imports that were concentrated on final users in European Russia. Of course, there is no reason why the most economically efficient regional allocation of a given set of imports should correspond to the regional pattern of production of the exports that 'paid for' those imports. In the case of Russia, the concentration of population and industry west of the Urals made some such redistribution entirely sensible. The sense of grievance in most fuel- and raw material-exporting regions was not alleviated, however, by considerations of that sort. As information about the outside world became more readily available during the 1970s, people in Surgut and Nizhnevartovsk noted that, during a boom in the world oil market, Saudi Arabia, Houston and Aberdeen were flourishing places. West Siberia was not, even by Soviet standards.

Moscow continues to commandeer hard currency for centralized imports. The scale of such importing, however, is being reduced. In 1992 centralized imports (mainly of machinery and food) were 59 per cent of all non-CIS imports; in 1993 they were only 41 per cent, of a much-reduced total (*Russian Economic Trends* 2:4).

Two factors seem likely to produce a certain regional reallocation of trading patterns.

First, the adaptation of Russia's product-mix away from value-subtracting[9] manufacture and toward fuel and raw material extraction and primary processing is already evident, despite the lack of substantial new investment (see Hanson 1994 for evidence, and McKinnon 1991 for an exposition of the idea of value-subtracting activity in communist economies). It is likely to continue. Many Russian policy-makers claim to be horrified at the loss of high-tech jewels in Russia's industrial crown, and the tendency to become a hole-in-the-ground economy. The jewels are probably far fewer than they think, however, and several hole-in-the-ground economies are a great deal more prosperous than Russia. Thus economic activity in general may tend to become more concentrated on natural-resource regions.

This tendency might also apply to agricultural regions, but with quite different implications for trade. The development of the farm sector is likely to be a matter of import-substitution behind protectionist defenses. The tariffs and quotas would be keeping out products dumped by West European and American producers over-producing behind their own protectionist defenses—a sad, wasteful business, but not Russia's fault.

The second tendency is likely to be toward trade liberalization and therefore the reduction of centralized imports. Import subsidies were abolished with effect from January 1994. Export taxes and quotas are supposed to be

9. Roughly: producing output that is worth less at world market prices than the world-market value of the materials used in the production process.

abolished by January 1996. Some important quota controls were dismantled in early 1994. Import tariffs remain, and some have recently been raised, but that has chiefly to do with the move away from direct central control of importing.

Both these tendencies, insofar as they continue, are likely to lead in the short term to some greater linking of regional imports to regional exports. Insofar as the weight of raw-material regions in the whole economy increases, that will mean simply that the weight of their import demand will increase. Insofar, however, as internal barriers within the economy are broken down, and Russia really becomes a single market, there should not be administrative tying of imports to exports, region-by-region.

FOREIGN INVESTMENT. The volume of foreign investment into Russia is extremely small, with a wide variance amongst estimates of its size. What there is, is chiefly direct investment, though portfolio investment is becoming possible as privatization proceeds, and foreigners' access (often through proxies) to voucher auctions also increases. But this flow, whatever its real dimensions, is far smaller than has been the outflow of capital from Russia over the past three years. In general, it would be hard to underestimate its importance.

Potentially, however, foreign investment could be of the greatest value, partly as a source of capital funds from abroad that do not bring future balance-of-payments burdens with them in the way that loans do, but above all as a vehicle for technology transfer. So far as their regional impact is concerned, data on numbers of joint ventures registered, though problematic,[10] give some indication of the pattern. One thing that is clear is that liberalization has brought a rapid diffusion of joint venture registrations away from Moscow (see Table 5).

The geographical diffusion of joint venture activity clearly reflects the opening-up and regional devolution that has occurred in the Russian economy since the end of communist rule. But it is noticeable that there is only one region in common between this list and the short list of eight regions with high all-round privatization indicators (Chapter 4, above). That is the city of St Petersburg. It looks as though the factors determining joint venture location so far have little to do with those affecting the rate of privatization.

Moscow city exemplifies this: a conspicuous laggard in privatization, it remains the leading location for joint ventures. It was suggested earlier that in Moscow there is even a trade-off between the two: that the lure of access to

10. Because they do not measure the volume of activity but do include joint ventures that have been wound up or were ever only nominally operational, and do not cover a number of other means by which foreign investors can now operate in Russia.

Table 5. *Distribution of operational joint ventures in the top 10 regions for joint venture operation, 1989 and mid-1993 (percent)*

	1989 (n=322)	Mid-1993 (n=4138)
Moscow	82.6	31.8
St. Petersburg	7.1	14.0
Krasnodar	0.3	3.0
Karelia	0.9	2.8
Murmansk	0.6	2.2
Novosibirsk	0.3	1.5
Samara	0.3	1.4
Komi	0.0	1.4
Moscow oblast'	0.9	1.3
Bashkortostan	0.0	1.3

Source: Database developed by M.J. Bradshaw.

hard currency suggests alternatives to privatization for those who control state assets in the capital city.

Institutions that cross regional borders

The creation of a single economic space in Russia depends chiefly on private initiative. It also depends on regional governments' showing less initiative. Traditionalist leaderships in such regions as Ul'yanovsk generate regional trade barriers. Their price controls and rationing stimulate an outflow of food and consumer goods to higher-price regions. They then intervene with border controls to impede this outflow, and with ration coupons for local residents to prevent outsiders' benefiting from the controlled prices.

There are a few cases of regional governments acting in ways that lower regional trade barriers. One example on a small scale is the Shakhovskoi rural district of Moscow *oblast'*. Here the leader of the Democratic Party of Russia, Nikolai Travkin, conducting an experiment in reform from below that is even more grass-rooted than Yavlinsky's and Nemtsov's in Nizhnii Novgorod, has amongst other things attracted capital from Siberia (Teague and Hanson 1992). On the whole, however, regional government activity probably tends, with one qualification to be noted later, towards autarky.

The pervasive nature of that intervention is reflected in the regional price and money-wage differences described above. These differences extend to regional differences in interest rates and privatization-voucher prices.

The development of commodity exchanges, multi-plant firms and distribution networks that cross administrative boundaries, as well as the development of efficient interbank clearing systems, insofar as they go ahead, should break down these barriers. To some extent, they already have. That regional differences in voucher prices are not larger than they are, given the wide range of regional variations in the ratio of locally issued vouchers to the book value of privatizable assets, indicates that quite a lot of cross-regional arbitrage has been going on.

One proposed new institution, much discussed in Moscow, might seem to belong to this boundary-crossing category. This is the Financial-Industrial Group, or FIG. The FIG would be a large commercial grouping, probably geographically extensive, somewhat resembling a Japanese *keiretsu* group, containing a bank, several production and research units and perhaps a distribution network. Both Yeltsin and Chernomyrdin have said the government should foster FIGs. Legislation about them specifies that they should normally not be more than 25 per cent state-owned, and that proposals to form a FIG should be vetted by the State Anti-Monopoly Committee (*Kommersant daily* of 14 and 15. vi. 1994).

Whether FIGs would be favorable to liberalization in general may be doubted. The fact that the FIG idea is said to be popular with senior managers of state and ex-state enterprises will arouse the suspicions of any economic liberal. It is all too easy to see the Financial-Industrial Groups as an insider's dream, disposing, with no legislative safeguard, of both market power and heavyweight muscle in lobbying for subsidies. So far, however, FIG figures suggest they are largely a figment of the old guard's imagination. Only four had been registered by Summer (*Kommersant daily* 14 and 15.vi. 1994).

One response that a number of local leaderships have made to the confining pressures of provincial autarky is the development of regional economic associations spanning several administrative territories. One of their purposes in doing this has been to unite in order to create a greater weight in lobbying for such hand-outs from Moscow. There are nine regional associations. They include the Siberian Agreement, and groupings in the North Caucasus, along the Volga and among central Russian oblasts. As already noted in Chapter 2, however, the center resists formalization and consolidation of such groupings. Moreover, several of them have been weakened by internal discord. A study by Petrov and Treyvish (1994) concludes that the Far East is the most likely of any of these super-regions to be able to consolidate and act as a unit. This is partly because of the relatively weak nature of its economic ties to more westerly parts of Russia. Its situation both provides an incentive to gain more autonomy for itself, and reduces the leverage of Moscow in deterring such a development.

It must be said, finally, that the secure establishment of a single economic space and, above all, of a reasonably well-functioning market economy will do more to hold Russia together than political pressure or the manipulation of tax breaks and subsidies by Moscow.

Conclusion

This survey of the Russian regions as players in the Russian economic game has sought to bring out three points.

First, relations between regional and national government are both chaotic and critical to the whole process of policy-making in Russia. This is not true in the smaller East Central European countries, where the re-creation of genuine local government now looks more like a return to a humdrum working arrangement.

Second, the prospects of any one region in Russia are especially hard to forecast, since so much depends on the particular path that national policy takes, and that in turn is highly uncertain.

Finally, and perhaps less obviously, there is a suggestion that in Russia at present the aspirations of political liberals may be at odds with the aspirations of economic liberals. In my concluding remarks, I shall focus on this last point.

On the one hand, most democratically elected Russian regional legislatures tend in some (not all) ways to resist policies designed to create an effective market economy.

On the other hand, some of the localities where there has been electoral support for democrats, rather than traditionalists—chiefly in large cities—may prove to be the areas that will suffer most from further decontrol and tighter money. Cities and regions with concentrations of better-educated people have tended to support modernizers against traditionalists. These better-educated people also tend to be employed (or, nowadays, to have been employed) in research and development and science-based manufacturing; yet the sad truth is that much of Russia's 'advanced' industry faces sharply decreased demand (especially for military hardware) or is value-subtracting, or both.

If one were to set aside the economic changes still to come, it would be easy to specify the kinds of institutional change that would help to reduce the tensions between regions and the center. One set of institutional changes tending in this direction would be liberal, the other authoritarian.

Liberal changes would be: a new or modified constitution that clarified the division of powers between regions and center; a strengthening of the judiciary; the development of political parties with networks of regional branches that carried real weight locally; associated with this, the election of reform politicians at local level, in place of members of the old elite (though with the 1994 round of local elections incomplete and showing continued electoral support for the *nomenklaturshchiki*, this prospect is remote); the establishment of a transparent and generally acceptable grant equalization formula to determine the pattern of regional reallocation of public funds; the development of an efficient, national tax service; the further growth of economic institutions that are non-state and whose operations cross regional boundaries (firms with subsidiaries, banks with local branches, commodity exchanges serving a large area, and so on).

Some changes of a liberal kind have already been promised. Before the next national parliamentary elections (scheduled for 1995) there are to be elections in the *kraia* and *oblasts* to elect heads of administration. Heads of administration will have to be elected, not just presidentially appointed, as at present, in order to take up their seats in the Federation Council after the 1995 elections. Some observers, however, doubt whether these changes will be implemented. Indeed, some are skeptical about the prospects of any elections' being held in the near future.

Authoritarian changes that would scale down the center-region problem can be easily described. They would come down to the development (some would say the further development) of authoritarian presidential rule, using security services and regional prefects to impose policies across the country, and making elections at all levels an ineffective sideshow. This sort of change would by definition be incompatible with the politically liberalizing institutional changes listed in the previous paragraph. It would not be incompatible with the changes in economic institutions also listed there—though the need for the center to be seen to be fair in its regional resource reallocation would be less pressing.

It follows that institutional developments that fell between these two scenarios would be the most likely to leave center-regional conflicts unresolved, or exacerbated. In effect, the pendulum swings between top-down and bottom-up development that we have seen in 1992-4 amount, unfortunately, to this sort of unhappy medium.

Even if Russia continues to muddle along rather than pursue a consistently more liberal or more authoritarian path of change, however, political fragmentation does not seem very likely. The republics, though they constitute a problematic and divisive territorial arrangement, are mostly not well placed by location or ethnic mix to seek full independence (see Chapter 1 above). Most larger territorial groupings, or clusters of administrative territories, contain internal divisions that would hinder their acting as a unit (e.g., the North Caucasus), or have economies whose transport and general input-output dependence on the rest of Russia is high (Petrov and Treyvish 1994). In Petrov's and Treyvish's well-founded judgment, the one possible exception is the Russian Far East.

The national policy-makers nonetheless face a real dilemma in their dealings with the regional politicos. If, as seems likely, the tightening of monetary policy is maintained through the remainder of 1994, plant closures and redundancies will sharpen the resistance of many regional leaders to the center and its stabilization efforts. Resistance from local elites will be more staunchly supported than before by their electorates. This will probably be the case even in areas where support for the modernizers has hitherto been strong.

Negotiating these hazards without either resorting to authoritarian rule or abandoning macroeconomic stabilization probably requires a more systematic regional policy. So far, government subsidies and soft credits have been handed out on a first-come-first-served basis, modified by the principle that he who shouts loudest shall receive. The alternatives are not so much between a regional policy and an austere abstention from government hand-outs, as between a regional policy and wasteful and indiscriminate hand-outs.

Part of this policy would be regional in effect rather than in design. The provision of an effective social safety net and employment service (already an area in which Western assistance is being received) would yield regionally differentiated flows of unemployment benefits as unemployment developed at different rates in different places. The calculation of nominal benefits that would give the same real 'floor' income in different regions is extremely difficult because of the large differences in price levels across the country. But a continuation of the tendency to devolve such social spending responsibilities to the regions would be a recipe for trouble, as the divergences in their public revenue bases increased. In short, a consideration of the regional issue gives added strength to the case for the development of a proper national social safety net, and for World Bank and other Western assistance with that development.

Another element in such a policy would be the establishment of the national taxation service and the regional grant equalization process discussed earlier. In other words, regional reallocation of public money needs to be primarily an outcome of general, nationwide rules of the game, not an exercise in picking branch or regional winners. Such an exercise remains exceptionally difficult in the circumstances of incomplete liberalization and a fragmented economic space.

So far as Western business involvement is concerned, the picture given here may help a little in location decisions. I believe, however, that the main lesson from a cool consideration of Russia's regional muddle is that the prospects of development in any particular place in Russia still depend overwhelmingly on the resolution of the great uncertainties that attach to economic development in Russia as a whole. In particular, successful financial stabilization would transform investment prospects across the whole country, to a degree that dwarfs the present differences in prospects between regions.

References for Part 1

Andrle, V., 1976, *Managerial Power in the Soviet Union*, Farnborough: Saxon House.

Bahry, D., 1987, *Outside Moscow*, New York: Columbia University Press.

Berkowitz, D., 1993, *Price Liberalization and Local Resistance*, Washington, DC: National Council for Soviet and East European Research.

Boycko, M., et al., 1993, 'Mass Privatization in Russia,' paper presented at the meeting of the OECD Advisory Group on Privatization, 2-4. iii. 1994.

Bradshaw, M. J., and Hanson, P., 1994, 'Regions, Local Power and Reform in Russia,' forthcoming in R.W. Campbell, ed., *Issues in the Transformation of Centrally Planned Economies. Essays in Honor of Gregory Grossman*, Boulder, CO: Westview Press.

Campbell, A., 1993, 'Local Government Policy-making and Management in Russia: the Case of St Petersburg,' *Policy Studies Journal*, 21:1: 133-41.

CEER, 1994, 'Russia's Regions,' *Central European Economic Review* (of the Wall Street Journal Europe) 2:2 (Spring): 12-15.

Gazaryan, A., 1993, 'Political and Economic Issues in the Re-creation of Lithuanian Local Government,' mimeo.

GKStat 93, Goskomstat Rossii, *Osnovnye polkazateli sotsial'no-ekonomicheskogo razvitiya i khoda ekonomicheskoi reformy v Rossiiskoi Federatsii za 1993 god*, Moscow: Goskomstat, 1994.

GKStat Jan 94, Goskomstat Rossii, *Sotsial'no-ekonomicheskoe polozhenie Rossii. yanvar'1994*, Moscow: Goskomstat, 1994.

Goetz, R., and Halbach, U., 1993, *Republiken und nationale Gebietseinheiten der Russischen Föderation*, Cologne: Bundesinstitut für ostwissenschaftliche und internationale Studien.

Gorod Sankt P: *Gorod Sankt-Peterburg. 1993*, St Petersburg: Mayor's office, 1994.

Hanson, P., 1993a, *Local Power and Market Reform in the Former Soviet Union*, Munich: RFE/RL Research Institute, RFE/RL Studies.

Hanson, P., 1993b, 'Local Power and Market Reform in Russia,' *Communist Economies and Economic Transformation*, 5:1: 45-61.

Hanson, P., 1994, 'The Russian Budget Revisited,' *RFE/RL Research Report* 3:18: 14-21.

73

Helf, G., and Hahn, J.W., 1992, 'Old Dogs and New Tricks: Party Elites in the Russian Regional Elections of 1990,' National Council for Soviet and East European Research, mimeo.

Horrigan, B., 1992. 'How many people worked in the Soviet defense industry?' *RFE/RL Research Report* 1:33: 33-40.

Kirkow, P., and Hanson, P., 1994, 'The Potential for Autonomous Regional Development in Russia: the Case of Primorskii Krai,' *Post-Soviet Geography*, XXXV; 63-89.

McAuley, M., 1992, 'Politics, Economics and Elite Realignment in Russia: A Regional Perspective,' *Soviet Economy*, January-March: 46-89.

McKinnon, R., 1991, *The Order of Economic Liberalization: Financial Control in the Transition to a Market Economy*, Baltimore, MD: Johns Hopkins University Press.

MinFin VE 94, Ministerstvo Finansov Rossiiskoi Federatsii, 'Rossiiskie finansy v 1993 godu,' *Vosprosy ekonomiki* 1994:1: 3-86.

Nemova, L., 1993, 'Rynok truda,' *Ekonomika i organizatsiya promyshlennogo proizvodstva*, 1993:10: 39.

Oates, W.E., 1992, 'Fiscal Decentralization and Economic Development,' *National Tax Journal*, XLVI:2: 237-44.

Petrov, N., and Treyvish, A., 1994, 'Riski regional'noi dezintegratsii Rossii,' Moscow: mimeo.

RazvReg 93, Goskomstat Rossii, *Razvitie ekonomicheskikh reform v regionakh Rossiiskoi Federatsii v 1993 godu*, Moscow: Goskomstat, 1994.

Rutland, P., 1993, *The Politics of Economic Stagnation in the Soviet Union. The Role of Local Party Organs in Economic Management*, Cambridge: Cambridge University Press.

Teague, E., 1993, 'North-South Divide: Yeltsin and Russia's Provincial Leaders,' *RFE/RL Research Report* 2:47 (26 November): 7-24.

Teague, E., 1994, 'Russia's Local Elections Begin,' *RFE/RL Research Report* 3:7 (18 February): 1-5.

Teague, E., and Hanson, P., 1992, 'Nikolai Travkin Attempts Painless Economic Reform,' *RFE/RL Research Report* 1:38: 39-45.

Tolz, V., 1994a, 'Russia's Parliamentary Elections, What Happened and Why,' *RFE/RL Research Report* 3:2 (14 January): 1-9.

Tolz, V., 1994b, 'Problems in Building Democratic Institutions in Russia,' *RFE/RL Research Report* 3:9 (4 March): 1-8.

Vneshneekonomicheskie 1993, *Vneshneekonomicheskie svyazi Rossiiskoi Federatsii*, Moscow: Goskomstat.

Wallich, C.I., 1992, *Fiscal Decentralization: Intergovernmental Relations in Russia*, Washington, DC: World Bank, Studies of Economies in Transition, no. 6.

Williamson, J., 1992, *Trade and Payments after Soviet Disintegration*, Washington, DC: Institute for International Economics.

Wishnevsky, J., 1994, 'Problems of Russian Regional Leadership,' *RFE/RL Research Report* 3:19 (13 May): 6-14.

Zaslavsky, V., 1992, 'Nationalism and Democratic Transition in Post-communist Societies,' *Daedalus*, Spring: 97-123.

Table A1 *Unemployment and short-time working by region, end 1993*
(% of economically active population)

	Unemployed	Short-time work	Combined
Russia	5.1	5.3	10.4
NORTH			
Arkhangel'sk	4.7	3.2	7.9.
Karelia	5.4	3.9	9.3
Komi	3.6	2	5.6
Murmansk	5.5	1.4	6.9
Vologda	2.9	5	7.9
NORTHWEST			
St Petersburg	7.1	5.1	12.2
Leningrad	6.3	6.6	12.9
Novgorod	5	5.9	10.9
Pskov	4.9	8.8	13.7
CENTRAL			
Bryansk	3.9	6.5	10.4
Ivanovo	4.5	16.3	20.8
Kaluga	4.3	8.9	13.2
Kostroma	4.5	7.1	11.6
Moscow	6	3.8	9.8
Moscow City	4.6	2	6.6
Orel	3	5.8	8.8
Ryazan'	4.2	5	9.2
Smolensk	4.2	6.2	10.4
Tver'	4.9	5.8	10.7
Tula	4	5.3	9.3
Vladimir	4	12.3	16.3
Yaroslavl'	5.1	9.1	14.2
VOLGA-VYATKA			
Chuvashia	4.6	14.7	19.3
Kirov	3.9	8.6	12.5
Marii El	4.4	8.8	13.2
Mordovia	4.1	13.4	17.5
Nizhnii Novgorod	4.1	6.2	10.3
C. CHERNOZEM			
Belgorod	3.3	7.2	10.5
Kursk	2.6	13.4	16
Lipetsk	4.7	5.3	10
Tambov	3.6	8.5	12.1
Voronezh	4.5	4.8	9.3
VOLGA			
Astrakhan	6.3	2	8.3
Kalmykia	7.2	3.8	11
Penza	4.7	9	13.7
Samara	3.5	5.1	8.6
Saratov	5.4	5.3	10.7
Tatarstan	3.3	4.7	8

Table A1 *(Continued)*

	Unemployed	*Short-time work*	*Combined*
Ul'yanovsk	3.8	5.7	9.5
Volgograd	5.2	8.6	13.8
N. CAUCASUS			
Dagestan	13.5	3.9	17.4
Ingushetia		4.1	4.1
Chechenia			0
Kabardino-Balkaria	9.2	5.4	14.6
Krasnodar	6.2	3	9.2
Adygeya	7.3	5.3	12.6
North Ossetia	10.2	7.5	17.7
Rostov	5	6.2	11.2
Stavropol'	5.4	3.4	8.8
Karachai-Cherkessia	5.4	5.7	11.1
URALS			
Bashkortostan	4.3	4.4	8.7
Chelyabinsk	4.6	8.3	12.9
Kurgan	4.4	4.3	8.7
Orenburg	4.5	3.8	8.3
Perm'	4.6	7.6	12.2
Sverdlovsk	5.1	8.4	13.5
Udmurtia	4.2	6.8	11
WEST SIBERIA			
Altai Krai	4.6	6.5	11.1
Altai Republic	6.1	2	8.1
Kemerovo	5.1	3.9	9
Novosibirsk	5.5	4.5	10
Omsk	4.8	5.7	10.5
Tomsk	7.7	5.3	13
Tyumen'	5	2.2	7.2
EAST SIBERIA			
Buryatia	6.4	5.1	11.5
Chita	4.2	3.2	7.4
Irkutsk	4.4	4.6	9
Krasnoyarsk	4.1	4.1	8.2
Khakassia	3.2	3.7	6.9
Tuva	6.8	1	7.8
FAR EAST			
Amur	4.5	3.2	7.7
Kamchatka	5.7	2.2	7.9
Khabarovsk	5.3	3.1	8.4
Magadan	6.1	0.9	7
Primorskii	4.9	3.3	8.2
Sakhalin	6.8	0.2	7
Sakha (Yakutia)	3.3	0.5	3.8
Kaliningrad	5.4	4.8	10.2

Source: *RazvReg 93*, Goskomstat Rossii, *Razvitie ekonomicheskikh reform v regionakh Rossiiskoi Federatsii v 1993 godu*, Moscow: Goskomstat, 1994.

Table A2 *Budgets and farm privatization by region, 1993*

Region	Revenue (bn Rb)	Expenditure	Balance	Private farms no. of units	1.194: Ave. size	Total ha.	Rural pop. (000s)	Units per 000 pop.
RUSSIA	25589.5	26878.4	−1288.9	272783	3830	11516966	39431.7	6.9
Arkhangel'sk	195.8	225.4	−29.6	1113	14	15582	414.5	2.7
Nenets	9.1	18.6	−9.5	25	23	575	...	...
Karelia	164.1	175.3	−11.2	693	17	11781	206.2	3.4
Komi	263.2	319.1	−55.9	644	18	11592	310.9	2.1
Murmansk	273	273.8	−0.8	60	12	720	81.6	0.7
Vologda	231.6	253	−21.4	1956	30	58680	460.1	4.3
St Petersburg	962.4	928.2	34.2	...	...	...	...	...
Leningrad	247.2	248.5	−1.3	4454	11	48994	566.2	7.9
Novgorod	107.7	133.1	−25.4	2874	19	54606	220.4	13.0
Pskov	99.2	132.4	−33.2	2903	19	55157	296.3	9.8
Bryansk	144.4	165.7	−21.3	1830	24	43920	464.7	3.9
Ivanovo	124.9	139.5	−14.6	1233	20	24660	238.5	5.2
Kaluga	118.7	131.8	−13.1	1779	27	48033	289.5	6.1
Kostroma	122.3	142.4	−20.1	1108	37	40996	27.1	40.9
Moscow	1097.9	1048.8	49.1	5567	10	55670	1358.4	4.1
Moscow City	2959	2814.8	144.2	...	...	...	...	...
Orel	121.4	144.5	−23.1	1755	51	89505	343.3	5.1
Ryazan'	191.8	177.7	14.1	1954	38	74252	443.4	4.4
Smolensk	152.3	155	−2.7	3183	52	165516	359.7	8.8
Tver	186.8	208.5	−21.7	3574	31	110794	462.5	7.7
Tula	204.8	206.2	−1.4	3184	31	98704	341.9	9.3
Vladimir	204.3	197.2	7.1	1921	17	32657	332	5.8
Yaroslavl'	263.6	262.1	1.5	1904	25	47600	283	6.7
Chuvashia	142	171.9	−29.9	863	7	6041	543.6	1.6
Kirov	198.7	214.5	−15.8	1192	48	57216	196.3	6.1
Marii El	82.5	130.1	−47.6	1170	14	16380	291.5	4.0
Mordovia	96.8	129.5	−32.7	1507	27	40689	402.8	3.7
Nizhnii Novgorod	744.7	675.3	69.4	3450	20	69000	821.6	4.2
Belgorod	218.1	208.3	9.8	2765	24	66360	510.7	5.4
Kursk	166.5	165.6	0.9	2044	57	116508	543	3.8
Lipetsk	214.3	206.3	8	1720	47	80840	459.5	3.7
Tambov	139.6	156.8	−17.2	4666	35	163310	561.7	8.3
Voronezh	277.6	281.4	−3.8	3064	44	134816	964.8	3.2
Astrakhan	104.4	130.2	−25.8	1842	122	224724	334.8	5.5
Kalmykia	36.8	64.1	−27.3	1547	440	680680	201	7.7
Penza	137.5	153.3	−15.8	2760	38	104880	569.9	4.8
Samara	732.9	700.5	32.4	5099	44	224356	643.1	7.9
Saratov	326.6	333.2	−6.6	13023	63	820449	712.7	18.3
Tatarstan	874.6	778.9	95.7	724	34	24616	995.9	0.7
Ul'yanovsk	272.3	245.4	26.9	1793	31	55583	411	4.4
Volgograd	322.7	327.3	−4.6	10614	84	891576	689.3	15.4
Dagestan	99.6	217.5	−117.9	11366	3	34098	1124.4	10.1
Ingushetia	9.6	31	−21.4	2131	16	34096	736.1	2.9
Chechenia	...	...	0	...	...	...	...	...
Kabardino-Balkaria	58.4	100.4	−42	470	11	5170	316.3	1.5
Krasnodar	710.2	668	42.2	18690	15	280350	2267.4	8.2
Adygeya	37.7	61.9	−24.2	1282	13	16666	207.5	6.2
North Ossetia	49	86.3	−37.3	934	12	11208	199.7	4.7
Rostov	484.3	497.1	−12.8	12431	42	522102	1413.5	8.8
Stavropol	269.3	302.9	−33.6	19594	21	411474	1212.1	16.2

Table A2 *(Continued)*

Region	Revenue (bn Rb)	Expenditure	Balance	Private Farms No. of units	1.194: Ave size	Total ha	Rural Pop (000s)	Units per 000 pop
Karachai-Cherkessia	32.4	51.1	−18.7	749	12	8988	226.9	3.3
Bashkortostan	1253	1008	245	4646	23	106858	1441.6	3.2
Chelyabinsk	626.2	631	−4.8	7022	58	407276	693.5	10.1
Kurgan	134.9	147.7	−12.8	5132	60	307920	505.8	10.1
Orenburg	266.9	270.5	−3.6	6074	82	498068	793.2	10.1
Perm'	444.9	460.8	−15.9	4803	26	124878	708.9	7.2
Komi-Permyak	10.4	29.7	−19.3	299	24	7176	...	...
Sverdlovsk	821	804.1	16.9	3119	29	90451	598.7	5.2
Udmurtia	207.2	235.8	−28.6	3166	21	66486	496	6.4
Altai Krai	300.1	429.6	−129.5	6645	102	677790	1284.3	5.2
Altai Republic	24.5	51.9	−27.4	909	120	109080	146.1	6.2
Kemerovo	569.1	755.8	−186.7	3217	33	106161	405.4	7.9
Novosibirsk	316.7	337.8	−21.1	5847	58	339126	718.9	8.1
Omsk	321.3	411.2	−89.9	7424	55	408320	706.1	10.5
Tomsk	138.2	187.4	−49.2	2158	50	107900	379.7	5.7
Tyumen'	295.3	320.7	−25.4	4835	37	178895	747.7	8.3
Khanty-Mansi	739	707.2	31.8	1280	46	58880	...	...
Yamal-Nenets	265.7	276.1	−10.4	61	113	6893	...	...
Buryatia	128.7	201.1	−72.4	2770	66	182820	428.8	6.5
Chita	144.5	176	−31.5	1863	136	253368	481.2	4.6
Aga-Buryat	6.2	14.9	−8.7	333	216	71928	...	...
Irkutsk	433.6	475.4	−41.8	2780	31	86180	582.6	5.9
Ust'-Orda Buryat	11	24	−13	669	37	24753	...	...
Krasnoyarsk	514.4	506.1	8.3	4849	37	179413	838.4	5.9
Khakassia	76.7	90.7	−14	1087	37	40219	161.8	6.7
Taimyr	11	25.7	−14.7	...	...	...	...	...
Evenkii	4.4	14.1	−9.7	88	51	4488	...	...
Tuva	33.6	69.5	−35.9	2103	95	199785	159	13.2
Amur	152.7	193.7	−41	3385	97	328345	366.4	9.2
Kamchatka	101.6	171.3	−69.7	749	28	20972	80.3	10.5
Koryak	12	42.1	−30.1	98	17	1666	...	...
Khabarovsk	378	445.7	−67.7	1818	25	45450	312.3	5.8
Jewish	28.7	44.2	−15.5	722	32	23104	74.2	9.7
Magadan	128.4	169.8	−41.4	315	36	11340	43.8	7.2
Chukchi	45.7	100	−54.3	30	15	450	32.9	0.9
Primorskii	467.8	532.3	−64.5	4998	16	79968	511.8	9.8
Sakhalin	173.2	234.7	−61.5	1033	13	13429	106.1	9.7
Sakha (Yakutia)	549.4	521.7	27.7	2728	42	114576	369.6	7.4
Kaliningrad	168.9	169.7	−0.8	2524	16	40384	199.3	12.7

Sources: *GKStat Jan 94*, Goskomstat Rossii, *Sotsial'no-ekonocheskoe polozhenie Rossii. yanvar'1994*, Moscow: Goskomstat, 1994. *RazvReg 93*, Goskomstat Rossii, *Razvitie ekonomicheskikh reform v regionakh Rossiiskoi Federatsii v 1993 godu*, Moscow: Goskomstat, 1994.

Part 2

MONOPOLY AND COMPETITION POLICY IN RUSSIA

David Dyker and Michael Barrow

Perhaps the biggest *microeconomic* problem of transition to a market economy is obtaining the economic and political benefits of competition in an economy that starts from a highly monopolized position. These benefits can arise in two ways: from the active promotion of competition and from the regulation of the abuse of monopoly power. In the West there is now a great deal of experience with competition policy, but this may not provide a suitable model for the Russian situation, given the latter's particular characteristics. Among these we might cite the highly integrated structure of industry (including so-called 'dwarf-workshops'); the 'mind-set' of Russian managers and politicians who are unused to promoting or working in a competitive environment; and the weak or inappropriate judicial and administrative systems.

Because of these (and other) characteristics, a policy such as regulation (e.g. of prices) may actually hinder the competitive process since it will potentially reduce the incentive to enter the industry and, furthermore, it is likely to have the generally undesirable effect of making the regulated firm or industry *more* dependent upon the state.

There is a need, therefore, for a pro-competition policy (concentrating, for example, on barriers to entry) rather than an anti-monopoly policy. The former takes account of the dynamic nature of competition and the need for structural change, while the latter risks maintaining the existing, inefficient structure. Inevitably, this will have to be a political as well as an economic strategy, in opposition to powerful vested interests. Current Russian policy (for example, the creation of 'financial-industrial groupings') is moving in the opposite direction to this and is likely to reinforce the tendency towards cartelization. If Russia is eventually to gain the benefits of competition this policy will have to change. Such a change may be forced upon the country by the pressure of economic circumstances.

Monopoly in Russia: The Basic Features

Defining the problem

It is a commonplace of contemporary Russian studies that monopoly is in some sense a defining problem of the transition period. On both economic and political levels, in terms of central planning and the one-party system, the old Soviet regime is seen as the epitome of monopolism. And while the pluralization of the Russian political system cannot be doubted, the new economic system seems to have done little to change the structural patterns inherited from the old. Yet when we begin to dig deeper, we find that the issue of monopoly and competition in the Russian economy, at first sight so black-and-white, is in reality complex, even ambivalent. It is in the dimension of policy that this emerges most clearly. But even in relation to basic facts, there is plenty of scope for diverse interpretations.

> The great mass of industrial production capacity [in Russia] continues to be concentrated in large enterprises. About 2 per cent of industrial enterprises (those with more than 5,000 employees) account for more than 40 per cent of the total volume of output, and for more than half industry's aggregate profits . . . Many sectors are characterized by oligopoly, with manufacture of a particular product concentrated in three or four very big enterprises . . . A distinctive feature of the [Russian] oligopoly situation is bilateral monopoly, where on a particular market there is just one producer and one buyer. ('O sotsial'no-ekonomicheskom . . . ', 1994, p. 7)

> If we define oligopoly quite liberally to mean four or fewer firms in an industry, we see . . . that, while 26.4 percent of industries in [the] sample are oligopolies, they

only account for 1.1 percent of all these firms and 1.9 percent of all this employment. At the same time, 70.3 percent of firms and 41.8 percent of employment falls in enterprises in industries which have more than 100 firms. The highest employment mean is in the industry category with five to ten firms, and . . . the plurality (and one-third of all) extra-large firms are in industries with 21 to 50 firms. Mammoth monopolies simply do not dominate the civilian industrial sector . . . U.S. and Russian industrial structures are actually quite similar . . . . (Brown et al., 1993, pp. 20-21)

These two statements, at first glance in total contradiction to one another, are in fact perfectly consistent. The first is a valid statement about enterprises and products. The second is an equally valid statement about firms and industries. Products as diverse as trolley buses, potato-harvesters, motor scooters and coal-cutting and tunneling machines, to mention only a few, are manufactured in a single enterprise in the whole of Russia. Engines for lorries are made only by the Zavolzhye engine factory and bought only by the GAZ vehicle factory. Heavy locomotives are produced only by the Novocherkassk electrical equipment factory, and the output is bought up completely by the Russian Railways Ministry. But naturally, when we move up to the industry level and apply much more highly aggregated categories, the picture changes radically. There are many enterprises that produce transport equipment, many that produce agricultural machinery, and many that produce mining equipment; and there are, of course, no big firms in Russia to merge these enterprises into Western-type conglomerates (although conglomerates do exist in Russia, as we shall see later). So it is hardly surprising that a comparison between Russia and the USA in terms of industry/firm statistics yields no evidence of relative over-concentration in Russia.

Our two quotes also tell us a great deal about the Russian economy. The absence of large firms, the importance of (relatively large) single-product enterprises, the segmentation of markets—all of these are features of an economy *in transition*, an economy still only a few years out of a system of central planning which dominated for 60 years. The structure of the Russian economy remains largely that bequeathed by central planning.

The distinctive feature of the Russian economy is not simply the high degree of concentration of production but also its artificial character, which in practice has retarded the transformation of the technical and technological basis of production and preserved its backwardness . . . Monopoly in Russian conditions is not only a feature of the economic position of individual enterprises; it is a property of the economic system itself, inherited from the mechanisms of administrative-command regulation of the economy. (Starodubrovskaya, 1994, p. 4)

In analyzing monopoly and competition issues in Russia, then, we must keep the unique circumstances of the Russian economy firmly in view—and that means judging monopoly and competition policy issues against the yard-stick of the overriding goal of constructing a stable market economy, with all the *political* as well as economic complications that involves. This does not mean, however, that the experience of the developed industrial countries in this connection should be ignored. On the contrary, the recent history of Western Europe in particular is rich in material relevant to our theme—the control of natural monopolies, the special problems of competition policy in the context of privatization, the attempts to prevent the abuse of emergency trade restrictions to buttress monopoly advantage. Our approach is, then, to try to place the issue in perspective, nationally and historically as well as globally, and indeed to show how those two dimensions may, in certain critical connections, actually meet. We begin with a brief review of the relevant legislation.

The legal framework

The first major step in the construction of a Russian monopoly and competition code was actually taken in the last months of the existence of the Soviet Union. In August 1990 the USSR Council of Ministers adopted a general declaration on monopoly, and created the State Committee for Anti-Monopoly Policy and the Support of New Economic Structures (GKAP—henceforth Anti-Monopoly Committee). These measures reflected the increasing concern being felt in the final years of *perestroika* about the implications of partial decentralization, as enterprises born of central planning began to use the new freedoms granted them by Gorbachev to test their market power (Yakovlev, 1994, pp. 34-5). It must be stressed, then, that the origins of Russian monopoly and competition policy lie not in some blueprint for a competitive, market economy, but rather in the unforeseen complications of an unsatisfactory compromise between central planning and market principles.

The first major piece of legislation to emerge specifically from the Russian authorities was the law 'On competition and the control of monopoly on product markets', promulgated in the spring of 1991. Then in October 1991 a state register of enterprises with monopoly power was set up, and in December of that year regulations on the control of monopolists' prices were issued. Further legal provisions established that the criterion for registration as a monopoly should be control of more than 35 per cent of a given product market. In May 1992 revised regulations on price control were issued. Then in August of that year a new provision established maximum profit levels for enterprises classed as monopolists (Yakovlev, 1994, pp. 36-7). Once again, we can detect a certain ambivalence in this series of legislative acts. Recognizably based on Western experience of monopoly control, they nevertheless included a number of features which seemed to originate from a much more *dirigiste* concept of monopoly control. Was this simply a reflection of the fact that the Russian economy in 1992 was still a kind of half-way house between central planning and the market? Or did it represent a real ambivalence in relation to the *goals* of monopoly policy—whether to build a 'well-ordered' or a genuinely competitive economy? We return to this question later on.

The legislation of 1992 still provides the framework of monopoly and competition policy in Russia. A new dimension was introduced in late 1993, as Russia and its CIS partners struggled to breathe life into the CIS Economic Union, which had been agreed on in principle in October 1993. A conference of CIS Anti-Monopoly Committees held in Almaty in mid-October proposed (perhaps rather predictably) a coordinated CIS policy on monopoly, and more concretely the creation of an interstate council on anti-monopoly policies and an international center for problems of competition policy. A meeting of the Coordinating and Consulting Committee of the CIS of 15 November 1993 is reported to have reached agreement on coordinating monopoly policy, presumably on the basis of the recommendations of the Almaty conference. It is not clear that much progress has been made on this dimension since then, and there is certainly little immediate prospect of significant CIS policy coordination on monopoly and competition matters—or indeed on any other matters. But the mere fact of *recognition* of the importance of the international dimension of the monopoly problem did, in itself, represent an important evolution in the approach to the issue.

On 8 December 1993 the Presidium of the Russian Cabinet approved a state program for the demonopolization of the economy. The new program laid down the following principles:

— Permanent price control should be imposed only on natural and state-owned monopolies.
— Price regulation in relation to temporary monopoly advantage should be imposed on an *ad hoc* basis by the government.
— Priority demonopolization measures should be adopted in relation to trade, construction, communications and transport (apart from railways).

— State monitoring of the privatization process from the point of view of competition policy should be enhanced.
— Regional barriers to free trade within Russia should be removed.
— Steps should be taken to excise financial, economic, organizational and legal barriers to free entry.

Although it exhibits substantial continuity with past legislation, the December 1993 program does break new ground in stressing the importance of looking at privatization and competition policy together, and of making markets more contestable, whether on a regional or sectoral level. In so doing, it reflects the content of much of the critical literature that has appeared on the subject over the past year or so. Yet at the same time some of its elements are certainly susceptible to a *dirigiste* interpretation. Thus the ambiguity that was so marked in the early stages of Russian anti-monopoly policy formation is still present.

Clearly Russian monopoly and competition policy has evolved over the past three years or so. Its evolution has, however, been a complex and far from linear one. There is no *a priori* reason to believe that the trend will be any different in the near future. It is vital, then, to understand the special factors which condition this key element of economic regulation in the Russian case, in order to assess how changes in the overall policy environment may affect monopoly and competition policy, and how far models and lessons from Western experience can illuminate the debate.

Russian anti-monopoly policy in context: the legacy of the Soviet Union and the realities of transition

FROM REPRESSED TO OPEN INFLATION Long before the collapse of the Soviet Union, the aggregate wage bill was far outstripping the volume of consumer goods available. But fixed prices meant that the excess demand could not find expression in open inflation. The result was ever-lengthening queues, and eventually a kind of 'galloping repressed inflation' which forced Soviet citizens to spend half their lives looking for something to spend their rubles on. This combined with the very nature of central planning, and insensitivity to user needs, to produce a strong seller's market. Since the collapse of the Soviet Union, escalating budget deficits, combined with substantial price liberalization, have turned galloping repressed inflation into an open inflation which has teetered on the verge of hyper-inflation. The degree of excess demand generated by those fiscal deficits and loose government credits has to a great extent reproduced the seller's market of the Soviet era. In that context there is a sense in which *everyone* is a monopolist, and it is perhaps not altogether surprising that Russian anti-monopoly policy has often seemed to reduce to not much more than price control.

THE SPECIAL PROBLEM OF BARRIERS TO ENTRY The kind of pattern cited at the beginning of this paper—where just one, or possibly two or three enterprises manufacture a particular, specific product like potato-harvesters—could hardly arise in a Western economy, or if it did it would quickly be transformed. Since many basic process technologies are common to whole spectrums of products (e.g. the entire range of agricultural machinery or motor vehicles, or machine tools), any firm holding and exploiting a temporary monopoly over production of a specific product manufactured through one of those basic technologies would quickly find itself beset with competition from other firms in possession of that basic technology. If the firm in question enjoyed some genuine technological advantage in the application of the basic technology to this particular production line, it might take potential competitors a year or so to emerge as actual competitors. The fact that such a temporary monopolist might therefore enjoy super-normal profits for a couple of years would be seen as an incentive to competition rather than a distortion of monopoly.

It hardly needs stating that the pattern of monopoly-by-product is a direct result of the organizational imperatives that ruled Soviet central planning. The essential hierarchy of the system, which ran from central planners to industrial ministries down to enterprises, could only work if enterprises only produced one main category of output, since ministries had to translate production targets by product group into targets for individual production organizations. Over-centralization made the task a colossal one even with grossly simplified procedures. Multi-product production profiles at enterprise level would have made it simply impossible.

But there was another side to Soviet industrial reality. While most enterprises produced only one main line, the deficiencies of central planning, particularly when it came to supplies of components, spare parts etc., of 'fiddly little things that don't count in the plan fulfillment report', meant that most enterprises ran a whole range of 'dwarf-workshops'—to make the crucial supplies that others could not be trusted to deliver. Thus most Soviet engineering factories, for example, made their own nuts and bolts. The Soviet system has bequeathed to Russia, then, not just a monocultural mainline production pattern, but also a remarkably broad range of medium-level technological capability in most enterprises and a unique pattern of vertical integration—particularly in the engineering industry. On that basis one would expect the inherited pattern of monopoly-by-product to disappear quite rapidly, as enterprises brought their whole panoply of capabilities, now free of the bizarre constraints of central planning, into full play. This has emphatically not happened. So in order to understand why it remains so difficult to contest markets in Russia, one needs to look beyond the Soviet legacy, to the nature of the Russian economy-in-transition itself.

The following elements seem to be of critical importance here:

— Especially in the early period of transition, enterprise managers continued to orient their strategies mainly to output—as a way of maintaining employment—rather than to profits. This put a premium on the preservation of existing, i.e. Soviet, supply patterns. Some enterprises even offered price incentives for the maintenance of traditional links, which made new entry particularly difficult.

—This orientation was reinforced by more subtle, 'mind-set' factors, which have been described as follows:

There were additional barriers associated with the distinctive corporate ethic . . . To expand their field of operations, to enter new markets, to 'take bread from their neighbor' was an infringement of the unspoken norms of their mutual relations and could lead to a sharp deterioration in the 'offender's' relations with his colleagues. (Starodubrovskaya, 1994, p. 6)

— Politicians, and particularly local politicians, continue to view the issues of exit from, and entry into, given markets, as coming within the range of their prerogatives. In regions dominated by elements of the old Communist Party *nomenklatura*, politicians and industrial leaders often work together very closely, to maintain general levels of economic activity and employment, but also to use established monopoly positions as a basis for personal enrichment and the raising of public revenue. This can result in a quite heavy regional segmentation of markets (Dyker, 1993). Once again, elements of continuity with the old Soviet system can be clearly discerned.

Previously, under the administrative-command system, markets were divided into fragments on the instructions of Gosplan and Gossnab—the fragmentation was along the lines of division between ministries and only in a few cases according to the territorial principle . . . Now practically everywhere there is a trend towards regional segmentation of markets, which of course impedes the development of competition on a national scale. (Capelik, 1994, p. 19)

— Mafia elements play the same game as the politicians, though their goals are, of course, limited to personal enrichment. Protection racketeering, for instance, seems to be almost universal in the restaurant business. The implications for free entry hardly need spelling out. Mafia activity is concentrated on retail sectors. It is not clear how active organized gangsters are in the building industry.

THE CENTRAL ROLE OF LOBBYING   Of all the characteristic features of democratic politics, lobbying has, perhaps, taken root most rapidly and deeply in post-Soviet Russia. But the Russian style of lobbying owes at least as much to the old Soviet 'market in bureaucratic approvals' (*ekonomika soglasovanii*— see Naishul', 1991) as to the traditions of Westminster or Capitol Hill.

Enterprise directors are well organized for lobbying. The various kinds of combines which have arisen out of the previous administrative structures maintain the organizational and personal links between enterprise directors which were formed under the old system. Usually they are headed by people who held quite high positions in the former administrative hierarchy, which of course facilitates the task of defending the interests of enterprises. The traditions of corporatism, so characteristic of the administrative-command system, the close and long established links between the enterprise directors and the political elite, make it easier to form new combines, including those with a political purpose. (Starodubrovskaya, 1994, p. 7)

Is Russian-style lobbying an effect, or a source, of monopoly power? In the case of the Russian aluminum industry, heavily cartelized under the umbrella of the 'Aluminum' joint-stock company, and able, through its political muscle, to gain blanket exemption from export duties from the Russian president himself (Dyker, 1994, p. 50), the answer is clear: an effect. In this case lobbying is used by an existing monopoly to ensure that its super-profits are not creamed off by the state. But lobbying is often targeted at creating the monopoly advantage in the first place. A good example comes from the area of commodity exchanges, one of the earliest market forms to develop after the collapse of central planning.

By spring 1991 the commodity exchange business in Moscow was dominated by the *Russian Commodity Exchange* (RTSB) and the *Moscow Commodity Exchange* (MTB), which were competing fiercely. The RTSB's reaction to this situation was to lobby the Russian parliament to grant it a monopoly of commodity exchange business. The parliament in the event refused. RTSB then tried to persuade MTB into a merger, but that ploy failed too. The story illustrates graphically the importance of lobbying in *building* monopoly positions. It also demonstrates that lobbying does not always work (see *Rossiiskaya Ekonomika . . .* , section 5.2). But the Russian economy is one in which licensing of one kind or another is absolutely pervasive. Under the regulation on the licensing of economic activity adopted in June 1993, regional authorities have the power to create regional monopolies by granting single licenses (Capelik, 1994, p. 22). Against this legislative background, the scope for lobbying against new entry is obviously extensive. The success rate of such lobbying seems, on the basis of casual empiricism, to be fairly high.

Natural monopoly in Russia

When we survey the Russian industrial scene as a whole, we are struck by how unique many of the monopoly and competition problems are. When we turn to the issue of natural monopolies, we seem to be on much more familiar ground, though even here we must be prepared for 'local color'. We pick out three key case-studies here: fuel and energy, alcohol, and agricultural procurement. The first can be taken as an example of natural monopoly on account of economies of scale and indivisibilities; the second of natural monopoly on account of external diseconomies; and the third, most controversially, of 'natural' monopoly on account of the peculiarities of the Soviet/Russian background.

The fuel/energy complex

Since the break-up of the Soviet Union, the Russian oil industry has fragmented, largely along regional lines. While the different Russian oil companies certainly cooperate for certain purposes, they do not appear to run a cartel as such. The pattern in the Russian gas industry has been quite different. Here Gazprom, the successor organization to the old gas ministry, retains a substantial degree of operational control over the entire Russian gas business, and surely qualifies as a classical monopolist. But it is not a 'nationalized industry' in the British sense. Rather it comes into that category—all too predominant in Russia—of 'spontaneously privatized' industry, where the old managing elites have largely arrogated to themselves effective ownership rights. No evidence has come to hand of Gazprom's using its monopoly position to extract better prices for gas from the government (fuel prices are, of course, state-controlled). But its attempts to restrict foreign investment to purely marginal developments in the Russian gas industry reflect a degree of countervailing power and political muscle that would not be available to, say, an individual oil company which must constantly look over its shoulder to see what other companies are doing.

The privatization of RAO EES (Russian Joint-Stock Company Unified Electricity System) also leaves a number of critical questions relating to monopoly policy unanswered. Shares in the company, which employs 1.2 million people and unites 72 independent oil companies representing the main elements in the Russian electricity grid, went on sale in 1994. The relationship between RAO EES and its subsidiaries remains unclear. How can they all be joint-stock companies? What powers will regional governments have over local companies? What is clear from the mode of privatization of RAO EES is that the Russian government is aiming to exercise 'public interest' control in two ways—through public holdings of shares, and through price control. The thinking behind this approach must be something like the following: in the context of widespread spontaneous/*nomenklatura* privatization of natural monopolies, it is better to privatize the monopoly intact, and explicitly, and then introduce explicit forms of government restriction on the operational freedom of the privatized company.

Another possible approach to the natural monopoly problem in sectors like electricity and gas would be to seek to separate off ownership of the network from the merchant function. This makes good analytical sense, but has a rather mixed track record in the West. In the UK, the recently privatized gas industry has not so far generated much competitive pressure. In principle, independent suppliers of gas should be able to use the British Gas transmission network, but so far the terms on which this has been offered to them have been unattractive, in spite of regulation by Ofgas. The UK electricity industry provides a more hopeful outlook: in this case the generation and distribution components of the business were privatized separately. Electricity generation *is* subject to competition (*pace* any reservations there may be about the 'dash for gas' form of generation) and regulation focuses upon the transmission network, which constitutes a natural monopoly. The lesson appears to be that even if there is an industry which is a natural monopoly, some parts of it may be open to competition, and regulatory activity should be aimed at ensuring that the benefits of feasible competition are obtained.

The alcohol industry

Mikhail Gorbachev's ill-fated anti-alcohol campaign of the mid-1980s had only a marginal effect on the problem of alcohol abuse in Russia, but it did result in a mushrooming of illicit distilling. After the break-up of the Soviet Union, and substantial, if erratic, deregulation of retail trade, the sale of alcohol went through a process of dramatic pluralization. By 1992-3 a large proportion of total turnover in alcoholic drinks was being vended by private individuals at pavement stalls. High-quality imported brands were generally available at a price, but the provenance of much of what was being sold was dubious, and there were widespread suspicions of adulteration. Then in June 1993 President Yeltsin issued a decree 'On re-establishing a state monopoly over the production, storage and wholesale and retail sale of alcoholic beverages'. A corresponding law was adopted by the Russian Supreme Soviet in the following month, and the government adopted a follow-up resolution on 23 April 1994. The new legal framework for the trade in alcohol does not set up a physical state monopoly in the style of the French tobacco monopoly. Rather it seeks to introduce a strict licensing system.

It is obviously too early to say whether this piece of legislation is going to improve the health of the Russian people. But a number of Russian monopoly experts have expressed considerable skepticism as to the true motivation behind the measure:

> These decisions will scarcely boost budget revenue very much, but they will do considerable harm to consumers. Strict regulation of enterprises in the alcohol business, licensing of their operations and other restrictions will make it harder for new agents to enter these markets and will retard the scientific-technical development of the sector, perpetuating the low level of efficiency characteristic of a few very large enterprises using obsolete production technology. These acts appear to be the result of strong pressure from the producers and wholesalers of alcohol, who are traditionally powerful in Russia. (Capelik, 1994, p. 22)

Be that as it may, there *is* a serious alcohol-related public health problem in Russia. In this case, having a monopolist (even a private one) controlling the market may be no bad thing. If this leads to higher prices and lower output, the traditional criticism of monopoly behavior, then this is hardly undesirable. Are there further advantages or disadvantages? Capelik points to the danger of perpetuating the low level of efficiency in the sector. One could, however, dispute whether it is desirable that scarce investment resources should be devoted to modernizing an industry which feeds the alcohol problem in Russia. In an economy with excess labor and a shortage of capital this would not seem to be the right way to improve the allocation of scarce resources.

Although Capelik argues that the state budget would not benefit by much, it is better that any monopoly rents should end up there than in the hands of private individuals. This suggests that licenses should be sold rather than given away, in the manner of a franchise. In principle, given enough bidders, any monopoly profits would be bid away and end up in the hands of the state, and the winning bidder would then act as a monopoly producer, with an incentive to monitor the market to ensure that its monopoly rights were not infringed. A model of this type comes from the UK, in the form of bidding for franchises to run regional television companies. The contract is awarded to the highest bidder in each region, subject to a quality threshold, with the Treasury receiving an annual payment from the franchisee. The quality threshold could also be applied in the Russian case, and it would be easier to monitor in the case of alcohol.

Likely problems with this proposal are a lack of bidders (even in the UK there was only a single bid for some of the TV franchises) and the possibility of criminal involvement. However, even with a single bidder there could be some benefits both to the Russian budget and to the health of the Russian consumer.

Agricultural procurement

The joint-stock company Rosskhleboprodukt, which has the status of a 'federal contract corporation' and is, as far as can be ascertained, 100 per cent state-owned, exercises effective control over the bulk of trade in grain, flour, pasta and similar products in Russia. It is able to do this partly because it is used as a channel for state subsidization of agriculture, but most importantly because it controls the great bulk of storage capacity for this kind of product. Thus monopolized structures created by the state on the wreckage of the old supply and disposal system continue to operate and distort the functioning of the wholesale market (Starodubrovskaya, 1994, p. 13). Note that Rosskhleboprodukt is a monopsonist (single seller) as well as a monopolist.

Here the 'natural' monopoly is in fact an extremely unnatural one, which can be expected, all other things being equal, to fade over time, as the transition process develops. Two policy problems arise: how to establish an interim scheme of regulation that will prevent Rosskhleboprodukt from exploiting its unnatural monopoly; and how to ensure that the unnatural monopoly does not survive any longer than is absolutely necessary. The second problem is essentially a political one, and can be subsumed under the general discussion in the succeeding sections of the 'integrity' of the government as regulatory guardian. The first is a more technical question, but one on which Western case-law obviously sheds little direct light. It may, nevertheless, be useful to consider the possibility of applying some of the Western experience of regulating monopolists/monopsonists to the Rosskhleboprodukt case.

Unfortunately, Europe cannot, by any stretch of the imagination, be said to provide an efficient model of agricultural production and distribution. In the US also, the system of agricultural subsidy and regulation is one based heavily on political lobbying. The omens are not good, therefore, for an efficient, decentralized system of agricultural procurement. In addition to political difficulties, a major monopoly element is the ownership of limited storage capacity and, perhaps to a lesser extent, of the means of transportation. This is analogous to problems with the deregulation of transport in the West: US airline deregulation did not result in a competitive market largely because of the advantages some airlines had from ownership of landing rights at important 'hub' airports. In the UK, competition in bus transport was hindered by the incumbent's advantage in having a network of city-center bus stations.

It may be helpful once again to distinguish the monopoly elements from the (potentially) competitive ones. The former could be retained in state hands, or franchised (and subject to regulation to ensure fair access), while the latter could be *made* competitive. The key, therefore, is equal access to storage and transport facilities. If the latter are potentially competitive, then the regulatory issue is in ensuring fair access to storage facilities (in a similar way to the important issue in telecoms regulation: access to the transmission network at fair prices to all). This also has the advantage of economizing on regulatory resources; it is unlikely that the regulatory authorities will be able to deal with all the regulatory issues, and thus focusing upon the most important ones is essential.

Lessons from Western Experience

Is Western experience useful?

Can the experience of Western economies with regard to competition be applied to the Russian Federation? It has been argued, both here and elsewhere, that it is critically important to take the particular features of the Russian experience into account. What does this mean in concrete terms? What are the main characteristics of monopoly, competition and competition policy in the West, and can they be adopted or adapted?

THE EXTENT AND CHARACTERISTICS OF MONOPOLY The quotations at the start of this paper show that some measures of monopoly power do not reveal much difference between Russia and, say, the USA in terms of industrial concentration. However, these measures of concentration do not capture well the *characteristics* of monopoly power, which are very different in the West from what they are in Russia. In fact, it is perhaps hard to recognize many of the features of Western monopoly in much of Russian industry. First, the Russian firm's monopoly position has traditionally been protected by law and has thus been unchallenged and unchallengeable. As we have seen, the peculiar features of the Russian transition process have tended to a great extent to preserve this situation. In contrast, in the West, most 'monopolists' do face a degree of competition, in the sense that they do have to take some account of other firms and other *potential* firms.

Western firms have to take *action* to erect or maintain barriers to entry to their industry. Sometimes this will mean the firm's investing in technology which improves the product from the point of view of consumers (e.g. Xerox photocopiers). Of course, this may not be incorporated into new products: a monopolist may patent a new product or process in order to deny it to competitors rather than to use it itself. New technology may bring about the demise of the monopolist if it proves impossible to control invention, innovation or diffusion. A good example is IBM and its introduction of the personal computer; it proved unable to withstand the onslaught of very many, smaller and more nimble competitors, even though it pioneered the technology.

The point of these examples is to show that Western monopolists are not necessarily sleeping giants, but are compelled actively to protect their position—even though this activity may not always be socially beneficial. Furthermore, it is difficult to maintain a monopoly forever, even without government intervention. By contrast, in the former USSR, firms did not have to worry about even the *threat* of competition, nor about government intervention, for the government colluded in its monopoly position. In some ways this might have been an advantage: the firm did not have to engage in socially wasteful activities such as advertising or 'defensive' patenting. However, on balance it appears that the disadvantages significantly outweighed the advantages.

A further contrast is apparent from the above description: although a Western monopolist might raise its price and cut output, it has some incentive to act as a reasonably *efficient* monopolist. That is, given the level of its output, it uses the right quantities of inputs; it is technically efficient if not allocatively so. Of course this may be tempered by the preferences of management for goals other than profit, but such preferences are limited by the external vigilance of shareholders. Soviet firms had much weaker incentives to be technically efficient, with a control system more akin to British nationalized industries, for example. Furthermore, in the former Soviet Union, firms were not free to set prices, and therefore could not raise them to take advantage of a captive consumer.

These contrasting conditions are highlighted if we ask where the monopoly rents end up. In the West, higher profits drive up the share price, so that the real beneficiaries are those who hold shares when the monopoly is created. Another group which may benefit are employees. They are in a reasonably powerful bargaining position where monopoly rents exist, and may be able to stake a claim to part of them. A good example of this is US airlines prior to deregulation in 1977, where even typists could earn a significantly higher salary than someone doing the same job elsewhere (see Bailey et al., 1985). Deregulation of the airlines led to bankruptcies, redundancies and lower salaries as the monopoly rents (arising out of regulation) disappeared. In Russia it is clear that workers do not on the whole benefit from any kind of monopoly rent, with poor working conditions and low pay an almost universal feature. Where, then, are the monopoly rents? Traditionally, they did not exist in a financial form, as they do in the West, because of strict control of prices. The contemporary situation is more complex. There is a good deal of successful rent-seeking in the Russian transition economy (including by Siberian gas workers), but rents still exist mainly in the form of inefficiency, chiefly overmanning, which would not be tolerated in competitive conditions.

THE DEFINITION OF COMPETITION Competition is, in some sense, one of the goals of restructuring; yet it is difficult to define it precisely in a way which is useful for policy matters. There are a number of ways of defining competition in theory:

— A starting-point is the textbook model of perfect competition, which is useful as an analytical device but not as the basis of a workable competition policy (see Bienaymé, 1993 and the comments by Williamson in the same volume). This theory rests upon a number of unrealistic assumptions and is static in nature. Competition is defined simply in terms of market structure alone: it is a market with a large number of sellers. Conduct follows from the structure of the market.

— An alternative to this is the 'Austrian' view, which sees competition very much in a dynamic framework, as opposed to the static model of perfect competition. Market structure is the *result* of the competitive process and monopoly is the reward for winning. The original European Community may have been influenced by this view: it foresaw competition arising between 'national champions' of Europe, the USA and Japan, with the result that the Treaty of Rome did not include any prohibitions on merger activity (an omission later remedied).

— The theory of contestable markets also challenges the idea that large numbers of firms are necessary for a market to work well. As long as there are low barriers to entry (and exit), it argues, then firms (even monopolists) are vulnerable to *potential* competition—'hit and run' attacks by competitors. This view leads to the conclusion that the focus should be on barriers to entry and exit, which might inhibit the competitive process. Where these exist, they should be removed, but otherwise the market should be allowed to work unhindered.

— A useful definition, particularly in the present context, is one highlighted by Williamson (1993): ' . . . a competitive firm is one that is *chosen* by many buyers' (emphasis added). Buyers have a choice, and it is this which disciplines sellers to act in ways which are in the consumers' interests. This aspect of competition was clearly absent in the former Soviet Union, and to a great extent still is in Russia. Williamson goes on to argue that competition is necessary (in the transition economies) ' . . . if markets are to create incentives to act in a socially beneficial way'.

Despite these differences of viewpoint, competition is *generally* seen as beneficial. Its particular benefits are ensuring an efficient allocation of resources, resulting in low prices for consumers, and also protecting freedom by avoiding concentrations of economic power (Jacquemin and de Jong, 1977). Whether resource allocation is efficient under competition depends upon factors such as returns to scale, externalities and research and development activities, but these are not seen as invalidating the general proposition. Protecting freedom means protecting firms from other firms, as well as protecting consumers, and this is reflected in French and German competition law, where the concept of 'dependence' is recognized. In the EC generally, small and medium-sized enterprises (SMEs) receive certain advantages under competition law because of their importance in avoiding concentration.

The benefits of competition are explicitly recognized in the policies of the USA and Germany, but France and the UK take a more cautious line. In the latter two countries competition is viewed as being broadly neutral: it may benefit the consumer or it may not, depending upon the circumstances. In the UK the 'public interest' is what matters. What that means in practice is that the competition authorities have discretion in deciding upon individual cases, and each is considered on its merits.

COMPETITION POLICY The benefits of competition are often clearer when we examine the alternative—some form of monopoly power. The disadvantages of monopoly are well known and documented, and competition policy is perhaps more easily defined by what is forbidden rather than what is encouraged.

In practical terms, competition policy usually has three components:

— Restrictions upon cartels or agreements between firms. For example, Article 85 of the Treaty of Rome prohibits ' . . . all agreements between undertakings . . . which may affect trade between member-States and which have as their object or effect the prevention, restriction or distortion of competition'. It goes on to list some practices which are expressly forbidden, such as fixing prices, restrictions on output and market sharing.

— Restrictions or prohibition of the abuse of a monopoly position. Article 86 of the Treaty of Rome prohibits ' . . . any abuse . . . of a dominant position within the common market or in a substantial part of it . . . in so far as it may affect trade between member-States.' Again, some particular practices are mentioned, such as imposing unfair trading conditions, or limiting production or technical development.

— Restrictions upon merger activity. As mentioned earlier, the European Union did not originally have any control over mergers, but this was changed by the adoption of the 1989 Merger Regulation. This prohibits mergers which create or strengthen a dominant position, and which would in turn inhibit competition.

Although these three aspects of competition policy have been illustrated by reference to European policy, similar illustrations could have been taken from individual countries' policies, with some differences of emphasis and interpretation. For example, the US Sherman Anti-Trust Act makes it illegal ' . . . to monopolize or to attempt to monopolize.' With the help of these three concepts, we can explore important themes of competition policy and investigate their relevance for the Russian Federation. We examine a number of key questions in turn.

Market structure or market conduct?

Is evidence about market structure all that is required to draw conclusions about monopoly power and abuse thereof? The answer provided by many countries' competition policies is that structure alone is not enough to prove abuse. The section of Article 86 cited above shows that as far as the EU is concerned it is abuse of dominance that matters, not dominance itself. In Britain, the competition authorities examine 'the public interest' (which is left undefined and hence can be widely interpreted) before deciding upon an issue. Thus the 'rule of reason' prevails, rather than there being a *per se* assumption of wrongdoing.

However, these matters are not entirely clear-cut. The European Court of Justice has ruled that a large market share alone can be construed as evidence

of dominance of the given market, i.e. that market structure is not entirely irrelevant as far as competition policy is concerned. Furthermore, the market
shares of other firms are also relevant—for example, a firm with 50 per cent of
the market may be dominant if no other firm has more than 10 per cent, but
not if another firm has 30 per cent.

One legacy of the USSR, as we have seen, is a particular market structure,
in which 'everyone is a monopolist'. Clearly, in this situation, competition policy in Russia cannot be based upon market structure alone, for on that basis we
would rapidly come to the conclusion that everyone is capable of abusing a
monopoly position. This would overwhelm any competition agency, and policy
measures would be likely to be indiscriminate and ineffective. In such a situation firms or industries should be dealt with on the basis of anti-competitive
conduct, ideally taking the worst abuses first. Being a large firm, or having a
large market share, should not be a sufficient condition for regulatory action.

DOES DOMINANCE HAVE TO BE PROVED BEFORE REGULATORY ACTION HAS TO
BE TAKEN? Is dominance a necessary condition for regulatory action to be
triggered? And following from this, should monopolies then be regulated, broken up, or is the best policy to prevent their occurring in the first place? Dominance may be defined as 'the ability to act substantially independently of
competitors' (DTI, 1992). Similar definitions appear in European regulations
and in the competition policies of France, Germany and the United States.
This accords with the idea of the competitive firm contained in the extract
from Williamson quoted earlier, in which firms have to compete to be chosen
by their customers.

According to Article 86 of the Treaty of Rome it is abuse *of a dominant position* that is prohibited, and this implies that the behavior in question could
not occur in the absence of dominance. Dominance is therefore a necessary
condition for regulation to occur. However, there are examples of dominant
firms' being penalized for behavior which could be pursued by a non-dominant firm, and which would then go unpunished. An example quoted by Fishwick (1993) is the *Michelin Nederland* case, where the company was fined for
a price discount scheme (based on a given dealer's annual sales) which restricted dealers' freedom to choose amongst rival suppliers. However, there is
no reason why such a scheme could not be operated by a non-dominant firm
intent on raising its market share.

In contrast to the position set out in the Treaty of Rome, no proof of dominance is required in the UK (Competition Act 1980) before action can be

taken. The UK authorities have argued (DTI, 1992, quoted in Fishwick, 1993) that oligopolistic conditions might in themselves lead to anti-competitive practices which would require the regulatory authorities' attention.

In the Russian context the important aspect of dominance is that it can apply to competitors and suppliers as well as to the ultimate customer. It may be argued that, in the short term, the most important aspect of competition in the Russian Federation is not the freedom of consumers to choose between different products, but rather that of firms to choose their suppliers. At present this is clearly not the case. This suggests that competition policy should focus on regulating situations where firms are in a position to exploit their suppliers or customers (other firms), and on encouraging new firms to enter the market, thereby offering a choice of suppliers.

WHAT FORM OF REGULATION OF MONOPOLY FIRMS IS REQUIRED? The United States provides the most powerful examples of the control of monopoly, where dominant firms have been broken up by the regulators to achieve a more competitive market structure. In Europe, by contrast, this rarely occurs and other means of regulation have to be used. Two interesting questions arise here: should regulation be permanent or temporary; and should price regulation be an element of it?

Examples of both permanent and temporary regulation can be found in the UK. It is envisaged that the newly privatized water industry will face permanent regulation because it is in the nature of being a natural monopoly (owing to the pipeline networks in place). However, even in this case some competitive features can be exploited, through the idea of yardstick competition. The water industry is divided into regional monopolies, each of whose prices are regulated. However, the price regulation depends not only upon the company's own costs, but on the costs of others as well. Companies therefore have an incentive to keep costs to a minimum (though it is permitted for some cost increases to be passed through directly to customers' bills). British Telecom is also regulated with regard to its price, but this is expected to last only until the gradual emergence of competition.

Where regulation exists, it usually takes one of two forms: rate of return regulation (familiar from US utility regulation) or price cap regulation (as applied using the RPI (retail price index) –X formula in the UK). Both of these formulae have been definitively analyzed theoretically, and there is some presumption in favor of price capping: it still gives firms some incentive to reduce costs, it focuses on what is important to the consumer, and it may be less susceptible to 'regulatory capture' since it is more transparent.

Another useful illustration of price control is the case of the British nationalized industries during the Conservative government of 1970–4, since it has some parallels with the Russian situation. As part of its anti-inflation policy, the government artificially restrained the prices of the nationalized industries (as well as of private ones) in order to try to change expectations about future price increases and hence influence the climate of wage bargaining. Whatever the success of the policy regarding general inflation, it had two other important consequences: it constrained *relative* price movements and it generated large financial deficits for the industries themselves.

From this brief outline, a number of lessons for Russian policy would appear to follow. First, regulation is itself anti-competitive; it is not a substitute for competition. As a number of commentators have pointed out, price regulation in Russia actually discourages competitors from entering the market. If market entry is influenced by an excess of price over cost, then price control is undesirable. If regulation is necessary, then it should be viewed as temporary and should aim at encouraging competition. There is an important difference between (pro-) competition policy and monopoly (regulation) policy and the former is better than the latter.

Second, price control has important implications for regulatory capture, which is surely an important aspect of the current Russian political situation. Price control increases the financial deficit of an industry and therefore increases the industry's dependence upon the state (this assumes, reasonably, that output prices are more strictly controlled than input prices). Price control therefore encourages political lobbying, which attempts to procure special advantages for the lobbyist and thus reinforces the industry or market structure. Perhaps even more important, it reinforces the existing *political* structure. Therefore there may be an advantage in abandoning generalized price control even if demonopolization has not occurred. This argument ignores the role of price control in combating inflation, but it does show that there may be a substantial cost to using it.

If price regulation is undesirable, then what kind of regulation should be enforced? From the previous arguments it follows that any regulation should aim to encourage competition. Examples of particular policies would be the elimination of barriers to entry, prohibition of onerous trading conditions such as refusal to supply, and prohibition of agreements which restrict competition, such as exclusive supply relationships.

AN EFFICIENCY DEFENSE? A question which arises at this point is whether there should be an 'efficiency' defense against regulation, to wit that the abuse of monopoly power or restrictive agreement actually benefits the competitive process and, ultimately, consumers. In the US there is no efficiency defense of cartel agreements between firms, but one can find examples in Europe. Under West German law, cartel agreements may be sanctioned if they improve the competitive process or increase the efficiency of the firms concerned. In the UK restrictive practices must be registered, but no action is taken if they are deemed to be in the public interest. In the EU there are 'block exemptions' for certain types of agreement (e.g. those relating to R&D), where it is felt that the agreement promotes economic progress. However, the agreement must not have the effect of eliminating competition, and it must be *indispensable* to the achievement of progress.

In Russia, the high degree of integration of firms implies less need for formal agreements, since the relevant linkages will be internal to the enterprise. It might therefore be safe to follow American practice and rule out the efficiency defense altogether, or to circumscribe its use narrowly. Any agreements that could be made are more likely to hinder competition than enhance it, so a blanket ban might not have serious economic costs.

INTERNATIONAL COMPETITION International competition is sometimes seen as a substitute for, or complement to, domestic competition. Where an economy is open, without significant trade barriers or an undervalued exchange rate, this is indisputable, and it makes little sense to draw conclusions about the extent of competition by looking solely at the degree of concentration among domestic firms. In the Russian case however, there remain significant barriers to the entry of foreign competition.

Administrative and political barriers apart, a major problem is the structure of domestic industry, which is vertically integrated to a high degree. We have already noted the existence of dwarf-workshops producing such mundane items as nuts and bolts. The important implication of this is that any foreign entrant will also have to be vertically integrated, for there will be few or no suppliers of vital intermediate components. This might discourage entry and therefore protect the domestic industry.

There is a further implication to the argument. If a foreign firm were to enter, it might wipe out the whole of the domestic industry, including the part that makes the nuts and bolts. If the domestic industry had not been so vertically integrated, part of it might have survived as a supplier or customer of the foreign entrant. Kay has highlighted this as one of the potential costs of monopoly, and provides examples from the UK. A major cost of monopoly can therefore be the long-term decline and eventual elimination from the market of the monopoly itself.

This suggests that vertical de-integration should be part of Russian competition policy, insofar as this is feasible (where the dwarf-workshop is geographically separate, for example). The economic relationship between the dwarf-workshop and its former owner would become based upon market exchange rather than command procedures. In the short run, transactions would continue between the two organizations, but each would be free to find alternative or additional customers and suppliers. Insofar as the products of these dwarf-workshops are standard items, one would be unlikely to encounter the sorts of moral hazard problems related to market transactions identified by Williamson (1975), because it is easy to define contracts for basic components like nuts and bolts in a very precise manner.

International competition may also be particularly important where there is no effective capital market to channel funds into suitable investment projects (Estrin and Cave, 1993a). In this case, domestic competition to incumbent firms is unlikely to be feasible, and foreign firms with access to their own capital markets would have to fulfill this role. But again there are barriers: foreign exchange controls and restrictions upon the ability to repatriate profits, and general uncertainty about regulations and taxation, are examples which are particularly relevant to Russia. Thus to be effective competition policy must be backed up by appropriate general economic policies.

MERGERS POLICY A merger is an alternative to an agreement or cartel arrangement between firms. Control of such agreements is likely to be weakened if there are no restrictions upon mergers. Most Western countries, including the EC/EU since 1989, have some sort of mergers policy. The EC Merger Regulation prohibits mergers which create or strengthen a dominant position, as a result of which effective competition would be significantly impeded. The German law is similar and in the UK there is a public interest criterion which is the same as that applied to monopolies. In the UK there is a presumption in favor of merger unless it is found to be against the public interest (the minister cannot prohibit the merger without an unfavorable report from the Monopolies and Mergers Commission, for example).

It is recognized that, in many cases, mergers can actually strengthen competition if they result in larger competitors for a dominant firm. This is recognized in German law (Katzenbach, 1990), in several cases investigated by the UK Monopolies and Mergers Commission, and by the EU, where SMEs are exempt from a number of aspects of competition policy. It seems likely that this sort of competition should be encouraged in Russia in order to challenge the incumbent monopolies. Competition policy should therefore have a market share threshold, with mergers below such a threshold not coming under scrutiny of the authorities. The main danger is of large companies merging in an attempt to preclude competition. This might occur particularly if a policy of vertical de-integration is pursued. Companies might try to replace the loss of one barrier to entry by another. We return to this issue later.

STATE AID With the increasing openness of markets there is greater emphasis upon the anti-competitive potential of state aid (which remains, of course, pervasive in Russia). A national government providing subsidies to its domestic industry has a similar effect to a tariff on imports insofar as it affects relative prices, and competition policy is increasingly taking account of this. Of course, a supranational agency, such as the GATT or the EU, is necessary to negotiate and enforce an appropriate competition policy here. The recent agreements concluded between the EU and the Czech Republic, Hungary and Poland envisage these countries adopting EU-type competition rules over a period of three to five years, which will include provisions relating to state aid. If Russia is to become more open and trade more with the West, then it is inevitable that it will eventually have to take account of such rules. The account of the Russian aluminum industry (below) illustrates this point.

Briefly, the EU position on state aid is that it is acceptable if it is compatible with the Community's objectives. This means that aid must not be given in order to maintain inefficiency, but it can be given for purposes such as raising productivity and competitiveness. In the future it is likely that such aid will be concentrated in the poorer regions of the Community, and will have stronger conditions attached, such as a time limit on the aid and an insistence on capacity reduction.

The problem of state aid is of a different order of magnitude in Russia, and is unlikely to disappear in the short term. It is a problem which goes beyond competition policy alone. We simply make the point here that competition policy should not place any constraints upon the speed with which state aids can be phased out. As we have already noted, price control is one policy which has the effect of increasing industries' deficits (and therefore the need for aid), as well as the intensity of lobbying.

Rules or discretion?

Comanor (1990) concludes that 'When competition policy is enforced through pre-determined rules, it has been far more effective'. Is this conclusion likely to hold for the Russian Federation as well? A related question con-

cerns the structure of the competition authority: should it have a judicial character, and should there be a separation of powers between investigator, judge
and jury?

Comanor reaches his conclusion by comparing different approaches. With
pre-determined rules, both the competition authority and firms know where
they stand and can act accordingly, usually in line with policy objectives.
Where discretion is favored, as in the UK, it is harder to predict the outcome
of any particular case, and firms do not know where they stand.

In the Russian case, this is as much a political as an economic problem.
There is no tradition of an independent judiciary, but there is a long history of
administrative decisions taken by unaccountable bodies. It is well known that
a market system needs a legal structure in order to work properly (for example, to enforce contracts), so that sooner or later Russia will have to have one
if it is to have an effective market system. The political imperative is therefore
to build up such an independent legal system, which would also oversee competition policy.

The lack of experience of competition policy also suggests that rules
should be as simple as possible to avoid the risk of misinterpretation (either
accidental or deliberate). These rules should be aimed at eliminating the undesirable practices which accompany monopoly power, such as price-fixing,
rather than monopoly itself. A judicial system is more likely to provide consistency than one like the British system, where individual decisions and occa-
sional reviews of the procedures are carried out by politicians. A rules-based
approach also seems preferable because its transparency lowers the risk of
regulatory capture by the industry. This is one of the major risks in Russia at
the present time, and therefore a policy which reduces its likelihood is to be
favored.

Summary

We may usefully summarize the lessons drawn from Western experience,
adapted for Russian circumstances, thus:

— Regulation can inhibit competition, but is required in cases of true natural monopolies, such as pipeline networks.
— General price control is undesirable as a component of competition policy (although it may be needed as part of an anti-inflation policy).
— Competition policy should focus on anti-competitive *practices* and not

on market structure. It should encourage competition (including new entry) as far as possible.

— International competition should be encouraged, and its impact upon domestic industry moderated through vertical de-integration.

— There should be a system of clear rules, giving little scope for discretion by ministers or officials.

— There should be transparency in the operation of the rules, which is best achieved by judicial backing of the competition policy.

CHAPTER THREE

International Experience and Monopoly Policy in Russia

Underlying weaknesses of monopoly policy in Russia

There has been much implied criticism of Russian monopoly and competition policies in the foregoing. It is now time to look at the whole gamut of anti-monopoly measures, and to try to systematize the critical points that emerge, as always looking at the issues against the specifically Russian background.

Management buy-outs and mergers

As we saw earlier, much of the privatization that has taken place in Russia has effectively taken the form of management/*nomenklatura* buy-out, often under the guise of employee buy-out. This is not necessarily and universally a bad thing in itself. But it does create problems in relation to monopoly and competition policy. We have already looked at the general, 'mind-set' dimension of this issue. Here we look at a more specific and more technical problem.

The process of privatization does not directly affect the degree of concentration of production and ownership ... It does, however, introduce the possibility of a reduction in concentration, as production units are hived off from enterprises. Equally, it may result in an increase in concentration through the formation of close financial links and the imposition of tight financial control. Given that large-scale privatization is implemented primarily through the transformation of state enterprises and associations into public joint-stock companies, anti-monopoly control over the

107

process of economic concentration resulting from the system of 'participation'—in effect, management buy-outs—takes on special importance . . . The record on the privatization of state enterprises shows that where enterprises are converted into joint-stock companies, there is no real change in the level of market concentration . . . At this stage the role of the Anti-Monopoly Committee is largely formal. Much more important is what happens after shares have actually gone into circulation. Unfortunately, the lack of any clear and unambiguous legislative mechanism for the regulation of mergers greatly complicates the work of the anti-monopoly agencies here. (Petrov, 1993, p. 20)

The problem is essentially a very simple one. Anti-monopoly scrutiny of privatization is understandably largely based on a 'snapshot' of industrial structure at the point of privatization. Petrov, himself an official of the Anti-Monopoly Committee, points up the importance of monitoring the *dynamic process* of privatization, as liberated enterprises begin to exercise their freedom to restructure. The problem of merger control is one we associate with advanced industrial countries. The paradox of the Russian situation is that, because of the concentration of financial power among members of the old elites, there is a real danger of a kind of politically-based cartelization of whole sections of the economy. The new privatization program adopted on 24 December 1993 seeks to attack the problem by strengthening safeguards against abuse of the position of dominant, minority shareholder, and by imposing restrictions on the activities of holding companies. Interlocking shareholding is now forbidden, as is the activity of unregistered financial-industrial groups ('Privatizatsiya: novyi etap', 1994).

Evidence from the UK privatization process suggests that it is best to decide upon ownership and market structure *simultaneously*. This can only be done at the moment of privatization (or, at the very least, it is easier to do it at this time). The UK electricity industry provides an example of break-up at the time of privatization, with generation being split off from distribution, and distribution itself being separated off into the national grid and the regional companies. In contrast, the gas industry was privatized in one piece, without any separation. There is much greater evidence of competition in the former industry than in the latter.

PRICE AND PROFIT CONTROL Restriction of freedom in relation to price formation and profit-making has, as we have seen, been a pervasive element in Russian anti-monopoly policy. It is an element which has attracted fierce criticism from Russian monopoly experts. Price control has proved to be ineffectual, even pernicious, on two counts. First, in conditions of general inflation, the price organs experience great difficulties in checking the justification for raising prices.

> It proved impossible in practice to check the calculations for items of cost not directly related to the particular kind of product. In a number of cases the relevant cost estimates are not available and price specialists have to set an arbitrary rate of growth in relation to the actual level in the preceding period. (Capelik, 1994, p. 28, citing experience in Yaroslavl province.)

In practice, adjustment of controlled prices has often been made with a considerable lag, so that firms on the monopoly register have actually been penalized. This has exacerbated the second big problem with price control as a weapon of anti-monopoly policy: it reinforces barriers to entry or, more correctly, reduces the incentive to overcome barriers to entry. If we are right in pin-pointing barriers to entry as the key competition problem in Russia, then we must roundly condemn the reliance on price control of Russian anti-monopoly policy. We must add that in attempting to solve the problem, the Russian authorities have tended to make things worse rather than better.

> It was in response to the administrative problems connected with price control in the given context that profit control was introduced as a major tool of anti-monopoly policy in mid-1992. The results were disastrous. A whole series of defects appeared, which were familiar from Western regulation theory and were confirmed in Russian practice. First, enterprises seek to magnify costs as much as possible, reducing profit to conform to the maximum permitted rate of profitability. In Russia this is aggravated by the fact that profit in relation to prime cost is used as the indicator to be regulated, rather than the rate of return on capital, as in other countries. The use of this simplified indicator is partly explained by the fact that the value of fixed capital still remains an unknown magnitude in Russia. But what happens as a result? Enterprises are given an increased incentive to raise expenditure, as current costs determine not only the numerator, as in the West, but also the denominator in the formula for calculating profitability . . . It is possible to reduce production, lower the quality of output or even simply refuse to produce regulated products . . . There are numerous ways of deliberately reducing the actual level of profitability. For example, enterprises ask their customers to delay payment if they are in danger of exceeding the maximum profitability. As a result, the rate of profit is brought within

the established limits and the payments for the output can be forwarded the following month. (Capelik, 1994, pp. 29-30)

These tricks may indeed be familiar from Western regulation theory. But
the alacrity with which Russian managers adopt them reflects the decades of
experience which most of those managers had, under the old Soviet system, of
simulating plan fulfillment, cooking the books, and generally improving the
recorded performance of the enterprise while damaging the public interest.
The moral must be that monopoly and competition policy, or indeed any other
element of economic regulation, must in contemporary Russian conditions be
based on the simplest and most transparent instruments. That will give the
best guarantees against manipulation by wily managers. It is in any case all
that the hard-pressed Russian civil service can cope with.

The international dimension

In the West, people are becoming accustomed to the notion that monopoly
and competition policy must globalize as business itself globalizes. The European Commission is the main generator and implementer of competition policy for all the EU countries, and the new World Trade Organization (WTO),
which succeeded GATT on 1 January 1995, is likely to play a much more active role in this area than its predecessor. One of the policy areas which both
the European Commission and WTO are likely to be much concerned with is
the abuse of anti-dumping provisions, or the imposition of voluntary export
constraints, as a tactic for building international market-sharing agreements. It
would be surprising if Russia found itself exempted from this pattern of glob-
alization of competition issues, just at a time when it is attempting to integrate
into the global economy. The history of the aluminum industry over the past
two or three years demonstrates emphatically that there has, indeed, been no
such exemption.
    As we saw earlier, the Russian aluminum industry is a powerful operator
on the domestic scene, capable of lobbying and pressuring the president himself. Internationally, the industry has made its mark through its exporting ex-
ploits since the collapse of the Soviet Union. The new pressure to earn hard
currency, and the collapse of domestic military demand for aluminum, have
given the Russian aluminum industry every incentive to go on an export drive.
But with Russian aluminum exports increasing by a factor of ten since independence, and the price of aluminum on world markets falling from $1.29 a

pound in June 1988 to 55 cents a pound in 1993 (Davies, 1993), the world aluminum industry, and in particular the European one, which is primarily affected by Russian exports, could hardly fail to react.

The European aluminum industry started to put pressure on the European Commission to impose emergency trade restrictions on Russian aluminum exports at the beginning of 1993. In August of that year the Commission imposed a quota of 60,000 tons on Russian aluminum exporters (roughly the average annual level of exports to Europe before the collapse of the Soviet Union); the quota was to run from 7 August to 30 November 1993. Under pressure from the industry, restrictions were then extended until the end of February 1994. Because the EU quota did not cover unwrought aluminum imported into the EU for processing and then re-exported, it had little real effect on the flow of Russian aluminum exports to Western Europe. But it was effective in delivering a critical message to the Russian producers.

The latter, for their part, did not remain passive in the face of all this. In April 1993 they created an *International Aluminum Committee* (Intercomalum), based in St Petersburg, bringing together all the CIS producers. The most striking aspect of this development is that membership of the committee also includes *the main Western producers*. Broadly based international membership, it is claimed, will facilitate foreign investment, including investment in environmental clean-up, and help the industry to 'organize itself in a structured way' (Gooding, 1993).

In early 1994 a deal was finally struck in Brussels. Russia agreed to cut production of aluminum by 500,000 tons in 1994, and to hold this lower level throughout 1995, within the framework of a worldwide agreement to reduce output involving all the main Western producing countries. The West has additionally promised investment of up to $1.5bn in the Russian industry (Vladislavlev, 1994); the United States has sponsored an equity investment fund for capital-intensive industries in Russia which would target the aluminum industry. The fund aims to raise $250 million, with backing by an Overseas Private Investment Corporation guarantee ('Aluminum pact . . . ', 1994). Mr Vahid Fathi of Kemper Securities comments that the Brussels agreement 'has the appearance of a cartel' (Morse, 1994).

There are many unclear points about the agreement. Governments have agreed to seek to cut production, not to limit exports. Given the extent of the collapse of domestic Russian demand for the metal, it is not clear that the agreement imposes much of an effective restriction on the Russian industry. And since neither Eastern nor Western producers themselves have explicitly agreed to anything, there must be some doubt as to whether discipline will be maintained, especially within the Russian industry. The Western commitment to invest in the Russian industry is vague. If, finally, it is true that 'all cartels cheat in the end of the day' (Morse, 1994), one may be inclined to discount the whole deal fairly heavily. If, on the other hand, the agreement does hold, it may be no bad thing for the Russian economy at large, assuming the investment component takes off and the Russian aluminum industry is effectively restructured and cleaned up. But cartelization abroad inevitably reinforces cartelization at home, and it is significant that the first reaction of the Russian government to the initial imposition of the EC quota in mid-1993 was to cut back sharply the number of organizations licensed to export non-metals. This is surely an area where public policy, at national and global level, needs to be more transparent. The new WTO will be expressly empowered to settle international trade disputes. It may be able to develop that prerogative into a tribunal which would judge anti-dumping issues and global competition issues together, matching at the policy-making level the reality of the business world. If it is to do so, however, it will need the active support of the EU, and of the governments of all the major economic powers, including Russia.

Conclusion: Is Russian monopoly policy a public 'good' or a public 'bad'?

One of the themes that has run throughout this paper is the deep ambivalence of much of Russian anti-monopoly policy. It is a sociological fact that many of the individuals who staff the anti-monopoly committees are strongly committed to market transformation. It is equally indisputable that in many cases established industrial interests have been able effectively to hijack anti-monopoly policy, and use it as a basis for market-sharing, cartelization, and raising new barriers to entry. That the system is so vulnerable to 'regulatory capture' seems to be a function of two main factors. First, managers who cut their teeth under the Soviet system are past masters at the art of manipulation of regulation. Secondly, the system of regulation itself is hopelessly top-heavy, in a rather characteristically Soviet way.

It may not be going too far too suggest that the whole emphasis of Russian monopoly and competition policy has been wrong. In a sense, the very title 'anti-monopoly policy' tells the whole story. The fact is that, as Brown et al. (1993) demonstrate, monopoly as such is not the key problem in Russia. Rather the problem is barriers to entry, and the fact that so much of the Soviet legacy conspires to make markets uncontestable. We would propose the abolition of the Russian Anti-Monopoly Committee, and its replacement by a Pro-Competition Committee, which would, in addition to regulating natural monopolies in a fairly standard Western style, attack the problem of barriers to new entry in the Russian economy at its very root. That means becoming deeply involved in politics, and taking on the most powerful vested interests in the country, including regional interests. Such a radical approach is, needless to say, unlikely to be feasible under the present Russian government. Rather it seems very likely that current policy, in its concern to reassert government control over 'strategic' investment through the creation of 'financial-industrial groupings', will in practice reinforce the tendency to cartelization (Starkov, 1994). But it is probable that economic pressures will push the Russian government back to a more radical policy strategy in 1995 or 1996. Pro-competition policy should be a central element of such a strategy.

References for Part 2

'Aluminum pact includes US sponsorship of fund', Reuter, 31 January 1994.

Bailey, E.E., D.R. Graham and D.P. Kaplan (1985), *Deregulating the Airlines: an Economic Analysis*, MIT Press, Cambridge, MA.

Bienaymé, A. (1993), 'Competition in theory and in the evolving real world,' in Saunders, *The Role of Competition*, London.

Brown, Annette N., Barry W. Ickes, and Randi Ryterman (1993), 'The Myth of Monopoly: a New View of Industrial Structure in Russia,' working paper, August.

Capelik (Tsapelik), Vladimir E. (1994), 'Should monopoly be regulated in Russia?' *Communist Economies and Economic Transformation*, vol. 6, no. 1, pp. 19-32.

Comanor, W.S., et al. (1990), *Competition Policy in Europe and North America: Economic Issues and Institutions*, Harwood Academic Publishers, New York and Melbourne.

Davies, J. (1993), 'Russian aluminium floods US market,' *Journal of Commerce*, 23 August.

Department of Trade and Industry (DTI) (1992), *Abuse of Market Power: a Consultative Document on Possible Legislative Options*. Cm. 2100, HMSO, London.

Dyker, David A. (1993), '*Nomenklatura* nationalism—the key to an understanding of the new East European politics?' paper presented to the conference Europe at La Trobe, La Trobe University, Melbourne, Australia, 5-9 July 1993.

—— (1994), 'Russian perceptions of economic security,' *Tokyo Club Papers*, No. 7, Tokyo Club Foundation for Global Studies, Tokyo, pp. 33-56.

Estrin, S., and M. Cave (1993), 'Introduction,' in Estrin and Cave (eds), *Competition and Competition Policy: a Comparative Analysis of Central and Eastern Europe*, Pinter, London.

Fishwick, F. (1993), *Making Sense of Competition Policy*, Kogan Page, London.

George, K., and A. Jacquemin (1990), 'Competition policy in the European Community,' in Comanor et al., *Competition Policy . . . .*

Gooding, K. (1993), 'CIS smelters marshall their defences,' *The Financial Times*, 15 April.

Jacquemin, A., and W. H. de Jong (1977), *European Industrial Organization*, Macmillan Press, London.

Katzenbach, E. (1990), 'Competition policy in West Germany: a comparison with the antitrust policy of the United States,' in Comanor et al., *Competition Policy* . . . .

Kay, J. (No date), *Competition Policy*. TSB Forum.

Morse, Laurie (1994), 'Aluminium shines for fund managers,' *The Financial Times*, 3 March, p. 29.

Naishul', V.A. (1991), *The Supreme and Last Stage of Socialism*, Centre for Research into Communist Economies, London.

'O sotsial'no-ekonomicheskom polozhenii Rossii v 1993 godu' (1994), *Ekonomika i Zhizn'*, No. 6, pp. 7-9.

Petrov, Andrei (1993), 'Privatization and anti-monopoly policy', *RFE/RL Research Report*, Vol. 2, No. 30, 23 July, pp. 19-22.

'Privatizatsiya: novyi etap' (1994), *Ekonomika i Zhizn'*, No. 2, 1994.

Rossiiskaya Ekonomika v 1992 godu (1993), Moscow, Institute for the Study of Economic Transformation.

Saunders, C. T. (ed.) (1993), *The Role of Competition in Economic Transition*, St Martin's Press, New York.

Starkov, D. (1994), 'Antimonopol'noe sito dlya superob'edinenii,' *Ekonomika i Zhizn*, No. 5, p. 11.

Starodubrovskaya, Irina (1994), 'The nature of monopoly and barriers to entry in Russia,' *Communist Economies & Economic Transformation*, Vol. 6, No. 1, pp. 3-18.

Vladislavlev, Georgii (1994), 'Rossiya atakuet mirovoi rynok tsvetnykh metallov,' *Finansovye Izvestiya*, No. 9, 3-9 March, p. 4.

Williamson, J. (1993), Comments, in Saunders, *The Role of Competition* . . . .

Williamson, O. (1975), *Markets and Hierarchies*, Collier Macmillan, London.

Yakovlev, Andrei (1994), 'Anti-monopoly policy in Russia: basic stages and prospects,' *Communist Economies & Economic Transformation*, Vol. 6, No. 1, pp. 33-44.

Part 3

PRIVATIZATION IN THE CIS

Michael Kaser

When radical progress towards economic transformation began in the post-Soviet states in January 1992, cases of 'shock therapy' were to be found in Poland (January 1990) and the then Czechoslovakia (January 1991). No Soviet successor government, however, administered more than a jolt—price decontrol at a stroke—and the Russian government was alone in adding current account convertibility and mass privatization. Momentous as each was in the light of the stagnant economy that Gorbachev had inherited and sought to reform, no actions of 1992-3 amounted to a 'shock', let alone to any 'therapy'. Monetary stabilization, which Central Europe quickly achieved, eluded all CIS governments until 1994, when the biggest (Russia) and two of the smallest (Kyrgyzstan and Moldova) brought inflation down to a tolerable range and relaxed enough controls for the EBRD to rate them as more than half-way towards the goal of a Western-type market economy. In Russia and Kyrgyzstan, as also in Uzbekistan, the privatization of some fifty per cent of state enterprises by the autumn of 1994 proved a major achievement in dispersing the control of the economy away from discredited central planning and bureaucratic ministries.

Individual acknowledgments are made in the notes, but the author particularly expresses his appreciation to the Series Editor, Alan Smith, and the members of a Chatham House Study Group, for their observations.

117

A difference from West European, and some Central European, disposals was the absence of prior financial or physical restructuring, partly because there was no money for it and partly in the interest of speed. In the event, the Russian privatization was the largest and quickest the world has known. By August 1994, just over half of state enterprises had been transformed and 40 million shareholders had been created. In common with other CIS privatizations, the Russian government offered neither restitution nor compensation to previous owners and made no attempt (save in the case of a foreign purchase) to assess the market values of state assets, because prices had been too recently decontrolled and were too inflationary to generate reliable indicators of profit on production or return on capital. By about the same date, five other CIS republics (Kazakhstan, Uzbekistan, Armenia, Tajikistan and Kyrgyzstan) had privatized a quarter or more of their state enterprises, mostly small establishments, reserving the larger for separate sale, including to foreigners attracted by commodities with export potential. Ukraine and Belarus made little progress until each elected a reformist president in July 1994. Everywhere housing is being sold off, mostly to occupiers, but private property in land remains contentious, with only Armenia, Kyrgyzstan and Uzbekistan creating a substantial independent farming sector.

The financial infrastructure for trade in property remains primitive throughout the CIS.

In Russia and Ukraine particularly, many commercial banks are penetrated by criminal gangs (as is much of the economy as a whole); marts for securities are not yet reputable stock exchanges; investment funds have been rocked by scandal; and prudential, regulatory and bankruptcy legislation is only gradually taking a role. The high proportion of shares held by management and workers ('insiders') protects employment (usually at inefficiency levels which could be maintained only by government subsidy, monopoly or non-payment of debts) and deters substantial foreign capital investment.

Privatization in the Post-Soviet Economy

The novelty of the privatization process

On the eve of the Russian revolutions of 1917 the world could be described as thoroughly capitalist. Lenin soon showed how quickly the ownership of land and capital could be transformed and the feasibility of an economic system in which the state held all but the most trivial of property rights. State socialism under a Marxist-Leninist dogma and authority was not as efficient as capitalism, but at the mid-point of the twentieth century one-third of the world population earned a modest living within it. Western mixed economies under Keynesian inspiration had by the same time both nationalized key industries and given wide scope to state entrepreneurship. It is only in the past fifteen years that governments have instigated a mass reversal of that trend. In all countries privatization embraced a political objective to 'roll back the state', that is, to weaken its economic power, and an economic expectation of enforcing market discipline on the enterprises affected, that is, of strengthening the economy. Additionally in the Soviet-type economies Western profit-seeking was admitted into what had been a region geared to group self-sufficiency. Such aims were tentatively embraced in the former Soviet Union by the *perestroika* of Mikhail Gorbachev, in order to jolt the economy out of the stagnation that characterized the Brezhnev period.

It was not until the political monopoly of the Communist Party was repealed and the Union split into fifteen independent states[1] that these three aims were vigorously pursued—so vigorously, in fact, that Russia has since independence achieved the largest and quickest privatization in history. No other member of the Commonwealth of Independent States (CIS), whose foundation in December 1991 dissolved the USSR, has been so sweeping or speedy in institutional change, but all have acknowledged the crucial role which privatization plays in the parallel and complementary transformations to a market economy and to more democratic forms of government.

Two of the three main functions of privatization were expressed by a Deputy Chairman of the Russian State Privatization Agency as "establishing a broad stratum of proprietors, the effective creation of a social orientation for a market economy, raising productive efficiency by the formation of a new ownership structure and the introduction through these new property-owners of a powerful social base for the market economy and of a democratic society."[2] State agencies in the Soviet system had held virtually all the property rights in the productive branches and had rigorously controlled the remainder (in the cooperative sector); private property was restricted to money,[3] personal chattels and small, owner-occupied housing. Demonopolizing property weakens the intervention power of the state and its functionaries, and affords those to whom property is transferred a vested interest in the new political system. It contrasts with the fostering of a private sector while state enterprises remain—the Chinese strategy discussed in Chapter 4. A crucial constituent in the Soviet Union was the demonopolization of politics achieved by banning the Communist Party, but nowhere in the CIS are there yet the many stakeholders in a democratic system to be found in the equivalent 'civil society' of most Western states. Ownership dispersion may thus perform a particularly important, if transitional, political function in setting up 'interest groups' opposed to a return to state dominance. This added influence does not diminish its economic role—the opening of enterprises to the rewards of efficiency and risk-taking and to the sanctions of misdirecting (or wasting) human, reproducible and natural resources. As the transformations began, an OECD symposium clearly formulated the goals of market-imposed discipline:

> Company managers, as agents of owners, are subject to contractual discipline enforced by shareholders; to take-over discipline enforced by potential bidders; and to bankruptcy discipline enforced by creditors. Managers of state enterprises are not subject to any such discipline, as they are subordinated to political authority and not to economically motivated shareholders; they are not subject to take-overs; and their losses are absorbed by automatic grants from the state budget.[4]

Microeconomic discipline was probably more needed in the CIS than in those other states which had been compelled to emulate its system for two reasons. One was that a 'market culture' was much further removed in time: Soviet central planning dated from 1930, but it was applied only after the Second World War in the Baltic states, Central Europe, the Balkans and Mongolia. The other was to reverse the decline in macroeconomic efficiency which characterized the Soviet period, and which resulted primarily from organizational inadequacy, the diversion of technology from civilian into military uses and the poor dissemination of innovative methods and products. Soviet growth was not 'intensive' but 'extensive'; that is, it was derived from adding more capital and more labor rather than augmenting their productivity: 'The reliance on growth through capital accumulation alone became more and more pronounced over time, reflecting some combination of slowing of labor growth, the slowing of technological catch-up and diminishing returns to capital.'[5]

The third outcome which privatization is effecting in the economies of the CIS is the inflow of external enterprise, bringing with it different technologies, more capital, complementary expertise (such as in marketing and in financial and consumer services) and access to new markets. Again, the former Soviet Union needed change because it had more comprehensively practiced trade self-sufficiency and technological self-reliance. Opening the economies to foreign firms can stimulate efficiency by competition with residents, whether privatized state enterprises or newly created private establishments, or by collaboration with them to achieve international standards. Together the changes assure the predominance of private incentives in the demand for and supply of resources and their demonstrable superiority in 'experimentation, learning and error correction.'[6] By and large, incompetence can be concealed in an administered economy, but is exposed by the diffusion of property owners and their agents and may be penalized as a consequence.

An environment of recession

Because, as just noted, the Soviet economy could grow only by increasing its labor force and investment (not, as with all Western systems, by enhancing their joint productivity), it had to assure the full employment of both its human resources and its capital stock. To promote structural and institutional change while keeping a high degree of labor and capacity utilization would patently have been facilitated by a buoyancy of demand at home and abroad.

Ideally, the necessary transfers could have been effected at only fractional cost. No such utopia was on offer: indeed the political revolutions of 1989–91 in communist-run societies took place when the world's market economies were in recession. This could have been turned to good effect by the 'advantages of lateness' (as Gerschenkron described for industrialization): the Communist Party of the Soviet Union was among the last to lose power—August 1991. As described below, the reforming economies of Central and East Europe had begun to implement their new strategies, although the size and heritage of the Soviet state posed issues that the early starters did not have to confront. The many foreign advisers (principally from the United States, the United Kingdom and Sweden) recruited at policy-making level included not only a Pole, but also Western economists with experience of Poland's 1990 'shock therapy'.

Indeed, the earlier political change of Central and Eastern Europe worked greatly to the disadvantage of the Soviet successor states in abruptly curtailing the economic relations of the USSR's sphere of influence. In the outermost circle the cessation of East-West strategic confrontation virtually eliminated the already shrunken trade with, and capital and military transfers to, selected states of the Third World. Within the 'socialist camp' not only was the CMEA dismantled, but all member-states without exception reduced demand and supply, because they were undertaking exactly the same transformation. Soviet economic unity within central planning was itself ruptured: for its first three years the CIS was a political and economic shell. Finally, the ethos proffered by advisers, international economic agencies and Western business was in the direction of freeing trade and payments. Certainly—as shown in the classification by the European Bank for Reconstruction and Development (EBRD)—it is integral to the final objective, but it can be argued that continued protection was needed for domestic industry and to check capital flight for at least some of the transition period. The reduction of import tariffs and the elimination of import quotas was more strongly urged by Western exporters at a time of recession than it might have been in more flourishing times. By the same token, Western governments in periods of lowered demand at home are prone to support domestic producers. The United Nations Economic Commission for Europe (ECE) in 1994 'compiled an inventory of some of the measures taken against eastern exports during the course of 1992-1993' and concluded: 'Thus, while standard measures of protection (tariffs and quotas) affecting the east diminished, contingent protection measures (anti-dumping and safeguard actions) were used more frequently, including by the EC against those countries with which it had Association Agreements.'[7] In 1993, the ECE found, such restrictive actions had been taken in 12 cases against East European imports and in 8 against those from former Soviet republics. Even without such added difficulties the redirection and revival of trade takes time, and the creation of competitive products and marketing outlets required resources and enterprise which were not abundantly available.

A further effect of the influence of general recession was the political decision throughout the CIS to privatize without previous restructuring (notably Russia), or to delay privatization altogether (notably Ukraine and Belarus). Western and some Eastern European privatizations (notably the British and Eastern German) were implemented only after being 'prepared for the market'—at considerable cost (well recouped in the UK, far from it in Germany). As noted below, no government money was put into advance preparation for transfer. One factor was the high inflation, released when prices were largely decontrolled on the very morrow of independence. This meant that reimbursement to the Ministry of Finance would be in depreciated currency; the decision to offer vouchers gratis was made at a denomination which was determined at an earlier level of inflation (so rapid was Ukrainian inflation that the first issue of vouchers had to be scrapped); there was a lack of substantial funds among potential buyers to pay for such pre-investment in their purchase prices and the size of budget deficits deterred such investments (especially in the Central Asian states). Even so, the Russian government hoped for some fiscal gain from privatization sales of enterprises in their original state, as the Minister of Privatization made clear.[8]

A turnaround of economic attitudes was involved in switching from supply to demand determination: the one constituent of 'shock therapy' which every CIS member implemented simultaneously (January 1992) was—as mentioned above—the liberalization of wholesale and retail prices. The 'shortage economy', with its queues and deficits in shops and hoarded inventories in factories, disappeared overnight and was replaced by inflation and speculation shading into crime. Corruption and 'rent-seeking' had been endemic when resources had been allocated by a bureaucracy, but were redirected and enlarged in conditions of an unregulated free-for-all. The constraints on private enterprise had been so severe under Soviet law and unconstitutional repression that its expression was mostly illicit. The authorized 'individual' sector was a weak foundation for speedy privatization (only 0.2 per cent of the population declared themselves to be occupied in the private sector for the 1989 census).[9]

Yet transformation there has been. The EBRD's estimates for mid-1994 put the share of the private sector in GDP for three CIS republics (Belarus, Tajikistan and Turkmenistan) around a mere 15 per cent; and five (Azerbaijan,

Georgia, Kazakhstan, Moldova and Uzbekistan) at 20 per cent; but there were two (Kyrgyzstan and Ukraine) at 30 per cent; Armenia stood at 40 per cent; and Russia at 50 per cent.[10]

Privatization as part of transition strategy

The degree of transfer of state to private property rights is a necessary, but not the only, measure of progress from a command to a market economy. First, there are other radical changes to be made and, secondly, the content of the privatization must be assessed in relation to the objectives of transition. The other components of the overall strategy have been classified by the EBRD into four groups, within which a graduation of four points assesses 'on the judgment of EBRD economists' the strength of establishment of a typical market mechanism. Together with privatization, their criteria may be briefly listed.[11]

Transition element	Mark	Description
Large-scale privatization	4	More than 50% of state enterprises privatized in a scheme that reflects support for corporate governance
	3	More than 25% privatized but with major governance issues unresolved
	2	Comprehensive scheme almost ready to be implemented
	1	Little done
Small-scale privatization	4	Comprehensive, well-designed program implemented
	3	Nearly comprehensive, but with important issues unresolved
	2	Substantial share privatized
	1	Little done
Enterprise restructuring	4	Corporate governance improved; financial discipline at enterprise level; large conglomerates broken up
	3	Structures created (e.g. bankruptcy legislation) and action taken to break up conglomerates
	2	Moderately tight credit and subsidy policy but little action on bankruptcy and conglomerates
	1	Lax credit and subsidy policy, few reforms to promote corporate governance

Price liberalization and	4	Comprehensive decontrol; anti-trust legislation
competition	3	Comprehensive decontrol
	2	Price controls for important categories
	1	Most prices controlled
Trade and foreign	4	Few import or export quotas; insignificant direct
exchange		involvement by state entities; almost full current
		account convertibility at unified exchange rate; no
		major non-uniformity in customs duties
	3	Few import quotas; almost full current account
		convertibility at unified exchange rate
	2	Few import quotas; foreign exchange regime not fully
		transparent (possibly with multiple exchange rates)
	1	Widespread import controls; limited legitimate access
		to foreign exchange
Banking system	4	Well functioning bank competition; prudential
		supervision
	3	Substantial progress on bank recapitalization, bank
		auditing and prudential supervision; significant
		presence of private banks; full interest rate
		liberalization with little preferential access to cheap
		refinance
	2	Interest rate significantly affecting allocation of credit
	1	Little progress beyond two-tier system

It may place CIS privatization in the context of these other paths for transition to cite the EBRD 'marks' for each element, as set out in Table 1 below, which lists states by size of GDP at currency conversions at purchasing power parity, estimated by the World Bank.[12]

The example of other transition economies

Between June 1989 (in Poland) and April 1990 (in Mongolia), the Soviet Union's 'fraternal parties' lost their political monopolies, and the pluralist governments of former allies began to demolish their command economies. There were some two years of experience on which new administrations in the CIS could draw as they themselves took steps towards marketization. The schemes noted below were in operation or under discussion by the time the Russian first stage was formulated; a variant not implemented at that time, for

Table 1. *Progress in transition in the CIS*

| | Privatization | | | | Trade | | |
	Large	Small	Restructuring	Price liberalization	& forex	Banking system	GDP ($billion)
Russian Federation	3	3	2	3	3	2	924
Ukraine	1	2	1	2	1	1	261
Kazakhstan	2	2	1	2	2	1	81
Belarus	2	2	2	2	1	1	70
Uzbekistan	2	3	1	3	2	1	55
Azerbaijan	1	1	1	3	1	1	19
Moldova	2	2	2	3	2	2	17
Turkmenistan	1	1	1	2	1	1	15
Georgia	1	2	1	2	1	1	13
Kyrgyzstan	3	4	2	3	3	2	12
Tajikistan	2	2	1	3	1	1	11
Armenia	1	3	1	3	2	1	9

Source: EBRD, *Transition Report 1994*, October 1994, pp. 10, 149–73.

example, was the scheme adopted by the Hungarian authorities, who avoided the use of vouchers by substituting interest-free but reimbursable loans to buy privatized equity.

BENEFICIARIES OF PROPERTY TRANSFER. The most radical of the methods of privatization, gratis distribution of equity by the issue of 'vouchers', had been proposed in June 1990 in a memorandum to the Polish Ministry of Finance by Roman Frydman and Andrzej Rapaczynski (shortly afterwards quickly known by being put to a conference of the World Bank).[13] The majority of transition states, including in the CIS, put vouchers into at least some part of their privatizations. Within the CIS, some used a certificate (the 'privatization cheese' of Russia), and others a credit in an escrow account.[14]

Restitution to previous owners or their legal successors was a keenly debated issue in the early debates on privatization in the eastern *Länder* of Germany, Czechoslovakia and Hungary. In its favor were a government's credibility on the protection of private property and a righting of their predecessors' wrongs, but on the other hand the search for claims and the uncertainty generated for new owners while they were investigated would slow the process.[15] Compensation in lieu to the expropriated owners avoided the latter obstacle. A combination used in Estonia was to give vouchers as compensation. In the event, all CIS governments declined both restitution and compensation on the grounds that confiscation was too remote in time and that most foreign owners had been compensated under Soviet bilateral treaties with affected persons' governments.

The group who chiefly benefited, at least in the first stage of Russian privatization, were the managers and workers of the privatized firm. Western privatizations had a tradition of concessional equity for employees and management buy-outs were a familiar part of financial intermediation. Yugoslav self-management had been much studied by Soviet commentators and after the eclipse of communist rule there was keen debate between an adaptation of worker-control (advocated by the then Deputy Prime Minister, Joze Mencinger, and the Director of the Slovene Development Fund, Uros Korze) and the public offering of equity (recommended by Jeffrey Sachs of Harvard University as government adviser). As discussed below in the context of actual 'insider' privatization, the considerations which particularly influenced choice within the CIS were political—both national and local—and social, in which the assurance of job security was highly ranked, together with an inheritance of leased enterprises, where managers and workers as lessees had gained a sense of ownership which they would not readily discard. Enterprise leasing was itself copied from Hungarian practice of 1980 onwards.

VALUATION Even with vouchers or employee shareholding, a value has to be attached both to the unit offered and to the property to be transferred; without them, purchasers have to be informed of the price to be paid or the value of the assets offered. In most transition states, including above all the Soviet Union, a lack of market-clearing prices both for assets and for their prospective outputs severely constrained any use of domestic values; world-market prices were little related to home conditions because exchange rates were overvalued and price relativities differed greatly. The Hungarian case-by-case method was a poor exemplar, despite a government policy for the previous decade of approximating home to foreign prices: one of the very first attempts to set a price included one for HungarHotels which was declared to be void for undervaluation by the Hungarian Supreme Court; four years later, a sale of the same HungarHotels was quashed by the government.[16] The Polish practice of employing Western accountancy firms was seen as too costly. For large economies such as Russia and Ukraine, there were too many state enterprises for expert assessment within any reasonable time-span.

An alternative which valued assets to be privatized relatively without a money *numeraire* was the 'points' system used in the then Czechoslovakia, whereby enterprises were ranked by the accumulation of 'points' allotted to them by holders of vouchers.

The eventual choice by the bigger CIS countries was to select the asset valuation at a base date on book value, as shown by state price-lists; this was unsatisfactory for many reasons, and the most that could be said for it was that it was available and uniform.

PREPARATION FOR PRIVATIZATION CIS governments had no need to examine East European experience in preparing state enterprises for the private sector because suitable restructuring had been the practice in market economies, notably in the UK in the 1980s. In post-communist conditions the individual tailoring of enterprises for sale by the Treuhandanstalt in the eastern *Länder* of Germany was an extreme example, but it also included contracts with purchasers to undertake further specified restructuring through specified investment amounts and not to reduce the workforce below specified minimums. As explained above, no CIS state undertook advance financial or physical restructuring. There were, however, some demergers and much divestment of social facilities. In auction sales competitive bidding included commitments on investment, employment, production and, where retained, the operation of social facilities.[17]

Furthermore, few enterprises were declared unprivatizable and therefore closed without privatization. The avoidance of unemployment nationally and the protection of individual workplaces was a potent consideration—by 1994 Russian unemployment was about one-third of that in the eastern German *Länder*—but a general renunciation of closure was characteristic also of Hungarian privatization.[18]

An even wider range of experience in privatization is, of course, also available from established market economies. A recent study concluded that 'the scale of the changes being attempted in Eastern Europe so dwarf what has been achieved even in Britain that any simple transfer of lessons is unlikely . . . This does not mean that learning is impossible, but it does mean identifying which elements in a particular case are peculiar, and therefore unlikely to be reusable in other circumstances.'[19]

Relics of the Soviet state

The process of privatization throughout the CIS was, above all, conditioned by characteristics of the Soviet heritage and needs to be judged in their light. The first proceeds from the general objective of reducing state power: the ideology of Marxism-Leninism dictated the politicization of economic decisions (epitomized in the language of battle, struggle and historical progression). The transfer of ownership depoliticizes economic decisions, while permitting the state to regulate those outcomes in the light of the public good.

In a second, but connected, trait, the hierarchical nature of the Soviet 'Partocracy' prolonged the 'petitioner' mentality that has been noted by economic historians as characteristic of some groups of prerevolutionary entrepreneurs, chiefly those connected with St Petersburg. The hold of the 'branch ministries' had to be broken, with their 'cozy relations' (Janos Kornai's term) with 'their' enterprises, extracting subsidies and 'easy' plan targets.

Thirdly, it was a 'state of the workers and peasants' and the slogan 'Workers of the World Unite' emblazoned newspapers virtually until the demise of the USSR. The enterprise was designed as the social focus of its staff, providing job security, health care, training and leisure opportunities: the commitment to employment was tantamount to a property right and privatization has, for this reason among others, favored 'insiders', managers and employees alike. For managers their ranking among the Soviet *nomenklatura* put them in a favorable position to empower themselves, both in official privatization and in its 'spontaneous' form.[20] Although long treated as second-class citizens, collective farmers[21] had the same job security. While this feature throughout the CIS reinforced their aversion to private farming, a more potent factor was the 'dependency culture' formed by the excision of peasant entrepreneurship in the 1930s ('dekulakization') and the hierarchical division of labor on the farm and of centralized supply and procurement outside it.

Fourth, because the writ of the state and the Party was absolute and often arbitrarily exercised, authority and rights were not duly delineated. The requirement of a market economy for information and for the predictability of rights and obligations demands the establishment of the appropriate legal norms and definitions. Even at the level of real estate, the ownership of urban land and buildings became the subject of much dispute as the properties were scheduled for transfer. In the countryside it was otherwise: each collective farm had a written *Akt* for its property and cadastral survey was meticulous, the remotest Central Asian village included. It is not too strong an interpretation to suggest that this is another element in the caution farmers show towards going private.

Finally, the militarization of the economy subsumed an ordering of priorities, quotas and rations that takes time to erode as the need for armed forces—thanks to the end of the Cold War—diminishes. The social consequences of manpower demobilization and of the conversion of the defense industry added to Russian and Ukrainian problems[22] as they confronted the need for momentous change in civilian economic institutions.

The political environment within which crucial decisions had to be made

on property rights was itself in rapid transformation.[23] Three directions of
change were fundamental as the Soviet state ended. First, and most obviously,
a unitary state (nominally a federation) diversified into a multinational group
of independent countries, some of which had to contend with internal fissiparity. Thus Russia's 89 main administrative regions distanced themselves from
Moscow in a wide gamut of variation. At one extreme was the self-declared
and hostile independence of Chechenia which the army was dispatched to sub-
due, and the large autonomies acquired by default in Bashkortostan, Tatarstan
and Yakut-Sakha. Elsewhere in the CIS, Ukraine was politically divided into
West, Center, East and Crimea; Georgia struggled against Abkhaz, Adzhar and
Ossetian separatism; Azerbaijan faced insurrection in Nagorno-Karabakh supported by Armenian invasion; Tajikistan fell into civil war among protagonists
of the former regime, of an Islamic renaissance and of democracy; and part of
Moldova separated itself into a Dniestr Republic. Ethnic rivalries were latent
in Kazakhstan and Uzbekistan, leaving only Kyrgyzstan and Turkmenistan as
states where internal divergence was no more than clannish, and Belarus as
the only potentially homogeneous country. Secondly, pluralist-democratic rule
began to replace Soviet-style authoritarianism, but here too the impact among
the successor states varied—least in Turkmenistan, most in the Slavic republics. Finally, the loss of imperial status brought change in political culture
as well as the rupture of economic relations that has already been mentioned.
Russian policy-makers had to fit themselves into a more modest place both internationally and within the CIS (a change that was seen as humiliating by
some shades of public opinion and by much of the armed forces), while the
non-Russian republics cherished their new-found national standing.

    These numerous interactions between social and political forces are asso-
ciated with a thorough change in property rights and with other measures
towards the creation of a market economy. Thus the appropriate term for the
national systems of the CIS in the mid-1990s is not 'adjustment' or 'transformation' but 'revolution'.

Notes to Chapter 1

1. Since they refused membership of the CIS, the three Baltic republics, Estonia, Latvia and Lithuania, are not discussed in this study. Notable coverage is found, for example, in Roman Frydman et al., *The Privatization Process in Russia, Ukraine and the Baltic States* (Budapest: Central European University Press, 1993), and Seija Lainela and Pekka Sutela, *The Baltic Economies in Transition* (Helsinki: Bank of Finland, 1994). Briefer studies are available in *IMF Economic Reviews*, no. 6, *Lithuania*, and no. 7, *Estonia* (both 1994); and *Latvia* (in preparation).

2. D. V. Vasil'ev, 'Basic Directions of the Privatization Program in Russia in 1992', in M.A. Deryabina (ed.), *Privatizatsiya: tseli i realnost'* (Moscow: IMEMO, 1992) p. 3.

3. Money in cash or in the only other permitted form, deposits in the State Savings Bank, was subjected to confiscation by currency 'reform' in 1947 and 1991.

4. D.M. Nuti, 'Privatization of Socialist Economies: General Issues and the Polish Case', in H. Blommestein and M. Marrese (eds), *Transformation of Planned Economies and Macroeconomic Stability* (Paris: OECD, 1991), p. 52.

5. William Easterly and Stanley Fischer, 'Growth Prospects for the Ex-Soviet Republics: Lessons from Soviet Historical Experience', in Abel Aganbegyan, Oleg Bogomolov and Michael Kaser (eds), *Economics in a Changing World*, volume 1: *System Transformation: Eastern and Western Assessments* (London: Macmillan, 1994), p. 78.

6. 'Arguments for Private Ownership', *EBRD Economic Review: Annual Economic Outlook* (London: European Bank for Reconstruction and Development, 1993), p.113 (q.v. for a fuller exposition of the issues discussed in this section).

7. Economic Commission for Europe, *Economic Survey of Europe in 1993-1994*: (New York and Geneva: ECE, 1994), p. 153.

8. Anatoly Chubais and Maria Vishnevskaya, 'Privatization in Russia: An Overview', in Anders Åslund (ed.), *Economic Transformation in Russia*, (London: Pinter, 1994), p. 94; Chubais, 'Main Issues of Privatization in Russia,' in Richard Layard and Anders Åslund (eds), *Changing the Economic System in Russia* (London: Pinter, 1993), cited in Pekka Sutela, 'Insider Privatization in Russia: Speculations on Systemic Change', *Europe-Asia Studies*, vol. 46, no. 3, 1994, pp. 417-35.

9. The share rises to 0.5 per cent if domestic staff, artists and actors are counted (*Narodnoe khozyaistvo SSSR v 1989g.*, Moscow, Finansy i statistika, 1990, pp. 26 and 275).

10. EBRD, *Transition Report* (London: EBRD, October 1994), p. 10.

11. Ibid., p. 11.

12. World Bank, *World Development Report 1994*, Washington DC, World Bank, 1994.

13. As stated in R. Frydman and A. Rapaczynski, *Privatization in Eastern Europe: Is the State Withering Away?* (Budapest: Central European University Press, 1994), pp. 2, 3 and 9.

14. On the initial preference in Russia for the escrow account and its substitution by voucher, see Morris Bornstein, 'Russia's Mass Privatisation Programme', *Communist Economies and Economic Transformation*, vol. 6, no. 4 (1994), pp. 419-58.

15. For a review of the arguments, see Stanley Fischer, 'Privatization in East European Transformation', in Christopher Clague and Gordon Rausser (eds), *The Emergence of Market Economies in Eastern Europe* (Oxford, Blackwell, 1992), pp. 230-1. For a list of governments accepting restitution and/or compensation, see UNECE, *Economic Survey of Europe in 1990-91* (New York, United Nations, 1991).

16. On early Hungarian denationalization and on the 1990 HungarHotels scandal, see Mario Nuti, 'Privatization in Hungary', in Michael Keren and Gur Ofer (eds), *Trials of Transition: Economic Reform in the Former Soviet Bloc*, Boulder, CO: Westview Press, 1992), pp. 193-202; and for the 1995 cancellation, see *Financial Times,* 13 January 1995. On the genesis of 'spontaneous privatization' in Hungary, see Nuti, op. cit., and Roman Frydman, Andrzej Rapaczynski and John S. Earle, *The Privatization Process in Central Europe* (Budapest: Central European University Press, 1993), pp. 132-3.

17. Bornstein, op. cit., p. 430, sets out these contracts in detail.

18. Frydman, Rapaczynski and Earle, op. cit., p. 123, point to the closure of only one firm, the Ozd Metallurgy Plant, at least in the first period of Hungarian privatization.

19. Michael Moran and Tony Prosser (eds), *Privatization and Regulatory Change in Europe* (Buckingham: Open University Press, 1994), p. 2. The book comprises papers on Germany, Great Britain, Italy, Czechoslovakia, Poland and Hungary.

20. For an early observation of this 'wild' privatization, see M.C. Kaser, 'The Technology of Decontrol', *Economic Journal,* vol. 100, June 1990, p. 611.

21. *Kolkhoznik* households were not issued with internal passports during the period 1932-76; their movement elsewhere than around their village was thus restricted.

22. Four-fifths of Soviet defense industry was located in Russia and most of the remainder in Ukraine.

23. A sketch of the history of property law from one revolution to another is given in V. K. Andreev, 'Metamorfozy prava sobstvennosti v Rossii i Soyuze SSR', *Gosudarstvo i pravo,* no. 3, 1993, pp. 40-48.

CHAPTER TWO

Privatizing the
Non-Farm Economy

The Soviet prelude

With Mikhail Gorbachev as Party leader (from March 1985), the Soviet authorities gradually widened the scope for a private sector. The first signs of what became the economic dimension of *perestroika* were modest: two large state enterprises in engineering, Togliatti and Sumy, were allowed to retain 70 per cent of their profits for self-finance (May 1985); and collective farms were allowed to sell 30 per cent of their output in urban cooperative shops at free-market prices (March 1986). The significance of these changes lay in the fact that they broke the complete financial subordination of the state enterprise and permitted farmers to sell through intermedaries other than the official procurement agency or by the laborious individual sale in *kolkhoz* markets. The next significant steps were the authorization of state enterprises to form joint ventures with partners from either capitalist or socialist countries, the conditions for the former being more restrictive (August 1986), and the bypassing of the monopoly of the Ministry of Foreign Trade (September 1986). The penetration of Western partners directly into state enterprises began to show the latter the prices, costing methods, financial service and marketing procedures of the capitalist economy from which they had been deliberately isolated since around 1930.

The first major change with respect to the domestic private sector, hitherto legally confined to peasants' household plots and *kolkhoz* market sales and to strictly controlled craft and professional cooperatives, was the authorization

Percentage of state enterprises privatized in the CIS (autumn 1994)

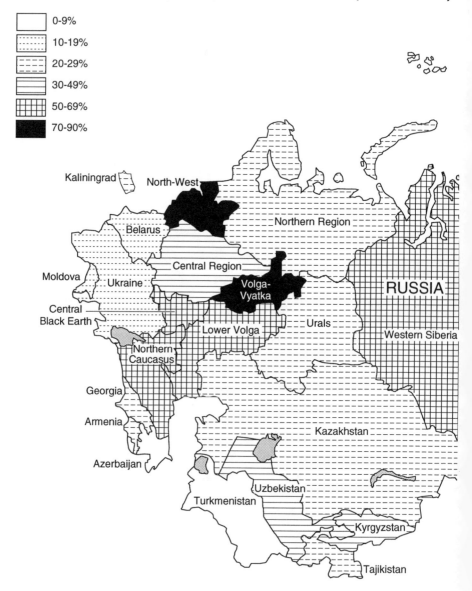

Legend:
- 0-9%
- 10-19%
- 20-29%
- 30-49%
- 50-69%
- 70-90%

Kaliningrad

North-West

Belarus

Northern Region

Central Region

Moldova

Ukraine

Volga-Vyatka

RUSSIA

Central Black Earth

Lower Volga

Urals

Western Siberia

Northern Caucasus

Georgia

Armenia

Kazakhstan

Azerbaijan

Uzbekistan

Turkmenistan

Kyrgyzstan

Tajikistan

of new-style cooperatives (November 1986), which soon became a channel for small-scale private activity. The Togliatti-Sumy experiment was greatly widened at the start of 1987 (to seven industrial ministries) and it was announced that it would be extended to all state production enterprises by 1990. This was followed by a Law on the State Enterprise which introduced, through a concept termed 'full cost-accounting' (*polny khozraschet*), some financial and managerial autonomy (and the election by the workforce of enterprise directors). A genuine private sector was granted a legal existence from May 1987: local councils could register persons in self-employment or in family businesses. The impact and the attitude of local authorities varied—such micro-business flourished in the Baltic republics but was restricted in Moscow. A Law on Cooperatives (May 1988) repealed the requirement of local authorization; the number of cooperatives quintupled in that year alone (to 75,000 throughout the USSR—many in the Baltic republics, few in Central Asia). Further laws and decrees enlarged the access of state enterprises to external partners: by May 1989 some 5,000 were registered for independent foreign trading and 460 joint ventures had been established. Finally, a compromise between private entrepreneurship and state ownership was offered (April 1989) in the form of leasing (*arenda*), whereby employees and managers could hire their enterprise on agreed financial terms and operate it during a set period (5 to 15 years) for their own profit. This was both a forerunner of 'insider' privatization and an opportunity for managers and others of the politically chosen *nomenklatura* to exercise business power.[1]

Privatization finally came to be official policy during the economic recovery program embraced (amid many unofficial alternatives and something of a compromise among them) by the Chairman of the Council of Ministers, Nikolai Ryzhkov, in December 1989.[2] It envisaged equality before the law for all forms of ownership and a substantial transfer of state into other forms of property. The remaining two years of Soviet administration brought a set of 'Basic Legislation' as a framework law from which the Union republics would derive their own laws: these were on land (March 1990), on property (June 1990), on entrepreneurship (April 1991), on destatization and privatization, on foreign investment and on the limitation of monopoly (all July 1991). The onus of privatization and associated changes was thus shifted to each republic.

The defeat of the attempted coup of August 1991 brought immediate liquidation of the institutions of the Communist Party and thus the withdrawal of its functions as economic coordinator between central decision-makers, between them and local agencies and enterprises, and between enterprises. The abolition of Gosplan and the diminution of the role of branch ministries further reduced institutionalized and informal coordination, including the use of buying agents (*tolkachi*, or 'pushers'). The aim in both cases was, of course, to liberate enterprises in the direction of the coordination of their decisions by market signals, and those who had been the agents of the previous system gravitated to new roles. Many, bereft of their functions, kept or took office in regional and local authorities or entered enterprise management; other agents turned to consultancy or crime.

The order of countries discussed in this chapter is, as already noted, by economic size, as measured by GDP in 1992 converted to dollars at estimated purchasing power parity. The only rerankings that would arise from repricing if conversion to dollars is at actual exchange rates[3] would put Georgia just above Azerbaijan and Armenia above Kyrgyzstan; the weight of Russia would then be 65 per cent of the CIS, rather than 62 per cent at purchasing power parity. The map at the beginning of this study shows, by country and within Russia by region, the share of state enterprises which had been privatized by the third quarter of 1994, as indicated in the country sections.[4] Two caveats should be entered: first, the statistics of all CIS countries are still in the process of capturing in data or estimates the magnitudes and trends of economic activity;[5] second, and in particular, the number of enterprises privatized by 1994 included many more small than large entities, and it is the mass privatization of big firms that patently has a preponderant effect in promoting a competitive market.

The Russian Federation

THE ENABLING LEGISLATION Russia, then the RSFSR, transmuted Soviet 'basic legislation' on privatization in a series of laws of July 1991, of which the chief was that on the Privatization of State and Municipal Enterprises.[6] Its two principal features, distinguishing it from corresponding measures in some other transition economies, were the establishment of dual agencies to effect the changes, separate from existing economic ministries,[7] and gratis 'vouchers' as the core mode of property dispersion. The State Property [Management] Committee (*Goskomimushchestvo*) began to function immediately and soon set up regional committees in all 89 constituent republics and other administrative regions (*oblasts*), in all cities with a population exceeding one million and in the town of Nakhodka.[8] It was to determine ownership of state enterprises between federal, regional and municipal bodies, effect 'corporatization' (joint-stock companies with all equity in public ownership), and list and select state enterprises for privatization.[9] The actual ownership and sales were in the hands of the Russian Federal Property Fund (*Rossiisky fond feder-alnogo imushchestva*).[10] The State Committee for Anti-Monopoly Policy and the Support of New Enterprise Structures was created in 1992 to keep a register of enterprises in a monopoly position in order to monitor, and if necessary to tax or demerge, their profitability; both at the central and the regional level it was to provide credits and technical support for new small enterprises. These three committees jointly founded (also in 1992) the Russian Privatization Center (*Rossiisky tsentr privatizatsii*) to manage foreign credits, grants and technical assistance for privatization.[11] An Institute for the Study of State Property management was mooted for establishment in 1995.

In the 1991 Law, the entitlements to purchase state assets were to be in the form of reserved (escrow) accounts credited to citizens in the State Savings Bank; but the distribution of entitlements was postponed when a Presidential Decree (December 1991) gave priority to the immediate privatization of retail and wholesale trade enterprises and certain other small entities (so-called 'small privatization'). Because supply enterprises were not broken up, the expected retailers' competition did not ensue; the result, after price decontrol, was severe inflation and output restriction.[12] Before the dissolution of the Union at the end of 1991 two further, Russian, measures widened the scope for private participation outside the state enterprise sector: the Housing Privatization Law and the Decree on the Liberalization of Foreign Economic Activity.

The Russian government had determined on a program containing elements of 'shock therapy' under the Deputy Premier, Yegor Gaidar, in October 1991. Price liberalization (effected on 2 January 1992), current account convertibility of the ruble (July 1992)[13] and the mass privatization described in this study were those to be rapidly implemented. The other constituents, notably macroeconomic stabilization, restructuring, monopoly regulation and financial intermediation, were to be on the 'gradualist' path. This slower pace of restructuring and financial intermediation was politically preferable because the government did not need to raise money 'up front', which would have required higher taxation, borrowing or inflationary finance (already huge because of subsidies to enterprises and to other CIS republics[14]); new capital would be raised by the private owner. It could secure worker acceptance of redundancy by phased layoffs, each group getting a better compensation package than if the enterprise were wholly closed. Distinguishing 'winners' and 'losers' was especially difficult in the immediate aftermath of chaotic Soviet pricing and procurement; with prospective viability uncertain, few mistakes might be made.[15] Moreover, the high degree of inherited disarticulation of

Russia from established market economies (the other transition economies not being immediately relevant) would delay penetration of perhaps the most potent of competitive forces: immediate efficiency gains from privatization are likely to be small and associated more with product market discipline—and especially increased exposure to foreign competition—than with the role of the capital market.[16]

LAWS FOR MASS PRIVATIZATION: THE FIRST STAGE   The crucial measures for what was to be the world's biggest and quickest privatization were enacted during 1992. At the beginning of the year only 70 enterprises were in private ownership by citizens and 922 non-farm enterprises were collectives; there were pending a mere 1,500 applications for privatization.[17] By the end of the first stage of large privatization there were 104,000 firms in private ownership; nine out of ten industrial workers were in private firms;[18] and Russia had a smaller state-owned sector than Italy.[19]

Detailed preparation for 'large privatization' began with a decree (January 1992) establishing rules for registering interest in privatization purchase, for valuation and for auctions and tenders. This was followed by Presidential Decree no. 721, which imposed 'corporatization', that is the removal of enterprises from the control of a branch ministry by transformation into a joint stock company. Enterprises (other than those in six specifically excluded categories) which employed 'on average'[20] more than 1,000 staff or had fixed assets valued in excess of 50 million rubles were required to corporatize. No requirement was laid on medium and small enterprises, but those with fewer than 200 staff and fixed assets of less than 1 million rubles could 'corporatize' by majority vote of the staff. The form of incorporation was an 'open joint stock company'—that is, one whose shares could be sold to the public; the 'closed' company (or 'partnership with limited liability') is limited to 100 shareholders and equity cannot be traded. The five categories of exception form the constraints on large privatization as it emerged later that year:[21]

—Radio, TV, pipelines, narcotics and toxic substances production, public utilities, gold and diamond reserves, natural resources (including those of the continental shelf) and specialized hospitals;
—Enterprises for which government approval to privatize must be given: armaments, energy, precious metals processing, banks, communications, printing and publishing and nonspecialized hospitals and sanatoria;
—Enterprises for which State Property Committee approval to privatize must be given: enterprises with a dominant market position, with more

than 10,000 employees or an asset value exceeding 150 million rubles, surplus military property, rail, air and sea transport, educational and research institutions, medical and pharmaceutical enterprises, spirits and tobacco, baby foods, and folk art and craft workshops;
—Enterprises for which regional State Property Committee approval is required to verify that a privatization accords with local privatization plans (local authorities may not impose further restrictions): public baths, waste treatment plant, pharmacies and socio-cultural enterprises;
—Social and cultural facilities of an enterprise may be separated off into another company.

In the event, a large number of permissions in categories (2) to (4) were granted;[22] many of those under (5) did not remain in their original uses. The Federal Property Fund became the first owner, possessing 25 per cent of the equity as 'Class B' non-voting shares, leaving 'Class A' for preferential distribution to staff and the remainder as common stock available for privatization.

When in mid-1992 the detailed program for large privatization was promulgated (by a Law and two Presidential Decrees of June and a Decree of August), it departed from the earlier plans by replacing as the citizen's instrument of purchase tradable vouchers instead of escrow accounts; by requiring mass transfer rather than a case-by-case selection; by valuing enterprises at January 1992 book value (without allowance for later inflation, which proved to be 1,949 per cent in wholesale prices that year) in place of estimated market value; by greater scope for 'insider' buy-outs; and by allowing land to be sold both with a privatized enterprise and 'for entrepreneurial use' (as distinct from agricultural or personal). Like the earlier legislation, the prudential and regulatory content was small.

Vouchers were termed 'privatization checks' and denominated as 10,000 rubles.[23] Consideration had been given to denomination as 'points' (as in Czechoslovakia that year), which could have had two advantages:[24] first, as the vouchers could be traded, their issue as points rather than in rubles would have prevented their adding to the money supply;[25] and, secondly, this would have obscured a fall in their exchange value (in fact their market price remained below par until October 1993 but peaked at 70,000 rubles just before their intended expiration in July 1994[26]).

The mid-1992 legislation may be summarized under seven heads.

— There could be no crossholding by state enterprises or institutions, because privatization shares may not be bought by enterprises more than

25 per cent owned by a state entity (as shown above, corporatization set a maximum of 25 per cent to state equity).

— Employees in a corporatized enterprise were entitled to choose by majority vote between three 'variants'. *Variant 1* (which was effective if no choice were made) gave 25 per cent of (non-voting) shares gratis to employees, who could buy a further 10 per cent for vouchers or cash at a 30 per cent *discount*; senior management could buy a further 5 per cent, and 10 per cent is offered at public auction for cash or vouchers. The controlling block of shares would be sold by auction or tender to a single investor or consortium. *Variant 2* (which proved by far the most popular) allowed employees to gain 51 per cent control by payment in money or vouchers, but at a 70 per cent *premium* on the book value. Up to 10 per cent could be sold at public auction for vouchers and the rest for cash, but the Federal Property Fund in most cases retained much of its holding. *Variant 3,* which required restructuring by management and employees, was little used.[27]

— By a later decree (October 1992, but in time for the sell-offs), 'voucher investment funds' could be established to acquire and invest vouchers and cash on behalf of individuals. At the end of the first stage, July 1994, there were over 600 such funds with some 40 million shareholders.[28]

— Uncorporatized state enterprises and the assets of liquidated enterprises were required to be sold by auction or competitive tender, organized by the Federal Property Fund in accordance with the plans approved by the State Property Committee (each at the appropriate federal or local level). The reserve price was 30 per cent below the determined book value and a prior deposit (equal to 10 per cent of the book value) was required.

— The 'incentive funds' fed from profits in proportion to the enterprise wage-bill under Soviet law (dating to the reforms of 1966, and in various guises back to 1930) could be applied to the cash purchase of shares by insiders.

— Enterprises leased under Soviet law could be bought by lessees on the terms of the particular lease, disregarding the time lapse then laid down (more than 80 per cent of such leases had envisaged reversion to lessees), but no new leases could be granted and enterprises unredeemed had to be privatized like an ordinary state enterprise.[29]

— Housing, whether state-, municipal- or enterprise-owned (in all, 2,400 million sq. m), is transferred gratis for a minimum living area (deter-

mined by the local authority) and the remainder occupied may be purchased at a price related to quality and size. As rents were decontrolled
at the same time a free market was promptly created.
— Money received for property was allocated to local, regional and central
government agencies on a predetermined scale; it did not go to the enterprise.[30]

Further legislation was added during the first stage, that is from the actual
issue of vouchers in late 1992 to its termination on 1 July 1994; at the last
minute, the validity of vouchers was prolonged to 1 September and then to 30
November. Perhaps the most important was a belated provision that large enterprises (with fixed assets, always at 1 January 1992 valuations, exceeding
250 million rubles) should effect their voucher auctions on an interregional
basis (Council of Ministers Decree of August 1993); only smaller enterprises
would run the sale in their town of location. This was intended to widen the
number of bidders and to reduce the power of local influences, including criminal elements that had physically threatened those who bid against their desired
outcome. This decree was linked to a Presidential Decree of the same date intended to protect the right of all citizens to 'equal opportunities to buy privatized properties within the entire economic space of the Russian Federation';[31]
infractions would be punished by exclusion from auctions. Another obstacle
to attracting a wide range of buyers was the requirement that only 30 days
could elapse between the announcement of a sale and the auction. In December 1994 the Chairman of the State Property Fund, Vladimir Sokolov, stated
that the period would be extended, with some discretion for each enterprise.
    It was also laid down in August 1993, as the first stage began, that 80 per
cent of the allocation of equity for sale had to be paid for in vouchers. As mentioned above, the State Property Committee (in its own Ordinance of October
1993) took a leaf out of the book of the German Treuhandanstalt (in the privatization of the Eastern *Länder*) by providing for the incorporation of restructuring investment in the privatization sale, and took it a stage further by another Ordinance on February 1994 by specifying a category of 'investment
tenders', the highest promised investment winning. To counter serious irregu-
larities in the registration of shareholdings (companies were known to have
simply deleted the names of owners they did not want), a Presidential Decree
of October 1993 put formal order into share registration and the provision of
information from company registrars. Special procedures were applied for privatization of enterprises in oil extraction and refining (November 1993) and
the gas monopoly, Gazprom (March 1994), with specified rights for citizens in

the territories where they operate. A similar favoring of local residents was also demonstrated in the legislation of the Autonomous Republics. Thus when 45 enterprises in Bashkortostan were scheduled for auction in late 1994, only vouchers issued within that republic would be valid. Chuvashia suspended all privatization from August 1994 and in January 1995 issued its own program for the year; higher proportions of equity were retained by the state than in the federal scheme and only the leasing of land occupied by firms was permitted, instead of the sale elsewhere being allowed.

THE RESULTS By the closure of the first stage on 1 July 1994, there were 40 million shareholders in Russia, more than in either the UK or the United States; of the 148 million vouchers issued, 144 million (97 per cent) had been invested and 44 per cent were held in the 630 investment funds (which are allowed to have up to a quarter of the equity of any single firm). A total of 103,000 state enterprises had completed the privatization procedure—47,000 in the first year, 1992; 41,000 in the second year; and 15,000 between 1 January and 1 July 1994. The pace had slackened as the program drew to its close: to the 14,659 privatized in the first seven months of 1994 may be added a further 13,367 in process, of which 50 per cent belonged to municipalities, 21 per cent to various regional authorities (*sobstvennost' sub"yektov federatsii*) and 29 per cent to the federal government. That distribution was much the same as shown in the year's completed privatizations. According to figures of 1 September, by which time 16,248 firms had been privatized, 49 per cent had come from municipal ownership, 24 per cent from regional bodies and 27 per cent had been federal property.[32] In the year-and-a-half of the first stage over 12,000 large and medium enterprises had been privatized at auction—bringing, with the 91,000 small businesses, more than 60 per cent of industrial workers into the private sector. In the small business group 74 per cent had been privatized (services 76 per cent; retailing 75 per cent; catering 67 per cent).

There was evidence of change brought about by transferred ownership. In 1993, 47 per cent of newly privatized firms had changed their product mix, 57 per cent had introduced new incentive-oriented remuneration and 60 per cent had laid off workers. Management was more or less the same, but there were three regions in which one in ten firms had ousted the former management. Two-thirds of those privatized in 1994 were profit-making. Of the proceeds from sales received in the first six months of 1994, 38 per cent had gone to local authorities, 25 per cent to regional bodies, 17 per cent to the federal government, 17 per cent to the state agencies responsible for privatization and 3 per cent to staff of the enterprises concerned. Few purchases had been made by foreigners in the primary sales, but a portfolio was being built up from initial buyers in secondary trading.

That 'insider' ownership had emerged as the dominant trend was evident from the choice of Variant II (51 per cent employee/manager equity) by almost 80 per cent of enterprises privatized in the first stage: Grigory Yavlinsky called them 'industrial *kolkhozy*',[33] but they may also be seen as preserving the 'traditional social relations of production, within which workers look to their line managers to defend their interests'.[34] Many such buy-outs had been achieved through closed auction, and even the open joint stock companies had outsider holdings rarely exceeding 30 per cent. By the end of the first stage many of such outside holdings had been pooled into 620 voucher investment funds (20 were deregistered by the State Property Committee for infringements of regulations).[35]

By the end of September 1994, 10.4 million dwellings in public housing had been transferred to the ownership of occupiers, which represented 31 per cent of the total area scheduled for privatization.[36] No real market in real estate had emerged by late 1994: there existed no enforceable mechanism for eviction; property rights were poorly defined and many local controls existed on rents and fees.

DISTRIBUTION BY BRANCH Because the selection of enterprises for privatization was neither uniform nor comprehensive—at least one went to court to protest at its privatization[37]—the distribution of vouchers or of auction cash does not necessarily reflect a ranking of preference among activities. In the first seven months of 1994, when some 16,000 enterprises were privatized, the branch absorbing most vouchers was fuel (3.6 million), followed by telecommunications (2.7 million), engineering and metal-working (2.2 million) and timber, paper and wood-working (1.1 million). Few vouchers were put towards retailing, but that branch garnered the most auction money (87 billion rubles). Together with catering, wholesale and retail trade got half of all the cash bidding (102 billion out of 204 billion rubles), but only 15 billion went into fuel and 12 billion into engineering and metal-working, or just a little more than went to construction (11 billion).[38] A clear picture must await completion of the second stage in Russia and reports of other CIS members as they achieve the transfers they plan.

A similar ranking may be found in the pattern of inflow of foreign investment.[39] In the first quarter of 1994, when $317 million was recorded as direct and $47 million as portfolio, almost half—$132 million—went to the fuel industry (above all, oil and gas); trade and catering (particularly hotels) followed, with \$35 million; timber and paper were third, with \$22 million; and engineering was fourth, with \$21 million.[40]

LAWS FOR MASS PRIVATIZATION: THE SECOND STAGE Of approximately 250,000 state-owned enterprises when Russia became independent, 130,000 had been privatized by November 1994, as the second major stage began; the remaining candidates for transformation include 30,169 in the 'large' category, of which some 5,000 are not yet corporatized.[41]

A decree of 24 December 1993 set out the second stage and in the ensuing months failed five times to secure a majority in the Duma. Eventually, on 22 July 1994, President Yeltsin took advantage of the Duma's recess to issue a new decree embodying some of the amendments proposed in parliament, pending later enactment as a formal law. Opposition in the Duma voiced three particular concerns:

— The Federal Insolvency Agency was imposing over-strict rules for indebted enterprises, which would in consequence be sold off on the disposal value of their property, not as going concerns; bankruptcies should be dealt with only by the courts on application by creditors.
— The State Committee on Privatization was a monopoly and might undervalue assets to secure quick sales.
— Foreign buyers were unrestricted and could purchase assets too cheaply.

Deputies in the Duma were also concerned that health care and education should not be privatized. The 44 branches for which privatization specifically is prohibited therefore include any institution which receives more than 50 per cent of its funding from the republican budget of the Federation. As in the 1992 decree, all mineral, forest and water resources, military property and most transportation facilities (including underground railways) are in this category. Among those which may be privatized only by decision of the Federation, 36 branches are listed, including commercial banks, printing and publishing enterprises, geological establishments and livestock and horse-breeding stations. For another 20 branches, privatization requires the express permission of the State Property Committee after consultation with the appropriate branch ministry. For all three groups, the decree set out four methods of partial privatization between outright prohibition and permission to go private: the state could retain a block of voting shares in one of three proportions (51, 38 and 25.5 per cent) or issue itself with a 'golden share' (*zolotaya aktsiya*). In order that these restrictions should not be indiscriminately applied, the decree specifies eleven branches (including communications, hydrocarbon and electricity industries and precious metal extraction and processing) in which the state equity of 51, 38 or 25.5 per cent may be held for no longer than three years, after which the shares must either be sold or be converted to a 'golden share'. As in the 1992 decree, the 1993 decree establishes branches (17) for which privatization must conform to plans agreed with the regional authority. It further specifies 11 branches within which privatization is mandatory, notably wholesale and retail trade, construction and building materials, lorry and taxi firms, food processing and consumer goods and hotels, motels and campsites. The decree establishes different procedures for 'state and municipal enterprises in *raions* of the Far North and similar regions'; this affects parts or all of twenty administrative regions. It aims to 'achieve a rational (*ratsional'ny*) union of the traditional economic activities of the peoples of the North with industrial production; to promote the rational employment of the population of and the social development of the regions; to create real conditions for the establishment of ownership rights for the population . . . and economic collectives among sparse peoples of the North.'[42]

The major difference between the second and the first stage is that all change of ownership will be for money and that the procedure is geared towards encouraging the concentration of share ownership so that equity-holders can effectively participate in enterprise governance. A two-thirds majority of staff has to approve the method of sale if the enterprise had a net asset value of less than 1 million rubles on 1 January 1992. Three procedures are laid down:

— *Variant 1* gives 25 per cent of all non-voting shares gratis to staff, up to a maximum of 20 times the legally established minimum wage plus, for staff, 10 per cent of voting shares with a 30 per cent discount (up to a maximum of 6 times the minimum wage); the remaining 65 per cent is auctioned.
— *Variant 2* allows no gratis distribution of shares but allows staff to take a 51 per cent holding of voting shares with payment in cash; the sales price must be approved by the State Property Committee; no deferred payment is permitted (as is envisaged in the other two variants);
—*Variant 3* allows staff to buy 20 per cent of voting stock at a discount of 30 per cent up to a maximum of 20 times the minimum wage, provided that an investor (who may or may not be of the staff) guarantees to the State Property Committee that the investment and other conditions laid down in an approved privatization plan will be fulfilled.

Any shares bought or received gratis may be sold by their owners without limitation: constraints are explicitly forbidden. This provision is intended to counter the pressure to keep insider ownership intact and the sometimes physical or criminal coercion exercised at auctions in the first stage for purchases to remain within the enterprise. Mandatory privatization is required of indebted enterprises declared bankrupt by the Federal Insolvency Agency. In order to limit monopolistic share purchase, no privatized enterprise may buy more than 10 per cent of the shares of another privatized firm. The registration of shares, the convocation of shareholders and the establishment of secondary markets are more protected than under the first stage. Whereas all the money (as noted above) raised during the first stage went to state agencies, 51 per cent of the revenue raised will be given to the privatized enterprise.[43] By the end of 1994 1,320 billion rubles had been received and 9 trillion rubles was anticipated for 1995. Ownership of the land on which enterprises stand will also be transferred.[44] Foreign purchasers are not subject to any discrimination but the sale to foreigners must be registered with the Property Management Committee; no local authority is allowed to impose its own restrictions on foreign owners. The Treuhand practice of tenders with guaranteed investment is followed in a new process of 'investment tenders'; funds received under such investment undertakings are free of tax, as are sums allocated to the Russian Federation in the form of foreign technical assistance and credits.

In advance of the final decree, the Chairman of the Council of Ministers, Viktor Chernomyrdin, defined policy on restructuring. After noting that some firms had successfully adapted to the new market conditions, he observed that the most numerous were those which could adapt 'and have some hope of succeeding. It is these enterprises which should get help from the government.' He stated that a list had already been drawn up of 'enterprises which are beyond salvation and should be closed down in accordance with the law on bankruptcy'.[45]

An implementation of bankruptcy procedures is among the functions falling to the State Property Committee as non-farm property changes are achieved—many enterprises in defense, aerospace, energy and transport would not be privatized, and the Committee would see to their more effective management. Other tasks would be the privatization of rural property, regulation of the securities market and post-privatization support (as envisaged in a Presidential Decree of 22 July 1994).

A THREAT OF RENATIONALIZATION As the result of ministerial changes in November 1994, the minister who had run privatization from the start, Ana-

toly Chubais, became the First Deputy Chairman in charge of the entire economy: this suggested a reaffirmation of reform policy, which nevertheless was
soon jeopardized by the consequences of the military intervention in Chechenia. His short-lived replacement as Minister for Privatization was not drawn
from reformers, being a provincial governor (of the Amur Region), Vladimir
Polevanov, who had supported President Yeltsin in the October 1993 crisis.
He caused great concern by claiming that privatization was endangering Russian security partly by the foreign ownership of shares in the defense industry
and in the production of strategic metals. In still broader terms, he was quoted
as saying that 'as day has night and life has death, privatization has national-
ization' and that the government should 'change its economic line and increase the state management of enterprises'.[46] Almost simultaneously a resolution of the Duma was published that declared the first stage of privatization
'unsatisfactory' and called upon the government to suspend the second stage
until a joint committee of the two could examine it.[47] Both Chubais and
Yeltsin forthwith reaffirmed their policy of the existing privatization program
and the President and Prime Minister made a joint public commitment to it.[48]
Chubais was explicitly set in charge of the agencies administering privatization and on 24 January Polevanov was dismissed.

His acting successor, Pyotr Mostovoi, the Deputy Chairman, observed that
in Polevanov's tenure, 'The decision-making process on privatization came to
a halt; the normal working relationship between the State Property Committee
and the State Property Fund was disrupted. Some of the damage can be fixed
in 24 hours, some will take longer.'[49]

Ukraine

LITTLE EARLY CHANGE In May 1994 *The Economist* headlined an article on
Ukraine 'How to Wreck an Economy'; in September another piece was
headed 'Hope at Last'.[50] The political stimulus for the change of prognosis
was the election in July of President Leonid Kuchma and the accord in September between members of the CIS to collaborate more closely; the economic stimulus was negotiation with the IMF on a reform program. On 27 October 1994 the Ukrainian government agreed on terms with the IMF 'which
could provide assistance over a 12-month period, through a stand-by arrangement in support of a strong program, of up to about $1.5 billion.'[51]

Until those changes there had been much legislation, but virtually no action, on privatization, against a background of hyperinflation, the collapse of

production and the annihilation of the post-ruble currency. Some measures were taken before the disintegration of the USSR. These composed a decree liberalizing foreign trade, allowing joint ventures and establishing the rights of foreign investors (October 1990); a Law on Ownership (February 1991) which established the equality of private, cooperative and state property but denied a right of private property in land, 'national wealth' and many specified branches of production; a Law on Enterprises (March 1991) which, with other legislation of the same period, set out nine forms whereby economic activity could be conducted. A feature of all these measures was the requirement for a mandatory collective labor agreement 'to regulate the production, labor and economic relations of the workforce and management and decide questions of labor protection, social development and the employees' participation in the use of enterprise profits if the latter is provided for by the enterprise charter.'[52] Greater participation by staff was laid down for enterprises more than 50 per cent owned by the state.

The external policy of independent Ukraine until July 1994 was sharply to disarticulate its economy and monetary system from that of Russia. In this period a Law on Leasing (April 1992) went beyond the earlier Soviet legislation in requiring a state enterprise to accept leasing if demanded by a majority of the employees, and a Law on Consumer Cooperatives (April 1992) changed the basis of profit distribution from the Soviet principle of labor contribution to a member's share; the Soviet Law on Producers' Cooperatives remained on the statute book. A Law on Bankruptcy (May 1992) was enacted, but scarcely applied, and one on Foreign Investments (April) permitted portfolio and direct investment, but attracted little inflow.

There had been a degree of wholesale and retail price liberalization in January 1992 (less than at the corresponding time in Russia, but more than in, say, Uzbekistan), and inflation became rapid and very serious. In order partially to compensate savers for the depreciation of their deposits, a novel procedure was embodied in the Law on Privatization Certificates, which accompanied the Law on the Privatization of State Enterprise Property (both March 1992). Each of the 52 million citizens of Ukraine would have a privatization deposit account opened in their name in the State Savings Bank for 17,000 rubles, to which would be added ten times the value of the citizen's personal deposit in that Bank on 2 January 1992 (the date of price liberalization) and twice any deposit made thereafter up to the date of the Law. The accounts—and the certificates which would later be issued in confirmation (for a small fee)—would not be tradable (unlike in Russia), and were to be applied to the purchase of at least 40 per cent (raised to 70 per cent in September 1992) of state enterprises to be privatized. Less than ten per cent of the population used these accounts to buy state property,[53] and the privatization accounts were released from escrow and could be used as ordinary (much depreciated) money. By the end of 1993 only 3 industrial enterprises out of 7,756 were private proprietorial and generated a mere 0.2 per cent of the country's industrial output in 1993 (two in Kharkiv and one in Lugansk); joint-stock companies, including those with equity wholly owned by the state, numbered 270, producing 4 per cent of industrial output; the 1,928 leasehold enterprises generated 22 per cent; state (republican) enterprises 74 per cent (4,844) and municipal enterprises 1 per cent (520).[54]

A further constituent of preparatory work was a series of decrees and implementing ordinances between July and December 1993 on corporatization, in pursuance of a Presidential Decree of June 'On the Corporatization of Enterprises'. Three classes were affected:

— state enterprises with assets no less than 20 million karbovanets ($60,000) on 1 January 1993;
— closed joint-stock companies with over 75 per cent of equity in state ownership;
— production and research organizations whose statute is not in accord with legislation in force.[55]

There was a provision that corporatization should not apply to utilities and transport which were monopolies or enterprises connected with agriculture.

Agencies were set up to manage the process: the State Property Fund of Ukraine for state (republican) enterprises, and regional privatization agencies in each region and municipality and in the Autonomous Republic of Crimea. A State Privatization Fund was created to receive the proceeds of privatization. Two ministries originally had oversight: the Ministry of Economy (with a Department of Property and Entrepreneurship) and the Ministry of Demonopolization and Destatization; a State Committee on Assistance to Small Businesses and Entrepreneurs was also established.[56] Under President Kuchma, however, control over privatization was shifted to the State Property Fund and put under the chairmanship of a convinced reformer, Yuri Yekhanurov. Investment funds were also authorized, but subject to individual licensing by the State Property Fund: they can issue shares in exchange for privatization certificates or money, and were forbidden to guarantee fixed dividends for their members (an abuse to which Russian investment funds were contemporaneously prone).

A trio of authors from the IMF and the CEPR summarized the 'political economy of immobilism' as, *inter alia*, supporting

> large rents from patently inefficient economic activities . . . An example in Ukraine is the profits available to agents who can obtain export licenses . . . A second example is the access that some enterprises have to highly subsidized energy imports . . . Other situation rents include the privileges and perquisites of enterprise managers [who] retain their elite position in society as state patriarchs of their collectives and are difficult to terminate given their close connection with decision-makers . . . The very novelty of the political game makes reaching a compromise on the implementation of stabilization very difficult.[57]

THE START OF MASS PRIVATIZATION The election of Kuchma to the presidency was not an immediate signal for privatization. A law was already in draft (described below) for implementation in 1994 but the parliament, dominated by conservatives, ruled its suspension until a list of enterprises of 'national significance' should be presented to it as excluded from privatization and the scope for foreign purchase should be greatly narrowed. The suspension was lifted in December 1994 when a list of some 6,000 (out of 83,000) was agreed as not subject to privatization.[58] By August 1994 only 10 per cent of all enterprises had been privatized (30 per cent if leased enterprises are counted)[59] and much small privatization was being blocked by local officials. In such circumstances only a few foreign firms had established themselves before the policy change brought by the 1994 election: 628 by April 1994.[60] German investment was the biggest inflow, but it aggregated only DM 92 million at the start of that year. External indebtedness continues to rise, at its greatest towards Russia; Ukrainian debts to non-CIS creditors (zero at the dissolution of the USSR, when Russia took it all over) aggregated $7 billion at the end of 1994.[61]

President Kuchma issued a series of decrees on mass privatization in the last week of November as part of a broader economic reform plan agreed, as noted above, with the IMF. A few days beforehand he had convened a conference of officials and other interested parties to explain the new objectives; the Chairman of the State Property Fund also spoke and stated that by 1 November 6,261 municipal and 4,100 republican enterprises had been either corporatized or privatized. The program, to start in January 1995, was as complicated as that proclaimed in 1992.

— Small privatization would be largely completed during the year; buildings would have to be either bought or leased for a minimum of ten years; money received would go to local government;

— Large corporatized enterprises would begin to be auctioned from 2 January 1995 in five regions (in Khmelnitsky, Kiev, Kirovograd, Zaporozhe and Zhitomir), as 'pilot privatizations' to familiarize citizens and to test the procedures; the rest of the country would start on 1 February and the process (initially affecting some 8,000 enterprises) would end on 1 June 1995.

— Each citizen would receive a privatization certificate of 1.05 million karbovantsi (by then about $11), non-tradable and usable only for purchase of shares, plus the value of Savings Bank deposits (and long-term insurance policies at the state insurance firm Ukrderzhstrakh) frozen at the time Ukraine switched from the ruble to the karbovanets, multiplied by 2,200 to account for inflation; the certificates would be valid until 1 July 1997;

— Enterprise directors have the right to buy up to 5 per cent of the equity of their firm; pensioners have similar privileged access to the shares in the enterprise from which they retired;

— Following the issue to privileged subscribers, staff of an enterprise may subscribe for up to 30 per cent of their enterprise equity; the remainder is to be auctioned to Ukrainian citizens, who may then sell on to foreigners on a secondary market to be established;

— The State Property Fund would be responsible for privatization preparations and auctions in association with joint regional committees on which local authorities were represented: all regions except Crimea, Kharkiv and Transcarpathia had already established these.

— Investment funds (of which 369 had been established by January 1995) could buy a portfolio with cash or contributed vouchers.[62]

Housing would be privatized in parallel: a fixed area could be purchased with special 'property checks', and further dwelling areas could be bought with privatization certificates.

Kazakhstan

The Kazakh government differentiated its three non-farm privatization schemes (small business, mass privatization and housing) from other CIS governments by choosing points (as in the then Czechoslovakia, later copied in Belarus) rather than money to denominate vouchers and by the compulsory use of investment funds (as in Poland) rather than direct purchase of equity;

reportedly it drew initial inspiration for an all-citizen voucher distribution from the example of neighboring Mongolia. It also took steps to assure to 'outsiders' control of privatized enterprises, which in most other members of the CIS went to 'insiders', and to attract foreign capital into the controlling equity.

Kazakhstan, then still part of the USSR, was the first Union Republic to create its own State Property Committee (January 1991) and began small privatization as early as August 1991. On attaining independence at the end of that year, the government formulated principles for voucher privatization, which has operated with the following characteristics.

— Of the two forms of privatization cheque, that designated an 'investment coupon' was distributed to all Kazakh citizens, those in rural areas receiving 120 points and those in urban areas 100 points. Distribution of coupons took place in late 1993.
— Investment coupons could be deposited only in 'investment privatization funds' and could not be traded or used directly to buy equity. So few coupons had been deposited in funds (a mere 15 per cent had been redeemed at the seven auctions by November 1994) that the government was compelled to waive deadlines for deposit and to offer a money value first of 4 rubles and then one tenge per point (a derisory offer, when a liter of petrol costs 6 tenge officially, and 12 tenge on the open market).
— By September 1994 144 investment privatization funds had been established, but some were so small that it was foreseen that about one-third of them would merge or be liquidated within a year. In the seven auctions to date only 30 per cent of the shares offered had been bought up. The share auction process was to be completed by late Spring 1995.
— Share trading is permitted only among investment funds, but a secondary market for shares is envisaged.
— The other form of privatization cheque is the housing coupon, the aggregate value distributed to citizens being equal to the estimated value of the public housing stock. Because many rebates were given on the estimated value of dwellings, and some tenants opted not to buy their accommodation, more than half of these coupons remained unspent, and were converted into investment coupons (although the government had expected them to be used for 'small privatization').

The differentiation between urban and rural recipients could have been ostensibly to compensate for different levels of living; it could also have been to promote President Nazarbaev's image among the 43 per cent of rural voters.

But a more apposite comment is that ethnic Kazakhs are predominantly coun-tryfolk and Russianized Kazakhs, Russians and Ukrainians live in the north-ern towns.[63]

In the Decree on the National Privatization Program (March 1993), state enterprises were classed into three groups: 'small privatization' applied to the 5,000 businesses with fewer than 200 workers; 'mass privatization' referred to the 850 firms with between 200 and 5,000 staff; and case-by-case privatization for the 100 enterprises with more than 5,000 employees (of which 25 were subsequently listed as open for a controlling foreign purchase, including the important oil and gas industries). The first step in the procedure was corporati-zation and, for the medium and large enterprises, the establishment of state holding companies (34 were created, covering three-quarters of industrial pro-duction) holding a majority of the government's one hundred per cent of the equity. The aim was not so much devolution as the assurance by ownership of previous contractual supply-sales relations.

Most of the 10,000 businesses which had been transferred to the private sector by 1 August 1994 were in the 'small' category. Only 21 per cent, how-ever, were fully privatized, partly because of the requirement that half the auc-tion price had to be paid in housing coupons and buyers were given time to ac-quire enough to make their purchase complete. Difficulties also arose because employees had unexpired leases on the equipment and challenged the legality of the sale, or because managers of the corporatized business who had been underbidders removed equipment before formal hand-over and had to be pur-sued through the courts.

In the medium-size category 10 per cent of the equity is passed to the em-ployees, 51 per cent is available for purchase by an investment privatization fund, and 39 per cent remains state property. The State Property Committee has not restructured before offering enterprises at auction and many sales have not gone through because of the enterprise's heavy indebtedness: the govern-ment, chiefly concerned with reducing the budget deficit in the interest of dis-inflation, has not made restructuring finance available.

Large enterprises are being sold individually, KPMG advising the State Privatization Committee. Although employees are also assured a 10 per cent stake, as in smaller enterprises, the overwhelming share is available to the buyer(s). Foreign purchasers are welcome and within the CIS Kazakhstan is second only to Russia in attracting them. Major deals include Philip Morris in-vesting $300 million in a cigarette factory, the Almaty Tobacco Combine, and associated tobacco plantations; the Bakyrchik gold mines; and large ventures in the oil, gas and pipeline industries.[64] On the other hand, Unilever was close to buying two margarine factories for $60 million, but could not obtain contracts for the supply of sunflower oil, and the sole facility in the former USSR producing vinyl fibers for the aerospace industry, Kustanai Khim Volokno, has found no buyer. The existing Kazakh oil industry is to be privatized in 1995 and Western advisers have been retained.[65]

In tandem with privatization and the influx of foreign enterprise, the Kazakh government is actively promoting an indigenous private sector. A 'State Program for Supporting and Encouraging Enterprise in Kazakhstan', promulgated in July 1994, requires completion of the legal and financial infrastructure of a developed market economy, based on the inviolability and protection of private property: there is room, it asserts, for 150,000 private businesses in Kazakhstan.[66]

Belarus

Like Ukraine, Belarus suffered two years of economic disorder, although inflation in 1993 (2,775 per cent) did not go through the roof (as Ukraine's did that year, with 10,155 per cent); similarly, presidential elections in July 1994 displaced a *nomenklatura* conservative, Vyacheslau Kebich, by one somewhat readier to privatize, Aleksandr Lukashenka. Progress to date has been slower than in most other CIS members, but the Minister for State Property and Privatization, Georgy Badzey, declared in October 1994 that the flotation of those republican and municipal enterprises scheduled for transfer would be completed by the end of 1995.[67] But not until 1997, the EBRD notes, would two-thirds of state assets be in private hands.[68]

In the Byelorussian SSR, the Supreme Soviet appeared to be in advance of the Union legislature. As early as October 1990 it resolved on a 'Program of Transition to a Market Economy', which specified 'destatization and privatization; economic stabilization and overcoming the crisis, demonopolization; support and development of entrepreneurship; and the restructuring of industry and of the economy as a whole.'[69] It formally copied Soviet basic legislation in 1991, enacting a Privatization Law and instituting a Committee for the Management of State Property and a State Property Agency. The chief purpose of these declaratory acts was to disarticulate the economy from the Union and to allow enterprise directors and the political *nomenklatura* to go their own way. The Law was used to issue leasing contracts to staff—272 enterprises were leased (with some 60,000 workers) during 1991-2, which effectively concentrated power in management. Little support was offered to independent business, and by the end of 1992 only 8 per cent of national output came from the private sector.

A gradual privatization process was initiated in 1993—by a law of 19 January 'On Destatization and Privatization of State Property' and three implementing Supreme Soviet Decrees of 16 June. The Law established two 'quotas' for citizens—one for state productive assets, the other for housing: privatization checks, respectively entitled 'Property' and 'Housing', would be issued with a timed validity. The aggregate value of 'property checks' was to equal half the book value of the assets to be privatized: the half not allocated gratis could be retained by the state, purchased by individuals, partnerships, private juridical persons, foreigners or stateless persons (within a separate law on foreign investment), or bought out by employees.

The points on housing checks were uniform, but the number required per unit of accommodation varied with size and quality. The points on property checks were more differentiated by recipient than in any other CIS state: they were distributed to adults basically on an age scale (20 points for those aged between 18 and 25, rising to 50 for those over 35). But a varied allocation was added under specified conditions. Thus, one point was added for each year of employment; 50 points were added for invalids and the disabled; and 15 for service in the Second World War (50 if disabled in consequence). Parents received 10 points for each child, but 30 were added for a deceased parent.[70] As in other CIS states, the State Savings Bank was made responsible for the issue of vouchers. Citizens could deposit their property checks in investment funds, of which 16 had been registered by the end of September 1994.

As elsewhere, the process with respect to the state enterprise begins with corporatization: 167 republican enterprises and 460 run by regional and municipal authorities were selected for the first stage. Some of the republican enterprises were divided into regional entities, and these are somewhat misleadingly included in the stated numbers. The government retains 50 per cent of the equity of each, selling off a tranche annually until its holdings are zero after ten years; 30 per cent are allocated to employees only by property cheese; and 20 per cent is auctioned to citizens, also by property cheese. No purchases are permitted to foreigners. Price Waterhouse has been retained for advice, but most offerings are unrestructured.

A new constitution (March 1994) guaranteed the right to private property (article 44); and accorded the president considerably greater power than previously (article 100). Lukashenka was elected with that authority, backed by a landslide vote of 80 per cent. He was, however, ambiguous on the pace of marketization. On appointment, he said he still favored 'a state regulated economy', declaring: 'I am ready to meet business people tomorrow and to say to them—help me out of our crisis. If they help me I'll help them. If instead they just think of ways to make a bigger profit, then they'll find it hard. [Privatization hitherto made] people feel it's all just a trick and only for criminals. But if there's a privatization that can be done in the interests of the people, then we would look at it.'[71]

Later he continued in the same vein: 'Privatization has turned into grabbing . . . A director has become a prince: he has today two Mercedes cars and five security vehicles . . . Facts show that not a single enterprise has become efficient. I cannot accept privatization for the sake of privatization.'[72] With such reservations by the highest officer of state, citizens have shown low interest in actually collecting their vouchers: of the 8 million entitled to receive them, 1,972,000 had applied by the end of October 1994; holdings of 40 million points were comprised in the 405,625 property checks already issued, of which just 1 million points had been applied to the purchase of shares.

Once an enterprise has been sold off—and by the end of October 1994 only 10 per cent of those scheduled had reached that status—foreigners may purchase shares on equal terms with citizens, but access usually depends on connections or bribery. In consequence most external capital has gone into direct investment. By September 1994 there were some 2,000 such firms, a quarter being wholly owned. Bureaucratic obstacles to their operation are considerable: Coca-Cola, with a 90 per cent holding with Kraynitsa of Minsk, had to cease production for a week because officials required completion of import forms (for the 'secret ingredient') in Byelorussian as well as in Russian and English.[73]

The privatization of small enterprises, against both vouchers and cash, is conducted separately by regional and municipal authorities. In the current first stage the target is disposal of half the assets, but by September 1994 only 17 per cent had been sold; of retail outlets, 30 per cent had been sold. Of enterprises under municipal owners, a mere 5 per cent had been sold. The State Anti-Monopoly Committee has drafted legislation to encourage the creating of new small businesses.[74] Municipalities are also selling building land. The International Finance Corporation is assisting in the small privatization program.

Uzbekistan

Seven weeks after its declaration of independence the Uzbek Supreme Soviet enacted a Law on Destatization and Privatization, whereby state productive assets were placed in the hands of a State Property Committee; it had earlier the same year established the legal bases for non-state enterprise by Laws on Enterprises and on Entrepreneurship (February) and on Cooperatives (June), and provided for a commercial banking system (February). The State Property Committee (adding 'and Privatization' to its title) was made responsible for the privatization program and for foreign participation therein by a Presidential Decree of February.

The first transfer of titles related to housing. The proportion of it in private ownership had been the highest in the USSR.[75] Householders were given (within certain limits) ownership of the property they occupied, although not of the land on which it stood. The transfer is now virtually complete.

Small-scale private activity, both legal and illicit, had been quite well-developed: 'Money-making, irrespective of its origins—or legality—always remained respectable in Uzbek society'.[76] The government's priority for small privatization, especially of retailing, was therefore welcomed and from late 1992 until mid-1994, 53,000 businesses had been sold or leased (mainly to employees).[77] The options open, under the 1991 Law, were leasing, transformation into a cooperative, sale by auction and sale by tender. No formal preference was accorded to employees, but Article 6 specifically encouraged it and authorized the use of retained profits and even of the amortization fund for a group buy-out.[78] Furthermore, share ownership by insiders of at least 25 per cent of equity (including any held by the State Property Fund) exercises control.[79]

Large-scale privatization was embodied in a Presidential Decree of March 1994. No vouchers are on offer and foreign buyers are welcomed, either to bid at auction or to negotiate individual purchase. The biggest purchase to date has been the 51 per cent of equity in the state tobacco monopoly by BAT Industries of the UK for a down payment of $60 million and $200 million over five years; each annual payment will bring a further tranche of shares, at the end of which BAT will have virtually complete ownership. Its Tashkent cigarette factory, renamed Uzbat, will be refitted, a new plant will be built in Samarkand and locally grown tobacco will be processed in its own works. As the law still does not allow private land ownership, BAT negotiated a 99-year lease for its factory sites at a predetermined rent.[80]

In all, 4,000 medium and large enterprises were scheduled for corporatization and sale of some equity in 1994; a number of branches will be unaffected —cotton plantations, the energy, metals, mining, pharmaceutical and 'high-technology' industries, and railway and air transport. The Commission of the European Union financed (with 900,000 ecus) three of the first sell-offs to test and establish procedures.

Taking into account these privatizations, direct foreign investment and the expansion of private activity, it is expected that the proportion of private to state productive assets will reach 50 per cent at the end of 1994 and 60 per cent a year later.[81]

Azerbaijan

A coup which changed the entire policy direction of the government in June 1993, a debilitating war with neighboring Armenia over Nagorno-Karabakh, inflation of 810 per cent in 1993 and 2,000 per cent in 1994 and conditions which President Heydar Aliyev described in late 1993 as 'a state of deepening economic crisis'[82] are scarcely propitious for systemic reform. A start has, nevertheless, been made with privatization.

During the presidency of Ayaz Mutalibov (May 1990 to June 1993), the Supreme Soviet enacted a Law on the Fundamentals of Economic Sovereignty (June 1991) which abolished central planning to leave economic decisions to enterprise directors, and which provided for an eventual privatization other than of land and the hydrocarbon and petrochemical industries. The first of these constraints was removed a year later and a law for the privatization of small state enterprises was passed by the National Assembly in January 1993, to be implemented by mid-1995. The coup intervened, but the victors (Heydar Aliyev was elected on 98.8 per cent of the national vote) retained most of the legislation on privatization: a program was launched in April 1994, also for completion in two years. A state enterprise is defined as 'small' when it has fewer than 50 staff, and the 8,000 to be sold constitute about 30 per cent of the total. The transfer of public housing to tenants also began.

The original scheme for gratis vouchers was not implemented, but 20 per cent of the equity in small privatizations goes gratis to employees; the State Property Agency may retain a proportion for the state (a majority in 'vital' enterprises) and then auctions the residue. The Prime Minister, Suret Huseinov, complained in July 1994 that managements were 'artificially' running down their assets in order 'to privatize them profitably', that is to buy them up at a lower valuation.[83] This practice has been noted in other republics of the CIS, but since there is no voucher system it benefits only insiders. Huseinov went on in effect to call for such a system: 'I do not oppose the privatization program, but this process should be conducted reasonably with consideration [for the] interests of all categories of Azerbaijan's population, and first of all of the invalids of the Karabakh war.'[84]

A government program formulated in April 1994 extended envisaged privatization to medium-sized state enterprises (50 to 300 employees) during 1996–8 and to large enterprises (employing more than 300) from 1998 onward.[85]

Although foreigners are not excluded from the purchase of privatized shares, the exclusion of hydrocarbons from privatization requires that entry to Azerbaijan's most salable products be by joint venture. A Western consortium's agreement with Prime Minister Abulfaz Elchibey was set aside at the coup, but was revived and revised by the incomers. The major charge was the entry of the Russian oil firm Lukoil with a 10 per cent stake: the British, United States and Turkish partners (led by British Petroleum) will invest \$7 billion over the term of the agreement, receiving 80 per cent of the production. The Azerbaijan National Oil Company transferred a quarter of its shares to the Iranian National Oil Company, partly because of a strong pro-Iranian element in external policy, but also because it was likely to find difficulty in mobilizing its own investment outlay. The first private company since the 1920s, MNM, established in December 1989, has extensive joint ventures with Turkish and Russian firms.[86]

Moldova

A Moldovan Privatization Law (July 1991) predated by a few weeks the declaration of independence: it excluded objects of national culture, state monopolies and defense and security enterprises, and deferred extension to the exploitation of natural resources, but established the legal framework for the sale of state assets. The civil war which left the Dniestr Republic in independent occupation of the left bank of the River Dniestr destroyed any early chance of domestic reorganization, but a Privatization Plan was launched in March 1993. Variant procedures were established for small and for medium and large enterprises, with public auction for the small privatization (900 enterprises in the first stage in 1993–4). For mass privatization the scheme is somewhat like the Russian one. In a first stage—two years from July 1994—vouchers were distributed (90 per cent of citizens had taken them by November 1994), their value being graduated according to the length of work service in Moldova (and not elsewhere). The second stage (1995-6) is likely to be solely for cash. Vouchers are in the name of the recipient and may not be traded, although they may be pooled in an investment fund. Auctions are solely for vouchers.

In 1994 the Ministry of Privatization and State Property scheduled 150 medium/large enterprises and 500 small enterprises for sale, and by July 1995 1,600 enterprises should have been transferred, making up 34 per cent of all state assets. By 1997 two-thirds of all productive assets in Moldova will be private.

As just noted, investment funds are authorized and 23 had been set up at the time mass privatization was launched. Enterprises connected with agriculture are in a separate category, with 20 per cent of equity given to employees, 50 per cent to suppliers and 30 per cent retained by the Ministry of Privatization. The fuel and energy utility, GPO, is also under a special dispensation: the government is to retain a controlling interest, and employees are given priority participation before the public's vouchers are accepted. A Deputy Premier, Ion Gutu, suggested in September 1994 that 'the government should take up to 20 per cent of the shares of some enterprises to sell them to foreign investors'.[87] Penfolds of Australia have established a large winery with their know-how, but foreign investment has generally been modest.

More than two-thirds of housing was by mid-1994 already in private hands and privatization of the remaining 350,000 dwellings in the public sector is to be assured. In the first half of 1994 80 per cent of the transfers were by voucher, 13 per cent with partial payment and 7 per cent with full payment.[88]

The quasi-independent Dniestr Republic boycotted the Moldovan privatization program and introduced its own, less comprehensive law; but by late 1994 no implementation had taken place.[89]

Turkmenistan

Turkmenistan has the smallest share of output generated in the private sector and had restricted privatization to retail trade, catering and consumer services by the end of 1994. As the Turkmen SSR it formulated property rights and allowed assets to be leased to foreign physical or juridical persons (October 1990), and liberalized these provisions on the eve of independence (November 1991). A Law on Destatization and Privatization (February 1992) closely followed the 1991 Soviet model in envisaging a voucher distribution for part of the equity offered, placed in escrow accounts in the State Savings Bank, and leaving the choice of privatization procedure to majority vote of the staff of the enterprise concerned. If they choose no method, one may be imposed by the Department for the Management of State Property and Privatization of the Ministry of Economy and Finance[90] or by the branch ministry responsible for the enterprise. Foreign purchases of shares were allowed, but a quota can be imposed. A Bankruptcy Law (June 1992) has been little applied to indebted state enterprises.

The exclusion of Turkmenistan's main resource, oil and gas, from privati-

zation means that 70 per cent of the value of the country's mining and manufacturing output will remain in the public sector. In a second stage, beginning
in January 1995, enterprises manufacturing consumer goods and building materials, processing farm produce and in transport would be privatized.[91] Citizens and foreigners could compete on equal terms, and the Treuhand practice
of investment contracts was to be followed; additionally guarantees would be
required on the purchase of raw materials.

Georgia

Pursuant to a Law on the Privatization of State Property (October 1991), a
State Committee on Privatization was established in 1992 and three paths of
property transfer were envisaged.[92]

— Public housing, in an already largely private dwelling stock, was the
  first group of state assets to be privatized, and the transfer to occupiers is
  now almost complete.
— Small state enterprises (with assets of less than 30 million rubles at the
  end of 1992 and fewer than 50 employees) were the next to be sold off.
  Of almost 5,000 such state businesses, some 37 per cent should have
  been privatized by the end of 1994.
— Medium and large enterprises will eventually be privatized in a program
  using vouchers, but it has not yet been launched. By mid-1994 only
  three of the over 900 enterprises in this category had been sold. Despite
  the passage of a Bankruptcy Law in 1991, little action has been taken on
  financial restructuring.

It is unsurprising that little change has been made in mass privatization. Hostilities in the break-away Abkhaz Autonomous Republic did not end until November 1993 and external relations, previously antipathetic to Russia, were
turned around by Georgian adherence to the CIS two months later. Inflation
that year was 2,656 per cent.

Kyrgyzstan

The Kirgiz SSR, as it then was, quickly followed the Soviet 'Basic Legislation', with its own Law on the General Privatization of Enterprises and on

Competition in July 1991; implementing decrees the following month set a start of January 1992 and a target of 35 per cent of eligible enterprises to be privatized by the end of 1993. A State Property Committee was established to operate privatization, which may be summarized under five heads.

— All Kyrgyz citizens received privatization certificates in the form of escrow accounts in the State Savings Bank. The sum incorporated a universal minimum, supplemented by a value calculated for those who were or had been in employment on the monthly earnings averaged over the previous five years and multiplied by years of service. This practice assured 'insiders' a higher entitlement. The accounts were to be converted into coupons which could be presented at auctions for purchase of shares.
— State enterprise management and employees are entitled to buy for certificates and/or cash up to 5 per cent of the equity of their firm if fixed assets per employee exceed 6,000 som ($1,000), but on a sliding scale up to 30 per cent if the asset/staff ratio is less than 1,000 ($170), purchasable with a 30 per cent discount.
— A further 20 per cent of equity is open to public auction against privatization vouchers and cash.
— The state retains a 50 per cent holding in enterprises for a transitional period.
— A special program (affecting 29 state enterprises of the ninety or so in serious debt by September 1994) is to float the shares of enterprises declared bankrupt.

By 1 August 1994, 65 per cent of Kyrgyz citizens had exchanged their privatization certificates for entitlements to shares (coupons) and a Presidential Decree extended the time limit for exchange to 1 October 1994. By July 230,000 shareholders had equity in 4,500 privatized firms, or 46 per cent of the total number of state enterprises. The IMF's agreement to the reform program, including privatization, and support for an independent currency which proved itself the most stable in the CIS, has attracted some Western direct investment. Price Waterhouse is advising the State Property Committee. The World Bank fostered capital inflow by convening a conference in Paris in December 1994 of investors from 27 countries; a mission from the US governmental Overseas Private Investment Corporation (OPIC) two months previously had backed the program; and Switzerland (Kyrgyzstan is sometimes termed the 'Switzerland of Central Asia' because of its democracy and enterprise) is providing financial and technical aid (agreed during President Akayev's visit to Berne in November).

The privatization program would have gone faster had acceleration not been opposed by a majority in parliament: new elections were held in February 1995, with the intention of resolving the issue. A Law on Privatization of the Housing Stock was vetoed by the President (August 1993), and this too awaits resolution by a new parliament.

Tajikistan

In terms of civil strife Tajikistan has had a worse experience than Azerbaijan or Georgia, for, after a lull in the first half of 1994, fighting broke out again in July. The government, installed by force in November 1992, has nevertheless made considerable progress in privatization. It inherited from Soviet times a Law on Property (October 1990), which besides formalizing private ownership rights, allowed joint ventures with foreign companies; and a Law on Destatization and Privatization (February 1991), under which a State Property Committee (established in August 1991) set out procedures for transfers out of public ownership. Under these Soviet provisions more than a thousand small firms (defined as employing fewer than 50) were leased to, or bought by, their managers and staff.

Under the 1991 law, leasing was also available to larger firms; these could also be privatized by corporatization—followed by sale (by installments if preferred) to the workforce or even gratis transfer (where few net assets remained) or by public auction. New momentum was given by the government in early 1994, and in the first half of the year 170 republican and municipal businesses were privatized—three times more than in the whole of 1993. By mid-1994 152 out of 1,304 medium and large firms had been privatized.[93] In so unstable a country foreign purchasers have not been attracted by the legal possibility of ownership. Public housing has mostly been transferred to occupiers.

Armenia

During its hostilities with Azerbaijan, the Armenian government has provided a sharp contrast in economic policy. A bastion of fiscal orthodoxy, it has brought the monthly rate of inflation down to 8 per cent (against an Azeri 60 per cent) and removed almost the last of its consumer subsidies. It stands out from all other CIS members in realistically expecting a balanced budget in 1995 and in making privatization a voluntary choice for the staff of an enterprise, but without further subsidization. The one lacuna in that connection is delay in parliament to the passage of a Bankruptcy Law and toleration of enterprise indebtedness through off-budget credits of the state-run banks. By mid-1994 about 40 per cent of GDP originated in the private sector, which employed some 35 per cent of the labor force.[94] The sector accounted for about two-thirds of imports.[95]

A Law on Destatization and Privatization of State Enterprises and Unfinished Construction Sites (August 1992, amended November 1993) established a procedure for divestment under a Committee for Privatization and State Property Management. Small-scale transfer began in the retail and personal services branch by preferential sale to employees, with auction for units not taken up. By the end of 1993 over 350 businesses had been privatized. Urban housing was already 30 per cent, and rural housing almost completely, privately owned before independence: the privatization program put a further 10 per cent into occupiers' hands by the same date.

Medium and large enterprises entered the program in July 1994, together with an extension to all other small firms. A total of 4,750 enterprises were then scheduled, of which 2,750 are classed as 'small', and the ten largest were being auctioned in the first half of 1995. The process follows lines used elsewhere in the CIS, save in the choice of transfer's being 'strictly voluntary' (of the 1,000 businesses to be privatized in 1994, 700 had already held assemblies and approved the change by mid-September).[96] The constituents of the process are:

— Some four million privatization vouchers have been distributed to all citizens and a further one million are to be given to state-enterprise employees to bid, if they so wish, for the 20 per cent of the equity of their own business reserved for them.
— Vouchers, valued at 10,000 drams (about $28), may be deposited in investment funds; regulations for their oversight were in principle more exacting than the Russian, but it was alleged that the market in vouchers was taken over by speculators, who in December 1994 were offering only 2,000 drams for a voucher.
— A pilot restructuring of three large, heavily indebted enterprises preceded the launch, but the government has still to issue directives on general financial restructuring. As 70 per cent of medium and large enterprises are scheduled for transfer, the cost to the government, and hence to its monetary policy, may have been underestimated.

Satisfactory as the progress seems to be, privatization and the rest of the radi-
cal reform program depend heavily on the continuance of President Levon
Ter-Petrosian and Prime Minister Grant Bagratian in office.[97] The nationalist
and populist opposition may succeed in the parliamentary elections set for
May 1995, and no peace accord has been reached with Azerbaijan, although
Armenian troops occupy Nagorno-Karabakh and the corridors to Armenia.
Military expenditure is a major rival to the cost of the privatization program.

Notes to Chapter Two

1. For a list of legislative acts on ownership, from the Lease Decree to the securities regulations of 1992, and for detailed accounts of the types of commercial property extant and of the privatization process up to late 1992, see Roman Frydman et al., *The Privatization Process in Russia, Ukraine and the Baltic States* (Budapest: Central European University Press, 1993), pp. 1-82.

2. This program was one of twelve economic plans considered by the Gorbachev administration in the later part of the *perestroika* period; none were implemented. They are tabulated and
discussed in Marshall Goldman, *Lost Opportunity* (New York: Norton, 1994), p. 76.

3. Product at current exchange rates is from International Monetary Fund, *Country Review*, for
the states concerned. For a discussion of the ratio between those rates and estimated purchasing
power parity (ppp) indices (which, adjusted for tradables and the ppp of the US dollar, yields a
'real' exchange rate), see M. Nuti in *International Economic Outlook*, London Business School,
June 1994; and J.S. Flemming and R.C.O. Matthews, 'Economic Reform in Russia', *National Institute Economic Review*, no. 149, August 1994, pp. 65-82. The 'real' exchange rate (allowing for
differential inflation in the ruble and in the dollar) is regularly reported in *Russian Economic
Trends*, Centre for Economic Reform of the Government of the Russian Federation and Centre for
Economic Performance of the London School of Economics (quarterly, with monthly updates,
Whurr Publishers, London and Lawrence, Kansas). At a conference of the Central Bank of Russia
and the Banque de France (Moscow, 16-17 January 1995), Marie Lavigne summarized a range of
calculations to indicate a ppp of 800-900 rubles to the dollar and an equilibrium rate of 4,000
rubles (personal communication).

4. The map of Russian regions showing percentage privatization is from *TACIS News*, no 3,
November 1994, p. 8, and is attributed to the State Property Management Committee and the
Russian Privatization Centre.

5. Brigitte Granville and Judith Shapiro, *Russian Inflation: A Statistical Pandora's Box*, Discussion Paper 53 (London: Royal Institute of International Affairs, 1994), documents one particular field; papers in *Economics of Transition* cover others (Kasper Bartholdy in vol. 2, no 1,
pp.111-16, and in vol. 2, no. 2, pp. 269-80; and Dariusz Rosati in vol. 2, no. 4, pp. 419-42).

6. For texts of the privatization laws and decrees on Russia, Ukraine and Belarus, thanks are
due to Dr Yuri Khromov (Russian Institute for Strategic Studies), Andrei Mitskevich (Supreme
Council of the Republic of Belarus), Inna Pidluska (Ukrainian Centre for Independent Political
Research) and Dr Christopher Smart (Russian State Property Management Committee).

7. The various agencies operating the privatization process in all 29 countries (the thirtieth
transition country, Mongolia, is not an ECE member) were listed in ECE, *Economic Survey of Europe in 1992-1993* (United Nations: New York and Geneva, 1993), p. 194.

8. 1992 population 166,000. Presumably chosen because of the paucity of large towns in the Russian Far East.

9. *State Property Management Committee of Russia*, official brochure, pp.1-3.

10. This was a marked difference from the Ryzhkov Plan of 1990 which foresaw sale (and hence control of privatization) by the branch ministries.

11. For their functions, operations and conflicts, see Bornstein, op. cit., pp. 425-6.

12. Roman Frydman and Andrzej Rapaczynski, *Privatization in Eastern Europe: Is the State Withering Away?* (Budapest: Central European University Press, 1994), p. 153.

13. On the unification of the exchange rate at auction-determined levels in the context of opening foreign trade, see *inter alia* Petr Aven, 'Problems in Foreign Trade Regulation in Russian Economic Reform', in Åslund, op. cit., pp. 80-93.

14. See particularly William Easterly and Paulo Vieira da Cunha, 'Financing the Storm: Macroeconomic Crisis in Russia', *Economics of Transition*, vol. 2, no. 4, pp. 443-65.

15. M. Dewatripont and G. Roland, 'Economic Reform and Dynamic Political Constraints', *Review of Economic Studies*, vol. 59, 1992, pp. 703-30; Dewatripont and Roland, *The Design of Reform Packages under Uncertainty*, CEPR Discussion Paper, no. 862, 1993; Roland, 'On the Speed and Sequencing of Privatization and Restructuring', *Economic Journal*, vol. 104, September 1994, pp. 1158-68.

16. Richard Hemming, 'Privatization of State Enterprises', in Vito Tanzi (ed.), *Fiscal Policies in Economies in Transition,*(Washington DC: International Monetary Fund, 1992), p. 84. The USSR was the most autarkic member of CMEA and Russia the most autarkic of the USSR.

17. Chubais and Vishnevskaya, op. cit., p. 94.

18. At end August *(Russian Economic Trends*, Monthly Update, 17 October 1994).

19. *The Economist*, 12 November 1994, p. 41.

20. Frydman et al., op. cit., p. 49, points out that 'average' was nowhere defined and that 'large' was defined as over 1,000 staff *or* assets of over 1 million rubles, while 'small' was up to 200 staff *and* assets of less than 1 million rubles.

21. This is a summary listing: a fuller list is given in Frydman et al., op. cit, pp. 47-8.

22. Of the approximately 6,000 Russian state enterprises with over 1,000 employees and 50 million rubles of assets, 2,000 were in the excluded categories (Frydman et al., op. cit., p. 53).

23. A mere $10 at the then ruling exchange rate, but this was irrelevant in auctions for which only vouchers could be tendered and because the nominal value of the enterprise was pre-set.

24. Maxim Boycko, Andrei Shleifer and Robert Vishny, 'Voucher Privatization', *Journal of Financial Economics*, vol. 35, April 1994, p. 260.

25. Lynn Nelson and Irina Kuzes, *Property to the People* (New York: Sharpe, 1994), ch. 4, state that Grigory Yavlinsky, an author of one of the most publicized reform programs under *perestroika* and a likely presidential candidate in 1996, argued against vouchers on this ground.

26. *Russian Economic Trends*, vol. 3, no. 2, 1994, p. 95; the price then dropped to 45,000 rubles when the expiry date was postponed.

27. This summary is from Pekka Sutela, 'Insider Privatization in Russia: Speculations on Systemic Change', *Europe-Asia Studies*, vol. 46, no. 3, 1994, p. 420.

28. EBRD, *Transition Report*, op. cit., p. 61.

29. Frydman et al., op. cit., pp. 20-22 and 63-4, gives fuller detail.

30. For the allocation (and a minor exception) see Bornstein, op. cit., p. 432.

31. *Izvestiya*, 13 August 1993.

32. Calculated from the numbers tabulated in *Sotsial'no-ekonomicheskoe polozhenie Rossii,* January-September 1994 (Moscow: Goskomstat, 1994), p. 58. Totals for 1992 and 1993 from *Russian Economic Trends*, vol. 3, no. 1, 1994, pp. 78-9, and for seven months of 1994 from ibid., *Monthly Update,* 17 October 1994. Other data from speeches of Anatoly Chubais and Maxim

Boycko (respectively, Chairman of the State Property Committee and Chief Executive of the Russian Privatization Centre) on 29 July and 29 August 1994.

33. Yuri Khromov, *Foreign Investments and Privatization in Russia*, mimeo, Russian Institute for Strategic Studies, Moscow, 1994, p. 3.

34. Simon Clarke et al., *What about the Workers? Workers and the Transition to Capitalism in Russia* (London and New York: New Left Books), 1993, p. 217.

35. N. Samoilova, *Kommersant*, 28 November 1994.

36. *Sotsial'no-ekonomicheskoe polozhenie Rossii*, op. cit., p. 61.

37. The Urals Emerald Mine, in the town of Asbest (*Kommersant*, 28 October 1994).

38. *Sotsial'no-ekonomicheskoe polozhenie Rossii*, op. cit., pp. 257-8.

39. An early advocacy of foreign investment as an important support for privatization is in Mario Baldassarri, Luigi Paganetto and Edmund Phelps (eds), *Privatization Processes in Eastern Europe: Theoretical Foundations and Empirical Results* (London: Macmillan, 1993)—papers of a conference in Rome, 1991.

40. Ibid., p. 54.

41. N. Samoilova, *Kommersant*, 8 November 1994; and *Business Central Europe*, June 1994, p. 20.

42. *Rossiiskie vesti*, no. 3 (427), 1994, Dokumenty, p. 7.

43. Proceeds from vouchers exchanged between 1 August and 1 December 1994 (under the prolongation authorized by Presidential Decree) will still go to the government bodies as before (*Rossiiskaya gazeta*, 21 July 1994).

44. Where municipal office space has been privatized, the recipient enterprise has been subjected—at least in some cities (including Moscow and St Petersburg)—to a high tax on the rent paid to the new owner by any tenant.

45. V. Chernomyrdin, 'No Exits on the Road to the Market', *Financial Times*, 16 May 1994.

46. *Izvestiya* and *Segodnya*, 30 December 1994.

47. Resolution no. 378-I dated 9 December 1994, published in *Rossiiskaya gazeta*, 21 December 1994.

48. *Financial Times*, 18 January 1995.

49. *Moscow Times*, 29 January 1995.

50. *The Economist*, 7 May 1994 (in a Survey entitled 'The Birth and Possible Death of a Country'); and 24 September 1994, of which the first line was 'The economic sick man of Europe may at last have a chance of revival'.

51. Address of Michel Camdessus, Managing Director of the IMF, to the Conference on Partnership for Economic Transformation in Ukraine, Winnipeg, 27 October 1994 (*IMF Survey*, 14 November 1994). Canadian Ukrainians have been in the lead of Western support for independent Ukraine.

52. Citation and detail of legislation from Frydman et al., op. cit., pp. 94-106.

53. Report of Yuri Yekhanurov, Chairman of the State Property Fund, to an International Conference on Transformation Processes in Ukraine, Kiev, 1-4 December 1994 (communication from Igor Egorov, Dobrov Steps Centre, Ukrainian National Academy of Sciences, in advance of the publication of the proceedings).

54. *Privatization in Ukraine*, vol. 3, no. 2, February 1994, p. 4; data for republican and municipal enterprises are for the first nine months of 1993, ibid., vol. 2, no. 9, December 1993, p. 4.

55. Ibid., February 1994, p. 5.

56. Frydman et al., op. cit., pp. 114-18.

57. Oleh Havrylyshyn, Marcus Miller and William Perraudin, 'Deficits, Inflation and the Political Economy of Ukraine', *Economic Policy*, no. 19 (October) 1994, p. 371. Havrylyshyn is Ukraine's Alternate Executive Director at the IMF.

58. Interfax News Agency, 7 December 1994 (BBC Monitoring Service, op. cit.)

59. If leased enterprises are included, the share was 42 per cent in industry and 67 per cent in construction.

60. Economist Intelligence Unit, *Ukraine, Belarus and Moldova*, Third Quarter 1994, pp. 24-5.

61. These data are from statements to the International Conference on Transformation Processes in Ukraine, December 1994, as communicated by Igor Egorov (see note 53).

62. *Financial Times*, 28 January 1995.

63. Adam Dixon, *Kazakhstan: Political Reform and Economic Development*, Post-Soviet Business Forum (London: Royal Institute of International Affairs, 1994), p. 18.

64. Together with Kazakh concerns, the Karachaganak gas deposit, requiring $6 billion investment, involves British Gas, Agip and Gazprom; Tengiz and Korolev oil, requiring $20 billion in the long term, involves the Chevron Corporation; the oil pipeline from Tengiz associates Russian and Kazakh state companies with Chevron and Oman Oil (100 per cent owned by the Oman government with the executive participation of a Dutch entrepreneur, Johannes Deuss).

65. Parisbas for Tengiz and Karazhan; Price Waterhouse for the Chimkent refinery; J.P. Morgan for Emba.

66. Kirill Nourzhanov and Amin Saikal, 'The New Kazakhstan: Has Something Gone Wrong?' *The World Today*, vol. 50, no. 12 (December) 1994, p. 227.

67. Reported by BBC Monitoring Service, *Summary of World Broadcasts: Former USSR*, 28 October 1994 (from Minsk Radio, 20 October 1994).

68. EBRD, *Transition Report 1994*, op. cit., p. 18; the original horizon for the two-thirds share had been 1999.

69. 'O khode ekonomicheskikh reform v Respublike Belarus', Government Statement of 28 March 1994.

70. *Zakon ab imyannykh pryvatyzatsyinykh chekakh*, 16 June 1994, article 7, which lists all the other supplements.

71. Quoted in John Lloyd, 'Belarus Pushes Russian Links', *Financial Times,* 13 July 1994.

72. Reported by BBC Monitoring Service, op. cit., 13 September 1994.

73. David Rudnick, 'Belarus: New President Keeps Investors Guessing', *Euromoney*, September 1994.

74. Ibid.; *Zvyazda* (Minsk), 24 September 1994 (cited by BBC Monitoring Service) and Economist Intelligence Unit, op. cit, p. 39.

75. 35 per cent of all housing space in 1977, double that in Russia—see Anthony Hyman, *Political Change in Post-Soviet Central Asia*, Post-Soviet Business Forum (London: Royal Institute of International Affairs, 1994), p. 28; the private share in urban dwelling-space (42 per cent) was the highest of all Union republics (*Narodnoe khozyaistvo SSSR v 1989g.*, op. cit., p. 166).

76. Hyman, loc. cit.; Nancy Lubin, *Labour and Nationality in Soviet Central Asia* (London: Macmillan, 1984), passim.

77. EBRD, *Transition Report 1994*, op. cit., p. 40; *Business Central Europe*, May 1994, p. 74.

78. Michael Kaser and Santosh Mehrotra, *The Central Asian Economies after Independence*, Post-Soviet Business Forum (London: Royal Institute of International Affairs, 1992), p. 45.

79. *IMF Economic Reviews*, no. 4, *Uzbekistan*, 1994, p. 12, fn. 19.

80. Neil Buckley, 'BAT-man's Opening', *Financial Times,* 19 June 1994.

81. Viktor Chzhen, Chairman of the State Property Committee, Uzbek Radio, 22 November 1994 (from BBC Monitoring Service, op. cit.)

82. Elizabeth Fuller, *Azerbaijan at the Crossroads,* Post-Soviet Business Forum (London: Royal Institute of International Affairs, 1994), p. 23, citing *Segodnya*, 28 October 1993.

83. Turan News Agency editorial report, 27 July 1994, in BBC Monitoring Service, op. cit.

84. Ibid. He added that he was opposed to the privatization of large enterprises.

85. EBRD, *Transition Report 1994*, op. cit., p. 18.

86. Basapress News Agency, 9 September 1994, cited in BBC Monitoring Service, op. cit.

87. Founded as ASINAM, MNM Holding is an acronym of the major shareholder, Mahmud Nadirolu Mamedov (Display advertisement, Survey of Azerbaijan, *Financial Times*, 7 March 1994).

88. Ibid., 16 September 1994; EBRD, *Transition Report 1994*, p. 30.

89. Economist Intelligence Unit, op. cit., p. 48.

90. A Ministry of State Property and Support for Entrepreneurship had a life of a few months until it was absorbed into the Ministry of Economy and Finance as two separate departments: one of State Property and Privatization and one of Support for Entrepreneurship (*IMF Economic Reviews*, no. 3, *Turkmenistan*, 1994, pp. 13-14). Turkmenistan is the sole CIS member to run privatization through a Ministry, rather than a quasi-autonomous State Committee.

91. ITAR-TASS, 29 November 1994 (BBC Monitoring Service, op. cit.).

92. Ibid., p. 24.

93. EBRD, *Transition Report 1994*, op. cit., p. 38.

94. Estimates of EBRD, *Transition Report 1994*, p. 16.

95. *Business Central Europe*, December 1993/January 1994, p. 74.

96. News conference of the Minister for Economy, Armen Yegiazaryan, *Respublika Armeniya*, 24 September 1994, cited in BBC Monitoring Service, op. cit.

97. See Jonathan Aves, *Post-Soviet Transcaucasia*, Post-Soviet Business Forum (London: Royal Institute of International Affairs, 1993), pp. 31-2.

CHAPTER THREE

Land Reform

The Annihilation of the Peasant

At the beginning of 1927, the Soviet peasant, whether Russian, Ukrainian, or of other nationality, had good reason to look forward to a tolerable future. The land was his; and he was reasonably free to dispose of his crop. The fearful period of grain-seizure, of peasant risings suppressed in blood, of devastating famine, were over, and the Bolshevik government seemed to have adopted a reasonable settlement of the countryside's interests . . . For the first time in history, almost all the country's land was in the possession of those who tilled it, and its product at their disposal.[1]

The collectivization process, begun ruthlessly in 1928, had the effect of eliminating the most competent part of the farm community . . . Systematically decimated and mismanaged, the countryside and its captive inhabitants underwent unprecedented degradation. The well-rounded and competent owner-farmer was replaced by a narrowly specialized *kolkhoz* worker tied to a particular sector of farm work.[2]

These two quotations may serve as a reminder of the catastrophe dealt to farming in the former Soviet Union by Stalin's collectivization and, in Central Asia, the forced settlement of nomadic herdsmen. The urgency of recreating incentives to good husbandry is recognized by all successor governments, but they are having to overcome many psychological and material obstacles to the crucial change—the privatization of land.

Lenin's decree 'On Land', promulgated immediately on his seizure of

169

power in 1917, prohibited private ownership of land but assured usufruct to those who tilled it. It thus differed from the agrarian reforms in the Central and Eastern European countries (Albania excepted) which emulated Soviet practice after 1945: large estates, if they had not already been dispossessed, were subdivided as the property of peasant households. The post-communist redesignation and restitution of title involves many practical problems, but an outcome is assured of a market valuation for land and the derivation of profit and of capital gain through commercial farming or development in alternative use; owners can exploit the land themselves, let it to tenants or sell up. The surrounding market economy provides the appropriate mechanisms, suppliers and customers.

All CIS governments on attaining independence were confronted by a need to restructure agriculture.

— In the sixty years since mass collectivization, land titles had been merged into those of *kolkhozy* or expropriated into state property, either as farms or in other uses. Any restitution to former owners would have been complex and costly, blighting the exploitation of disputed land. Titles were not revived even where historically less remote, as in western Belarus and Ukraine and in Moldova outside the Dniestr Republic, collectivized in the late 1940s.

— All Soviet farms were large ('giant grain factories' was once the ideal)—averaging 11,000 ha in Russia—and in principle open to adaptation directly as 'agro-business'. But they were overstaffed (360 full-time on that average), and job allocation was so differentiated as to inhibit single households from readily managing the range of activity demanded of an independent farmer.

— Both state farms and *kolkhozy* had a sole objective of fulfilling a target of deliveries to the state procurement agency and were successively exploited (under Stalin) and subsidized (under Khrushchev and Brezhnev) to ignore the cost of, and profit on, production.

— Even more than in state factories, farms undertook much social provision and were virtually the local government: there were about as many farms (51,200) as village and settlement authorities (47,100).[3] State farm directors and collective farm chairmen thus held extensive powers and, as a class, they are unwilling to surrender them.

— The autocracy of farm management and the network of contacts it had to develop among suppliers, recipients and funding agencies imbued subordinates with a 'dependency culture' and hence a fear of risk-taking outside the established order. The rural *nomenklatura* has played on these concerns to dissuade potential farm leavers.

— Previous sporadic attempts to instill personal profit motivation among the 'rank and file'—free farming during the War, the 'link' system in the late 1940s and early 1960s, group leasing in the 1980s—had proved nugatory or been repressed.

— Side-by-side with megafarms were dwarf-holdings on which highly intensive cultivation was practiced. Each member household of a *kolkhoz* or state farm had its own adjoining plot and four out of five city folk had access to land for growing food.[4] Consumption in the household took much of the output, but the sole selling outlet was the personal market stall, for any marketing service was forbidden as constituting 'speculation'.

— In common with state employees and pensioners, farmers have had their savings annihilated by inflation since January 1992 and possess inadequate capital to establish themselves on their own: farm buildings and equipment suited to large collective operations are costly or impossible to adapt for individual holdings.

— New calls on farm-household income reduce investible funds: the explosion of 'kiosk trade' has made a wide range of manufactures and imported consumer goods available where decrepit state and cooperative shops were monopolies; motor vehicles can be freely bought; local churches, stripped bare and often in a ruinous state, are being rebuilt.

— Finally, the lack of property rights was conducive to neglect of soil fertility and ecological conservation. As industry and mining lacked a capital market but had to achieve product quotas, so collective and state farms had no interest in keeping up the value of their resources and maximized crops to fulfill procurement obligations. Excessive cropping, subjection to short-term 'campaigns', inadequate capital works, salination after poor irrigation, gully and other erosion contributed to an environmental disaster.

A new legislative base

These profound defects were known through Western publications and Russian fiction (novels of the 'village prose' movement revealed the disastrous condition of rural life), but were only obliquely discussed in the official press.[5] What was needed was a recognized forum for farmers to express their views openly. The officially sponsored Peasants' Union heard such criticism in the later days of *perestroika*, but it was essentially a forum for the managers of collective and state farms. More significant was the legal recognition of AKKOR, the Association of Peasant Farms and Agricultural Cooperatives of Russia, in 1990. Boris Yeltsin, then Chairman of the RSFSR Supreme Soviet, declared the need 'to make the farmer, instead of a bureaucratic superstructure, the proprietor and to revive the peasantry in Russia—a stratum of people who will feed the Republic through their labor.'[6] The reference to feeding the nation was to the heavy cost of imported grain, but there was also great concern at the domestic subsidies paid out to the grossly inefficient 'agro-industrial complex'. Three laws, grouped as 'The Revival of the Russian Countryside and the Development of the Agro-Industrial Complex', were enacted at the end of 1990: the Law on the Peasant Farm, the Law on Land Reform and the Law on the Social Development of the Countryside. Peasant farms were accorded legal equality with state and collective farms, and individuals were allowed a leasehold (*arenda*) or possession (*vladenie*) of land, but not formal ownership (*sobstvennost'*). For the first ten years of tenure resale was permitted only to the village council. Republican legislatures were the vehicles because Union 'Basic Legislation' on leasing (November 1989) and on land (February 1990) had devolved that authority to them.

The Russian Law permitted the division of land and assets among member households of both state and collective farms, distributing shares according to length of service. Republics with a Turkic or Iranian ethnic minority took advantage of the Basic Legislation to redraft their own Land Codes (1989-91) but—except in Uzbekistan—in the opposite sense to the Russian. All forbade or severely restricted the buying, selling, mortgaging or bartering of land. The Kyrgyz Code and Land Law (both of April 1991) did offer a possibility of land division in the case of loss-making state or collective farms; Kyrgyzstan's mountainous terrain presented the same problems of maintaining upland agriculture as in similar territory throughout the world, where individual peasant husbandry can help to keep submarginal land in cultivation. Although faced with similar geomorphic constraints to Russia's, Armenia went much further than Russia in its land reform (January 1991), authorizing the dismantling of collective and state farms by decision of their employees; by September 1992 the greater part of arable land had been turned over to private owners and 300,000 head of collective livestock had been distributed. Many chose to reconstitute a state farm or *kolkhoz* as a voluntary cooperative, from which a household could withdraw with appropriate notice. By that date there were already 167,000 private farms, the only restriction on their property right being a three-year moratorium on the sale of land received under the reform.

The Russian Federation

Independence from the Soviet Union allowed legislatures throughout the CIS to attempt to repair—as far as laws can—the damage created by collectivization: some made little change, placing their hopes for a more efficient agriculture on a market environment for buying and selling farming equipment and farm produce; others went a long way in liberating the peasantry, but found them pusillanimous in accepting freedom. Sampling responses to the 1990 law, an inquiry had found a mere 17 per cent of employees of state and collective farms in favor of private ownership.[7]

In Russia the inalienable right to own land had to await the Constitution pushed through with a narrow (and some would say, questionable) popular majority in December 1993.[8] But as soon as he was in control of Russia President Yeltsin issued, in late 1991, a series of decrees intended to break up *kolkhozy* and state farms, notably that 'On Urgent Measures for the Realization of Land Reform in the RSFSR' and to create local Commissions on Land Privatization and Reorganization. General meetings of members of farms were to be held before 1 March 1992 to decide whether to distribute their land or to remain as collectivities; if only some wished to go private they could take a proper share of land and assets; the land remained on long lease but, with many restrictions, they could transfer title for payment. The hiring of labor by a private farmer remained forbidden. Every farm had to effect the reorganization then decided and to reregister itself as such by 1 January 1993—either as individual farmers or as a cooperative (which could take the form of a joint-stock company). In the face of substantial conservative pressure, the provision on reregistration was amended to allow acceptance of the *status quo*: this negated the requirement to submit new property relationships. In the event, out of the 77 per cent of state and collective farms which submitted for reregistration by the deadline, 35 per cent maintained their former status.[9]

The far-reaching Decree 'On the Regulation of Land Relations and the Development of Agrarian Reform in Russia' (October 1993) in effect repealed Lenin's decree of almost exactly 76 years previously. It recognized—as a new Constitution was shortly to do—private property in land and authorized the issuance of titles in the form of 'certificates of rights of ownership'. The ten-year moratorium on resale was abolished and a market in land was facilitated by protection of the rights of transactors. It established a Committee on Land Resources and Land Tenure Regulation, the Head of which is also the Chief State Inspector of the Utilization and Conservation of Russian Federation Lands; the chairmen of local land resource committees are accordingly also local land inspectors. The inspectorate issues certificates not only to individual owners, but also to each member of a voluntary cooperative showing the size of share, but without specifying boundaries, as in cases of separate ownership. As under the 1991 decree, a member of a cooperative (or, transitionally, a *kolkhoz*) may obtain a delineated parcel of land without recourse to a decision of other members. The decree eliminates all compulsory deliveries from farms, the bane of *kolkhozy* since the 1930s and even levied on household plots under Stalin. State farms are the subject of a separate decree (September 1992), whereby they may be auctioned as a privatized state enterprise or run as a joint stock company by the employees.

Six classes of person are listed in the main (October 1993) decree, five of whom may receive land: *kolkhoz* members; independent farmers; employees of state, factory and municipal farms; Cossacks; and citizens not previously engaged in agriculture. Foreigners may not own land, but companies with foreign ownership, like domestic companies, may do so. The specification of Cossacks is supplemented by regulations on 'procedure for providing Cossack communities with land' , since they were deliberately dispersed by Stalin and are a focus of a renewed nationalism. Citizens not previously engaged in agriculture must demonstrate ability in good husbandry before being allowed to buy land and may be dispossessed if standards are not maintained. As unemployment increases (it was 6 per cent in Russia in late 1994), workers are migrating back to villages with which they have social ties. Nikolai Komov, chairman of the Russian land resource committee, stated that 95 per cent of the land certificates had been delivered to recipients by spring 1994 and that a land market had been established, even if temporarily imbalanced between demand and supply.[10]

To encourage a rational distribution of property in state and cooperative farms and a market appreciation among buyers, the International Finance Corporation sponsored a pilot set of disposals of six farms in the Nizhny Novgorod region between January 1992 and March 1994. Of the four *kolkhozy* and two state farms selected, one of the latter withdrew: all decided to remain a group, one as a limited liability partnership, two as joint-stock companies, one as an association and one remaining as a *kolkhoz*.[11]

Such voluntary choice when in possession of detailed valuations and prognoses suggests that some of the advantages of scale can be combined with private incentives. Nizhny Novgorod was exceptional and there are many reasons why so few villagers have so far decided to go private. The main reason was the small size of the plot distributed: compared to a requirement of 50 to 100 ha for efficient small-scale farming, the average is 43 ha, but half are less than 20 ha. Private farmers had some machinery mostly purchased from the original *kolkhoz*, but there was no service through which more equipment could be bought.[12]

By 1 October 1994 there were only 285,600 private farmers in Russia, owning an agricultural area of 11.8 million ha (that is 41 ha per farm and 7 per cent of the national area).[13] Their share of main crops in 1994 was only a little higher than the previous year: 5.7 per cent of grain (compared with 5.2 per cent in 1993), 14.1 per cent of sunflower seed (9.9), 5.7 per cent of sugar beet (3.9) and 1.6 per cent of vegetables (1.0). Moreover, in the third quarter of 1994, for the first time, the number of peasant farms (*fermerskie khozyaistva*) dissolved (6,300) exceeded the number created (6,100).

Such a poor response to the offer of ownership and even retrogression may chiefly be attributed to sales problems. In order to stanch the large provision of subsidies to essential foodstuffs, the prices paid by government agencies (successors to the compulsory procurement bodies) were kept low and did not cover a farmer's expenses, particularly as the prices of farm inputs rose rapidly. The First Deputy Minister of Agriculture and Food, Vladimir Shcherbak, noted that more than 20,000 farmers had given up their land in 1994, mainly because the sale of produce generated insufficient income to acquire machinery. It is also known that if the farmer took produce to town markets for direct sale, transactions were often in the hands of mafia gangs, and protection money was exacted. While inflation remained high and interest rates at commercial banks were negative, farmers, with poor or no security, could not obtain credit.[14]

In December 1994 a Presidential Decree established a procedure for transforming state enterprises providing technical services to agriculture and processing farm produce into open joint-stock companies. In the processing group a proportion of shares will be earmarked for sale to farmers producing the material processed. As noted above, as non-farm property targets are attained, the State Property Committee is attending more to agrarian reform. But, as a revised Land Code is unlikely to be enacted before the December 1995 parliamentary elections, a proactive policy is ruled out before 1996.

Belarus, Moldava and Ukraine

The management and members of collective and state farms in Belarus and Ukraine have been still more reluctant to privatize themselves than their colleagues in Russia. The neo-communist agrarian *nomenklatura* was if anything more entrenched and more supported by their parliaments. With the election of more reformist presidents in July 1994, agrarian reform appeared on the government's agenda, but for much later resolution in Belarus than in Ukraine.

BELARUS. President Lukashenka is a former collective farm director and won his 1994 victory on a populist program: price subsidies for food keep both farmers and consumers content at a cost that contributes to a budget deficit estimated for 1994 at 21 per cent of GDP. Lukashenka inherited a newly enacted Constitution (March 1994) which reserved to the state the right to declare certain assets the exclusive property of the state (Article 13) and a 1993 Law on the Right to Property in Land which permitted leasehold; a later decree amended it to allow foreigners and foreign companies 99-year leases of land for their use. At the end of 1992 there were 2,100 private leaseholders, with an average of 20 ha apiece. The President made clear his caution on agricultural land soon after inauguration: 'We shall develop private farms, but not in a hurry, not without a selective approach, not as it has been done by people who do not know the value of the land and have never worked on it. Of course, it is possible to give away land to pseudo-owners, but by that we would push Belarus into even worse poverty. Where land is concerned, one should have a sober, calm, methodical, but resolute attitude.'[15]

UKRAINE. In late 1992 a Ukrainian decree allowed property title to tenants of rural household plots, which were simultaneously allowed to become double their previous legal size (from 0.25 to 0.5 ha). It gave them the right to sell, subject to a high tax decreasing to zero after six years' possession. This decree applied to 4.6 million in such households and hence began some restoration of genuinely private farming. The legal situation changed radically after the accession of Leonid Kuchma to the presidency. His decree 'On Private Ownership in Land' (November 1994) partly follows the corresponding Russian legislation: each member of an enterprise, cooperative or society (terms which embrace farms run by factories, state farms, *kolkhozy* and private farmers' associations) will receive from the State Committee on Land Resources a certificate of ownership to a parcel of land or to a share in group property. Such certificates may be traded, bartered, inherited or mortgaged. Members of existing state and collective farms are invited to take voluntary decisions on their mode of ownership, but there are size limits on any one individual's property. Parliament has, however, challenged the legality of the right to transact land, and implementation has been thereby delayed.

MOLDOVA. By contrast, Moldova was early in authorizing land privatization (decree of May 1992), while still within what was to be the Russian model. Collective farmers receive certificates of ownership and the farm is transformed into a joint-stock company: the share, but not a parcel of the pooled land, may be transacted; sale of the land involved is not permitted until the year 2001. Restricted permission may be given to the separation of holdings and dividends are calculated upon a uniform holding of 5 ha (irrespective of the actual share) and, as before, on labor contribution.

The Caucasian republics

ARMENIA. Mention has already been made of the privatization of land in Armenia even while a part of the USSR. The agrarian reform (January 1991) was rapidly executed and only experimental state farms and some areas which the government prefers to lease are not privately owned. Data for September 1993 showed 167,000 private farms and 9,500 cooperatives (from which any member may freely withdraw). There was, however, a three-year moratorium, just expiring, on the sale of land received under the decree.

GEORGIA. Georgia has achieved virtual privatization under leasehold, but continues to forbid private ownership in land. By mid-1994 over half of the republic's agricultural land was under private lease,[16] but a target of 96 per cent by the end of that year was judged 'unrealistic'.[17]

AZERBAIJAN. A Land Law, drafted in early 1993, is still under consideration in Azerbaijan, where the Commission of the European Union is encouraging change by the provision of advice and financial support. In August 1994 it was announced that 3 million ecus (of a total 1994 aid allocation of 12.5 million ecus) would fund three projects relating to agrarian reform, one of which would provide grants to newly established family farms.

Central Asia

It was to be expected that on independence Central Asian[18] governments would be readier than those of the Slavic republics to distribute land, for they have a young rural population, whereas villages in the Slav regions tend to be of the elderly.

KAZAKHSTAN. Kazakhstan has gone the furthest. Under legislation of 1991 land could be leased for up to 99 years as salable and heritable, but not mortgageable, and such leaseholds together with household plots already accounted the following year for one-third of the livestock and one half of plant output other than cotton and grain. Legislation of March 1994 went much further. It divides the land of a cooperative or state farm, as a joint-stock company, into four tranches: 20 per cent may be bought by the director personally; 29 per cent is available for purchase by other members, employees and pensioners; 20 per cent is to be auctioned to buyers who must be Kazakh citizens and have an education and work experience relevant to agriculture; and 31 per cent may be leased for a maximum of five years. The Kazakh Private Farmers' Association welcomed the measure, which buys off the *nomenklatura* opponents of agrarian reform—not only the director, but local officials who can buy in at auction or leasehold sale.[19] The state procurement agency, Kazkhlebprodukt, was turned in January 1994 into a joint-stock company and its monopoly was withdrawn. Finally, in December 1994 the Premier, Akezhan Kazhegeldin, unequivocally declared that the parliament would be asked to legislate for full private ownership of land in the republic.[20]

KYRGYZSTAN. The volte-face in Kyrgyzstan requires all *kolkhozy* to have been dissolved by the end of 1994 and all state farms by the end of 1995. When the Kyrgyz Land Code of 1972 was replaced (April 1991) it had maintained a complete prohibition on buying, selling, donating, mortgaging or barter of land.[21] Soon afterwards, however, a Presidential Decree (August 1991) allowed farmland to be held by individuals, either citizens or foreigners, collectives, including teams of shepherds (*chaban*), and companies (also either national or foreign-owned). A Law on Cooperatives (December 1991) set out terms on which farmers could establish voluntary groups. By mid-November 1994, the Prime Minister, Apas Dzhumagulov, announced that of the 21,700 farms in Kyrgyzstan, 17,000 were privately owned, and that by the end of the year all *kolkhozy* would have been dissolved. He said the same dissolution would apply to state farms, but President Askar Akayev, in a separate news conference (during a visit to the UN European Office, Geneva), said that 1995 was the target for state farm closure.[22]

UZBEKISTAN. Uzbekistan was the earliest to initiate land reform, distributing gratis to farm households the irrigated land of *kolkhozy* under a Land Law of 1989. In late 1991 the land of loss-making state farms (other than cotton plantations) was sold to staff or became *kolkhozy*. The land and assets of these and all remaining *kolkhozy* were to be divided among members by the end of 1993 but the process was still continuing in late 1994. The revelation that over a third of Uzbek state farms made a loss in that year and were heavily indebted indicated that that sector will readily be included in the general privatization of state enterprises.

TURKMENISTAN. The Turkmen Land Code of October 1990 defined land as 'the property of the whole people' and provided for usufruct to be leased to any person, citizen or foreigner, for a term of 25 years. A Land Reform Law (April 1992) allowed collective and state farms to be divided among those engaged in them as leaseholds-for-life and with a right of inheritance. Annual accounts for 1993, according to a speech by President Saparmurad Niyazov, showed that the number of profitable *kolkhozy* had declined and that that of loss-makers had risen (to 328 farms).[23] Concern at the subsidization involved must have been a factor in a decree (March 1994) requiring the dissolution of all *kolkhozy*.[24]

TAJIKISTAN. The rule of President Imamoli Rakhmanov in Tajikistan has not yet been sufficiently secure for legislative progress beyond the Land Code of December 1990, under which the state continues to be the sole proprietor of land, but allows leases of up to ten years on the decision of the local authority. A Land Reform was brought before the Assembly then extant (March 1992), but not proceeded with after it and the democratic-Islamic forces were overthrown by the neo-communist faction.

Notes to Chapter 3

1. Robert Conquest, *The Harvest of Sorrow. Soviet Collectivization and the Terror Famine* (London: Hutchinson, 1986), p. 13.

2. Kyril Tidmarsh, 'Russia's Work Ethic', *Foreign Affairs*, vol. 72, no. 2, spring 1993, p. 69.

3. On 1989 data there were 27,900 *kolkhozy* and 23,300 state farms, 43,100 village councils and 4,000 settlement councils *(Narodnoe khozyaistvo SSSR v 1989 g.*, op. cit., pp. 5, 501 and 509).

4. Sample survey of households in Moscow, St Petersburg and Russian regional and district capitals (Richard Rose and Yevgeniy Tikhomirov, 'Who Grows Food in Russia and Eastern Europe?' *Post-Soviet Geography*, vol. 34, no. 2, 1993, p. 122).

5. Some milestones were V. G. Venzher et al., *Proizvodstvo, nakoplenie, potreblenie*, Moscow, 1965; and Tatyana Zaslavskaya's confidential address to a Party Seminar in April 1983 (she cautiously released some of her ideas on farming expressed there in *Izvestiya*, 1 June 1985).

6. *Pravda*, 28 November 1990.

7. Ibid., 27 November 1990.

8. Article 36 states: 'Citizens and their associations are entitled to hold land in private ownership', but with the proviso that 'this does not damage the environment . . . [nor] violate the rights and legitimate interests of others.'

9. Anna Tyagunenko, 'Agrarian Reform in Russia', *Communist Economies and Economic Transformation*, vol. 5, no. 4, 1993, p. 462.

10. Reported by Radio Russia, 25 August 1994, in BBC Monitoring Service, op. cit.

11. A full analysis is in an unpublished MPhil Thesis at the University of Oxford: Gareth Williams, 'Agrarian Reform in Russia and the Nizhny Novgorod Land Privatization Project, 1990-1994' (April 1994); brief accounts are in *Business Central Europe*, December 1993/January 1994, p. 16, and *Financial Times*, Survey of Russia, 27 June 1994, p. vi.

12. Tyagunenko, 'Agrarian Reform in Russia', pp. 464 and 465; it provides a much fuller analysis of the reform than is summarized here.

13. *Sotsial'no-ekonomicheskoe polozhenie Rossii*, p. 43; *Rossiiskaya Federatsiya v 1992 godu*, Moscow, Goskomstat, 1993, p. 412.

14. Most of these points are from Tyagunenko, op. cit., pp. 464-9; the Minister's statement is from ITAR-TASS, 2 December 1994 (BBC Monitoring Service, op. cit.). Although mainly concerned with urban land, Vincent Renard, 'Emerging Land Markets in Eastern Europe', *Economics of Transition*, vol. 2, no. 4, pp. 501-9, notes that in Russia privatization has been delayed by slow land registration under a preference for a complex multi-purpose land information system.

15. Interview on television programme, 'Moment Istiny', on 1 September 1994 (BBC Monitoring Service, op. cit.).

16. EBRD, *Transition Report 1994*, op. cit., p. 24.

17. Economist Intelligence Unit, *Georgia, Armenia, Azerbaijan, Kazakhstan and Central Asia*, Third Quarter 1994.

18. The term *tsentral'naya Aziya* embraces Kazakhstan, while *srednaya Aziya* is limited to Kyrgyzstan, Tajikistan, Turkmenistan and Uzbekistan.

19. *Central Asia Newsfile*, April 1994, p. 10.

20. ITAR-TASS, 12 December 1994 (BBC Monitoring Service, op. cit.).

21. Kaser and Mehrotra, op. cit., p. 41.

22. Respectively Interfax News Agency, 21 November 1994, and Reuters News Service, 15 November 1994.

23. *Central Asian Newsfile*, May 1994, p. 10.

24. Ibid., April 1994, p. 12.

CHAPTER FOUR

The Problems

The new owners

Soviet Marxists castigated the market under capitalism as 'anarchy', where Adam Smith had seen an 'invisible hand' coordinating the self-interest of producers and consumers. The experience of CIS economies in their initial steps towards private-motivated marketization is nearer to the Marxist view. Reasons are mostly to be found in political change, but the atomization of ownership has brought an instability which deflects domestic and inward international investment. For various considerations, principally financial, restructuring before privatization (on, say, the Treuhand's practice in the eastern *Länder* of Germany) was rejected. The mass transfers to non-state owners offer capacity from some of which high returns could be drawn, if capital could be put in to mold production towards a new pattern of demand and to meet external competition. The new proprietors are not yet making such investment and a vicious spiral confronts all CIS states: the longer that adaptation of, and addition to, the capital stock is delayed, the more unstable their economies are likely to be, and hence the less attractive to investors.

Quite apart from the broad perspective of political and economic uncertainty within which they view all CIS states, investors rarely find the clear distinctions between state and private, and legal and illegal, operation which are (though not exclusively) normal practice in developed market systems. Until greater stability and certainty prevail, domestic savings will continue to escape abroad to a surer environment, and foreign investors will find better options elsewhere for their funds and expertise. The pervasive influences in-

The author appreciates the help of Christopher Davis (Wolfson College, Oxford), Ian Jeffries (University of Wales Swansea) and Vladimir Sobell (Economist Intelligence Unit) in providing documentation during a period when events and the literature are particularly dynamic.

hibiting domestic or foreign investors can be encapsulated in two words—
nomenklatura and 'mafia'.[1] Neither term applies universally, but both express
the empowerment of politicians and of criminals by the manner in which privatization has been effected.

INCOMPLETE DENATIONALIZATION. Much of the advocacy of 'market socialism' in the reforms of communist-period Eastern Europe and during Soviet
perestroika assumed 'commercial freedom' for state- or worker-owned enterprises. The concept was of 'denationalization' rather than 'privatization'[2]—
that is, of freeing the enterprise of its subservience to directives and officials in
the capital city, thus allowing it to conduct transactions directly with other enterprises to its perceived advantage rather than with contractual partners imposed by an obligatory plan, and to lay out its revenue for investment and remuneration as it chose. All the 'economic reforms' of the late communist
period made some obeisance to such demands—the Soviet Enterprise Law of
1987 was typical in this regard. Addressing a gathering of enterprise execu-
tives in December 1990, Mikhail Gorbachev claimed that 'planning had to be
relaxed to give enterprises oxygen and economic freedom'.[3]

In those last three years of *perestroika*, those who argued for privatization
largely, though by no means exclusively, still saw the process as 'denationalization'.[4] It was politically associated with decentralization, which culminated
in the break-up of the USSR and fissiparity in Russia, and with democratization in general.[5] The contrast with China is illuminating: that government, im-
placably opposed to democratization, has not privatized its large state enterprises, but has assured economic expansion exclusively from decontrolling
agriculture and retailing, harnessing private incentives to local-authority agencies[6] and admitting foreign capital within strict territorial constraints.[7] The
conditions obtaining in China were absent in the USSR of the late 1980s[8] and
a privatization unaccompanied by demonopolizing the Communist Party was
rejected by Russian reformers.

The dissolution of the CPSU and of the USSR and the devolution of power
within the Russian Federation[9] facilitated the control of regional and local
politicians and of managers in the name of dismantling the dictatorship of
Moscow. Such subsidiarity shows no sign of diminishing as the share of the
private sector in the economy enlarges. In provincial politics the weight of the
industrial *nomenklatura*[10] was traditionally substantial, but it increased as
control by the Party *obkom* disappeared and as regional separatists perceived
locally situated plants (disarticulated from the various ministries) as coming
under their remit. Provincial and local authorities in the former Soviet system

had had little say in non-farm enterprise since the *sovnarkhozy* were abolished in September 1965, but they will now remain important. "It is precisely the present turmoil of Russian political and economic change that gives the provinces their present position center-stage . . . Russia's turbulence . . . and the center-stage position of regional politics are not about to disappear overnight."[11] A similar dispersion of political power anticipated and followed independence in Ukraine. As early as November 1990 economic separatism was being advocated: 'There can be no one model for such different regions'. Regional devolution was a demand of the coal miners' strike of June 1993 and, as mentioned in Chapter 1, the implicit division of Ukraine into four regions persists.[12] Neighboring Moldova is of course actually divided.[13]

The employees of state enterprises generally acquiesced in the take-over by combinations of their own management and of local elites (often under new titles), partly out of familiarity, partly because they were insufficiently organized outside the workplace itself, due to the weakness of trade unions.[14] Labor mobility is hindered if wages exceed marginal productivity for reasons of 'insider' power.[15] In the post-Soviet situation 'membership of an enterprise structures a person's life much more than in the West . . . The alternatives to staying in the enterprise are poor . . . Retaining ties to an enterprise allows workers to continue using the enterprise's tools and equipment . . . and earn some additional income from petty jobs.'[16] Recession has made clinging to the enterprise still more attractive. The official Russian estimate for September 1994 is that 6.3 per cent of the economically active population was unemployed and that another 6.1 per cent was working part-time or on 'administrative leave' (unwaged but notionally on the payroll), aggregating 8.7 million persons.[17] The proportion is nevertheless well under the unemployment shown in countries where restructuring has preceded privatization—16 per cent of the workforce both in the German eastern *Länder* and in Poland. Irrespective of the arrangements which were introduced to support 'insider' privatization, staff have tended to identify their interests with those of management and through them with others of the local *nomenklatura*. The Russian enterprise in which the boundary of state, local-authority and private interest is obscure has been ironically termed *goskomchast'*, an acronym of 'state committee' and 'private'.[18] In the Central Asian states both the central and the local *nomenklatura* play a major role in enterprises which are neither fully state-owned nor fully privatized.[19]

There was already some cross-ownership among state enterprises beginning before privatization,[20] but the Soviet inheritance was of excessive vertical integration, engendered by considerations of supply security in a 'shortage economy'. The responsible ministries or the state property committees in the more industrialized CIS members have made efforts to 'unbundle' these before privatization.[21] In Russia the law prohibits any firm in which the state has more than 25 per cent equity from holding shares in a privatized company. Many corporatized firms are in such substantive state ownership, but the director operates them as if they were private. Thus Vagit Alekperov put together the most dynamic oil corporation, Lukoil, even though it is 50 per cent owned by the wholly state-owned Rosneft (to be reduced over three years to 38 per cent), and the 15 per cent in employee/management hands is of non-voting shares. The gas monopoly, Gazprom,[22] will remain 40 per cent government-owned even after the present, second wave of privatization: its Chairman, Rem Vyakhirev, is a leading entrepreneur. Privatization in Belarus and Kyrgyzstan gives 50 per cent of equity to the state, with the proviso in the former that 5 per cent is subsequently sold off annually; in Azerbaijan a majority state holding is to be preserved in any enterprise the government decides is 'vital', and the same is true of the Turkmen and Moldovan energy industries.

INSIDER PRIVATIZATION As was shown in Chapter 2, four out of five Russian firms privatized in the first stage chose Variant II, giving majority shareholdings to employees; in Ukraine the stage now starting allows management and staff 35 per cent; and in Tajikistan employee buy-out is the norm. Elsewhere the scope for insider control is legally narrower, but, in the absence of information and brokerage services, management and staff may be able to put together enough equity for effective control. A survey of 27 Russian enterprises undergoing privatization in March 1993 indicated that 'the choice of privatization option largely depended on managers' desire to maximize control in order to avoid the threat of change and to minimize the costs to employees. There was no evidence of serious dissent once management had recommended an option to the general meeting. For the enterprises visited, seven had chosen Option I and 14 had chosen Option II. Of the other six enterprises, five had yet to make a choice and one had become private prior to formulation of the options. No enterprise in the sample had chosen Option III and it proved impossible to obtain a clear official view as to its rationale.'[23] Because enterprises differed in recent profitability, and hence in the money available in the Incentive Fund, the inquiry found wide variation among them in the proportion of equity financed from that source (from zero to 100 per cent); there were also differences in the ratio of vouchers to cash buying, apparently because of the money put up at auctions by family members and the amount of outside vouchers brought in for the purpose.

Although no evidence was shown of underhand methods to assure management/employee control, there have been reports (concerning other privatizations) about threats of violence being uttered against outsider bidders at public auctions; in any event, holding the auction in the locality of the enterprise concerned reduced participation from elsewhere. Other reports speak of share registers being tampered with so that the holdings of outsiders are abolished or canceled on specious grounds.[24] At a late stage (Council of Ministers Decision of 10 August 1993), the Russian government required auctions of enterprises with assets worth over 250 million rubles to be effected on an inter-regional basis. The law, moreover, requires that companies with more than 1,000 shareholders must appoint an independent registrar, but this has been evaded. Another ploy has been not to advertise the availability of shares, although they were available on application.[25]

Management has also been known to exert pressure on staff to sell their equity to it.[26] Staff beneficiaries of gratis equity may be tempted to dispose of their holding for sums which are trivial in relation to the assets in which their shares participate. Low-price voucher selling (*vaucherny bestsenok*) is almost a compelling choice for the ill-paid, those owed wages, and those who realize that dividends will be slow in coming from their enterprise.[27]

Employee ownership in general encourages a wage level too high in relation to investment self-finance. Employment, on the other hand, is likely to be too high in relation to marginal productivity for some time after buyout, but as natural wastage occurs it may become too low in the light of efficient capital-to-labor ratios. Such experience as has been monitored of non-farm producer cooperatives in established market economies is inconclusive with regard to the incentive of profit-participation and the disincentive of free-riding in such sharing.[28] Recognizing these deficiencies, the architects of employee buyouts in CIS states may have argued on two grounds. The first is that the demand to sell shares would evoke a capital market that initially did not exist. The second is that insiders would not buy properties just for their scrap value,[29] thereby leaving a plant available for retooling or product change when new money could be attracted.[30] Cases have, however, been noted in Russia where employee-shareholders have blocked restructuring in favor of maintaining excess staff or investing in staff welfare facilities.[31] As transition progressed, the autonomous private sector has enlarged (in two republics, Armenia and Russia, to around half GDP[32]) and, by better wages or self-employment profit, attracts redundant labor out of insider-controlled firms.[33] It is also possible that remaining state enterprises could attract labor, in a more competitive environment and after restructuring.[34]

Most existing managements were able to retain command because of their own right to buy equity, their purchase of the shares of other staff and their place within the local *nomenklatura*. A trenchant analysis of experience in both CIS and eastern Europe concludes: 'The success of privatization will be short-lived if the process is conducted in a non-transparent way and if the process is managed as an opportunity for enrichment amongst a bureaucratic elite. In most post-communist countries, a number of joint stock companies of closed type have been created, the structure of which prevents shareholders from selling their shares and provides scope for directors of enterprises to exercise effective full control and sometimes to allocate themselves large, artificially created dividends.'[35] This situation contrasts with, for example, the far-reaching personnel changes among directors of state enterprises in Poland in the period 1990-1991.[36] But any generalization that management must be changed upon privatization is as unhelpful as 'to pretend that the transformation can be inaugurated in a *tabula rasa*, or to belittle the ability of those tainted by the old regimes to alter their behavior in a constructive manner'.[37] Evidence is cited of insider-controlled managements acting in a more market-like manner.[38]

Finally, the first stage of Russian privatization and those transfers imminent in other CIS states have been taking place when employee shareholders had little funds of their own to finance restructuring, needed because no government put significant money in before privatization. Inflation following the price decontrol with which each CIS republic began transition (January 1992) destroyed savings, and real wages had everywhere declined. Particularly among management, but doubtless also among workers, most personal funds were, or are being, used at auctions to supplement voucher bids for the respective buy-outs. In Russia's first stage, and apparently in other CIS privatizations, that money went to the government; only in Russia's second stage is it to be channeled back into the firm concerned. The procedure adopted until now brings no fresh investment, deters inflow from outside (either by share purchase or joint venture, domestic or foreign), and is a temptation to disinvest.[39] The third biggest repository of vouchers, AlfaCapital, would 'cold-call firms in target industries' to inquire about 'any unused or imported plant or equipment that can be sold in case of liquidation.'[40] One observer asserts that in Russia 'decumulation of capital is the rule rather than the exception'.[41]

CONCENTRATION OF OWNERSHIP The creation of investment funds should in principle diversify ownership away from management and introduce external controllers, better able to compare the operation of one firm with another and to exert shareholding influence. All CIS states permit their operation and, in the wake of some well-publicized scandals (described in the next section), are now more concerned with regulating them. In Russia, of the 147 million vouchers issued, 44 per cent were by the end of the first stage in investment funds: the average auction bid of 20 vouchers, when only one was issued per person, suggests both fund intervention and a concentration of shareholding (sometimes as vehicles for insiders to gain greater control). The legal limit of 10 per cent to any fund's holding in a single company constrained effective participation in governance, but was later raised to 25 per cent. As protection against fraudulent use of that participation, investment funds must be licensed by the State Property Committee. It withdrew its license from the temptingly named Nefte-Almaz-Invest ('oil and diamond investment'), but only temporarily, because it had 970,000 shareholders. In the second stage of Russian privatization, investment funds are no longer limited to a maximum holding in any one company, but they no longer have the privileged access to new privatizations which they had during the first stage. Of the 657 funds licensed at the end of that stage,[42] it is expected that many will merge.[43] Some may be delicensed for fraud or for mafia participation, and others squeezed out by an increased burden of taxation.

The largest Russian fund appears to be First Voucher Fund, which obtained some 4 million vouchers either deposited with it by shareholders or by purchase. It largely took shares in enterprises with substantial real estate value, including two modern hotels, the Cosmos in Moscow, and the Sovetskaya in St Petersburg, but is also in the fertilizer, jewelry and food business. By setting up its First Pension Fund it was able to finance investment in the International Business Center in Moscow.[44] The legal situation of MMMInvest, which gathered 3.1 million vouchers, is unclear; it declared that it had between 5 and the maximum of 25 per cent holdings in 28 companies, including oil, motor vehicle manufacture, tobacco, telecommunications and the big Moscow department store, TsUM.[45] The next largest, with 2.5 million vouchers, AlfaCapital, has bought into the food, cement, glass, chemicals, pharmaceuticals and electricity industries.[46] Despite the state's majority holding in these assets, it also bought shares in oil and in telecommunications.

BANK SHAREHOLDING In contrast to the limit placed on investment funds in Russia, there was no legal constraint on a bank's holding in an individual company.[47] Commercial banks therefore created their own investment companies or divisions to effect share purchase. Thus, DialogBank has an investment company, Troika Dialog, but AlfaBank maintains its AlfaCapital as an investment fund (with licenses both as a fund and as a stockbroker). Banks proliferated with remarkable rapidity throughout the CIS and have already raised gearing ratios to unstable heights. The evidence so far is that banks are not yet poised to assume the dominant role of investment bank participator long demonstrated historically in continental Europe and Japan.[48] Indeed, the trend seems more to be towards the 'Anglo-Saxon model', with banks holding two sets of equity—one for participation in restructuring and the obtaining of capital gains, and the other set of diverse minority holdings for speculative profit. Such at least are the declared policies of First Voucher Fund/First Voucher Bank and of Menatep.[49] One consideration is that the 'German/ Japanese model' presumes the sharing of inside information with the partici- pator bank, while the Slavic members of the CIS are more attracted to build- ing up their stock exchanges and opting for a level playing-field for investors, including foreign companies. In the Central Asian and Caucasian states, the weaker potential for dispersed share-ownership and the more influential role likely for transnational corporations in natural-resource exploitation could point to a useful countervailing role for domestic banks. There seems scant support for a proposal to bypass outsider governance in management by bank- creditor and employee-shareholder representation.[50] This is not the place to examine the broader implications, amply set out in two major studies,[51] of embracing an individualistic ('neo-American') rather than a solidaristic ('Rhenish') path. If anything, most CIS privatizations represent, in a certain resonance from the past, a variant, 'collectivist' model.

STOCK EXCHANGES With the disappearance of the Soviet Union and the de- struction of its supply system (administered by a central agency, Gossnab USSR, and the branch ministries), numerous commodity exchanges ap- peared—there were more than three hundred in the CIS a month or two after independence.[52] Mostly owned by large state enterprises concerned with the relevant products, they aimed initially only to match buyers and sellers in barter arrangements. Speculative dealers soon moved in and their scope widened to include securities. Their number soon shrank both by amalgama- tion and because the forum for commodity transaction became normal con- tracting. Those that remained formed the basis for stock exchanges.

By mid-1994 there were 70 authorized stock exchanges in Russia,[53] of which Moscow, St Petersburg, Yekaterinburg and Novosibirsk were the largest. The dealing total in 1993 was a modest $1 billion (which may be com- pared with $14 billion on the Prague Exchange), but is likely to be $3 billion in 1994,[54] particularly since the installation of Nasdaq-style trading.[55] Advising the State Property Committee, KPMG set up electronic clearing for St Petersburg, and Deloitte and Touche organized the other three majors. A consultant with the latter said that eventually all Russian share-trading would be unified.[56] A Stock Exchange and Securities Commission was established by Presidential Order in March 1993 to regulate procedures and to protect investors;[57] its power was enhanced by Presidential Decrees of October 1993 and June 1994. Following fraudulent deletion or alteration of stockholders, a State Property Register was established under the State Property Committee and company registrars were regulated by it; a Federal Commission for Securities and the Stock Market (headed by the First Deputy Prime Minister in charge of the economy) replaced an interdepartmental committee which had been relatively passive (November 1994). With effect from 1 January 1995 a license must be obtained to engage in professional activities on any Russian securities market; the Federal Commission on Securities and the Stock Market was authorized to issue temporary permits valid until 1 March 1995. The Czech Republic has established a 'dematerialized' national share register in the Ministry of Finance. Such a computerized register, neutrally held, should seriously be considered as an alternative to the trading of paper.[58]

In Ukraine a Law on Securities and Stock Exchanges (January 1992) has led to the establishment of seven exchanges, of which the Kiev-based Ukrainian Stock Exchange is the biggest, with 15 branches and over fifty registered brokers. An Uzbek Stock Exchange was established in January 1992, well in advance of a Law on Securities and Stock Exchanges (September 1993). A Moldovan stock exchange was founded in 1994 by a consortium of banks and investment funds. One in Kyrgyzstan was scheduled for opening in that year, pursuant to an enabling Law of December 1991 on securities and stock exchanges. Kazakhstan had legislation of about the same time (June 1991, amended in April 1993) but does not yet have an exchange in operation. The same is true of Azerbaijan and Belarus, with laws but no exchange as yet. In all these states and in Georgia, Tajikistan and Turkmenistan there is curb trading.

Fraud and crime

Confidence in investment funds and in securities trading in Russia was shaken by the scandal of AO-MMM in the summer of 1994. Sergei Mavrodi spent heavily on television advertising (reportedly $100 million) to offer huge returns on unbacked securities: it was no more than a pyramid scheme benefiting from the similarity of name with MMMInvest, which actually did buy shares from which a return could certainly be expected. AO-MMM sold bearer redemption certificates on which early buyers received a hundred-fold return after six months. With a face value of 500 rubles, their curb market price (they were never registered in any formal register) peaked at 115,000 rubles on the eve of a coordinated challenge from three government departments (22 July 1994)—the Ministry of Finance, the State Committee for Anti-Monopoly Policy and the State Tax Inspectorate—on various abuses and on tax arrears of 50 billion rubles. Mavrodi was arrested and remanded in custody, but had to be freed when on 30 October he won a by-election to the Russian Duma; his promise that on regaining freedom the company would buy back its certificates went unredeemed; the fate of the genuine shares bought through the sister company remains unclear.

AO-MMM was not the only fraudulent scheme: Russki Dom Selenga (the title a Russianization of 'selling'), licensed neither for securities nor as an investment fund, attracted over 1.5 million depositors before an injunction was imposed; TeleMarket, Tibet and Chiara were others whose certificates were redeemable only at the price the companies themselves determined. Provincial exchanges, notably the North Caucasian Stock Exchange, were especially targeted. A Georgian investment company, Achi, took some $10 million from naive depositors before it closed in August 1994 and its chairman decamped.[59]

The extreme indebtedness of companies to each other, to the banks and to government agencies has given rise to a different type of fraud. An inquiry into 15 companies by the Russian State Bankruptcy Agency revealed bribery to managers to ship goods for which their enterprise would be unlikely ever to be paid: the client got delivery for the cost of the bribe and the supplier listed the value of the 'sale' as unpaid debt covered by bank credit or state subsidy. Such 'invisible commissions' were paid on 375 billion rubles of deliveries by an oil refinery in Yaroslavl. A more serious aspect is that creditors complaining too insistently 'could wind up with bullets in their foreheads.'[60] Enterprise indebtedness in Russia amounted to 114.5 trillion rubles on 1 September 1994, of which 47 per cent was overdue; enterprises in other CIS states owed Russian enterprises on the same date 8.5 trillion rubles.[61] A Russian decree that came into effect on 1 January 1995 requires accounts for goods delivered under contract to be settled no later than three months after that delivery. In case of non-compliance, the Federal Insolvency Agency has the right to recover the funds.

By restricting in 1987 the opening of the private sector only to those not employed in the state sector—supposedly housewives, students and pensioners—the Soviet legislators also invited into it those who were already leading a deviant life and assured rich takings for the few who did enter it.[62] Those demobilized or deserting from the Afghan war added to prisoners released from the *gulag*—many inured to violence and having contempt for authority—were material for criminal gangs. Gorbachev's two years of alcohol restriction fostered criminality, just as Prohibition in the United States had done. When the Soviet government and Party disappeared, violence, with frequent murders, became a routine occurrence in Russian economic life. Virtually all retail outlets, and especially the many pavement kiosks, pay 'protection money' to gangsters. In an attempt to control kiosk and street traders, the Moscow City authorities required them to register: corrupt clerks soon provided names and addresses to mafia gangs and allowed inescapable extortion. 'Protection' was not only forced on petty traders: Moscow police reported 200 contract murders in the city in 1993, of which 20 victims were leading bankers. The Far Eastern region is said to be controlled by a 'criminal clique' ruling by violence and disposing of more than 200 privatized enterprises. Uranium smuggling has been suspected, though not proved to have originated in Russia or Ukraine. A Duma deputy, Andrei Azderdzis, was killed in April 1994, doubtless for publishing in his newspaper a list of leading members of ruthless organized gangs, of which there are thought to be 5,800 in Russia, each with more than 20 members. Among these, the ethnic Russians are forging links with the international criminal underground; some sixty Chechen gangs (30 members apiece) are, it seems, working by themselves in prostitution, smuggling, money laundering and counterfeiting, while Azeri and Armenian gangs dominate drug dealing. The Russian criminal economy was estimated at 0.8 per cent of GDP in 1992 and perhaps 1.2 per cent in 1993: this is of the order of that in the United States, but the danger lies in its rate of increase and the inhibition it exercises on productive entrepreneurship.[63] Such magnitudes are not to be confused with the 'second' economy—always significant in Soviet times and still continuing—of informal or illicit transactions; this probably adds about one-fifth to recorded GDP.

New measures to assist in tracing illegal transactions and to encash more tax liabilities were introduced in Russia in March 1994. A bank is forbidden to open an account without presentation of a certificate of registration for tax and must report to the State Taxation Inspectorate any transaction by a private individual (including non-residents) of the equivalent of $10,000 or more. The bank must deduct in favor of the Tax Inspectorate arrears of tax if the taxpayer's account is in credit in rubles (and since May in credit in any forex account held). At the end of December 1994 the Russian Duma had passed as a first reading a draft criminal code which for the first time introduced liability for the conduct of illegal business, the fraudulent obtaining of credit and the obstruction of lawful economic activity. On taking office in July 1994 the new Presidents of Belarus and Ukraine decreed strong anti-crime measures; in the latter there had been about 1,500 murders and drug raids netting 11 tonnes of narcotics.[64] At about the same time, a Georgian decree strengthened measures against the mafia, terrorism and bank fraud, but comment was that such efforts would be weakened by the poor pay and discipline of the police.[65] The pressure to reduce government expenditure for a lower budget deficit and the attraction of work in the private sector, often for security services, had reduced the effectiveness of policing and the criminal justice system everywhere in the CIS, but a general increase of resources in 1994 seemed to have begun to turn the tide on organized crime. There may, however, have been little improvement in the field of corruption: the Russian Interior Ministry suspects that at least 2,000 civil servants are corrupt.

Capital flight, illicit because ruble convertibility extends only to current transactions with non-CIS members, severely reduces investible funds for restructuring after privatization and, with respect to their governments, cuts the taxable base and limits their ability to service external debt. Part of the outflow is honestly gained money salted abroad to evade tax or—more importantly—to be more secure than in domestic economies with high inflation, depreciating currency and unpredictable or even retrospective tax legislation. Much, however, is simply money laundering, originating in criminal activity either in the CIS or elsewhere. Estimates vary, but in Russia it would seem that flight peaked in 1992, the year of maximum inflation. The IMF put it at $13 billion in 1992 and $8 billion in 1993; the Russian Customs Committee suggested unrepatriated export earnings as being between $15 and $20 billion in 1992, but $10 billion in 1993. Statistics supplied to the Bank for International Settlements show that depositors recorded as originating in the former USSR added $5.3 billion to their accounts in Western reporting banks in 1992 and $2.3 billion in 1993, but reduced this outflow by $0.6 billion in the first half of 1994. From January 1994 BIS data are available by member state of the CIS: deposits fell in the first half of that year in Russia, Azerbaijan, Georgia, Kazakhstan, Turkmenistan and Ukraine.[66] One explanation may be capital repatriation as investment and monetary conditions improved, but depositors may be running down their balances to clear debts or to purchase real assets. It could be, therefore, that these deposits, together with some of the borrowing from Western reporting banks ($55.7 billion[67]), may be returning as if it were foreign investment, while the ownership was by CIS residents. In the peak year of Ukrainian inflation one estimate has $12 billion escaping abroad; the BIS shows a decrease in deposits of $133 million in the first half of 1994. Kazakhstan, which shows a rundown of $109 million in residents' deposits in Western banks, had noted in the first half of 1992 exports of $400 million, of which only $125 was repatriated.[68]

In general, the term 'capital hover' has been applied to such externally held funds:[69] They may return when domestic conditions are attractive for investment. Insofar as the funds are held in profitable real estate (London residential property and Spanish land are popularly spoken of as favored) and equities (there are reports of purchases in other transition economies—eastern Germany, the Czech Republic and Hungary), there should be factor income once the assets are above board. A proposal to declare an amnesty, but subject to a tax upon repatriation, was suggested by the then Chairman of the Central Bank of Russia, Viktor Gerashchenko, in July 1994, but was not taken up (he was dismissed in October). From February 1994 Kazakhstan has allowed anonymous forex accounts for both residents and non-residents, mainly to attract flight capital from Russia.[70] Externally held money might also be driven back: the FBI has an investigation unit in Moscow to support its inquiry into mafia funds in the United States, and the UK National Criminal Intelligence Service told a news conference in Moscow that 200 'suspect' transactions, each exceeding £0.5 million, had been monitored. Estimates for the aggregate of funds held externally by residents of the CIS are in the range $50 to $60 billion, but cannot by their nature be accurately identified.

In addition, about $11-12 billion (or about as much as is circulating in rubles) are held within Russia, although transactions must formally be in rubles. About one-quarter of the banknotes are reportedly counterfeit, but what is genuine could purchase significant quantities of capital goods for enterprise restructuring if conditions were ripe. As it is, the 'dollarization' of the economy is of the order shown in Peru at the height of hyperinflation in 1990.[71]

The undervaluation of assets

An ideal sequence would have been to liberalize prices and allow factor prices to be influenced by product markets and external competition so that assets of state enterprises would approximate to their scarcity value. Both at the time and in retrospect it was not feasible in any CIS state, on at least two grounds: a capital market could not be established promptly, and product supply was highly monopolized (with a balance-of-payment constraint on import competition). The solution generally chosen was to use for asset valuation the book value on the eve of price decontrol, that is on 1 January 1992, despite the obvious reservation that the process of marketization will change the relative prices and costs on which each enterprise is valued.[72] Another serious flaw is that those prices bore no relationship to the relativities of effective (derived) demand; they had been built up from cumulative labor costs (the 'embodied value', following Marx) in manufacture or construction, periodically repriced at replacement cost.

Vouchers in Russia were calculated on the same value scale, but even by the time their value was announced (August 1992) inflation was 28 times (industrial prices) and 8 times (retail prices) the level on 1 January 1992.[73] By the time vouchers were being combined with cash for privatization purchases, the disparity was much wider. A still greater divergence had opened up between the ruble–dollar exchange rate of 1 January 1992 and that ruling by the date of each first-stage privatization and still more by its end in July 1994.

It was hence inevitable that the valuation of enterprises both in rubles and dollars for the purpose of privatization should be well below a realistic market valuation of the individual assets. A list of the five hundred biggest privatized enterprises issued by the State Property Fund used the free-market exchange rate averaged over the four weeks preceding each privatization date and valued those firms at $7.3 billion in aggregate.[74] As an indication of the concentration of Russian industry, the ten biggest were valued at $3.4 billion, or almost half the value of the top 500. The list also cited the workforce of each enterprise, from which it could be calculated that these 500 companies were valued at under $1,000 per employee, which may be compared to about $100,000 per employee in the United States.[75]

The valuation procedure itself explains some of the divergence, and the infamous overstaffing of Russian factories explains some more. Another explanation is that actual bidders feared that the insider dominance was so strong that they would not be able to realize the full value of their purchase.[76] This is partly borne out by the greater value shown by the shares in the secondary market—$16.1 billion at 1 November 1994, or 4.7 times the auction prices of various dates for the ten biggest enterprises. A related consideration is that nearly all medium and large enterprises have some social infrastructure which is both difficult to detach and whose upkeep in service involves continuing current outlay. Soviet health care, for example, was substantially based on the workplace—from small factory 'health-points' (*zdravpunkty*) to the clinics of large enterprises; crèches and kindergartens for staff were the norm and holiday facilities from child holiday camps to resort sanatoria were standard. The cost of their upkeep has risen and they can hardly be sold off—often they are dumped on the local authority. Of a nationally smaller number of hospital beds between 1989 and 1993, the proportion in enterprises dropped from 10 per cent to under 3 per cent. Some of the 'social space' has been simply shifted to production requirements.

Further factors in low realistic valuation are the volume of inter-enterprise debt, which would have to be cleared in any proper financial restructuring; the uncounted cost of repairing damage to the environment, about which a great deal of qualitative evidence is becoming available; and undervaluation of un-exploited natural resources.[77]

The valuation of natural resources would be a prime consideration for the less-developed CIS members, but their governments are offering exploitation on a royalty, production-sharing or joint venture arrangement and mostly privatizing their large processing and manufacturing facilities on a case-by-case basis in which international competition and/or tendering is being invited. No 'base line' of the Russian type for valuation is needed. The industrialized states—Belarus, Moldova and Ukraine—are having to confront the same problems as Russia in assessing the worth of installations, for which restructuring costs are high and heavy indebtedness to banks, the state and other enterprises has to be taken into account. Although Ukraine has adopted a later base than Russia for asset values, the date chosen (1 January 1993) was in mid-hyperinflation and hardly offers more rational price relationships. Ukraine also shares with Russia a major difficulty in valuing the defense and nuclear industries, the demand for the products of which has changed more radically than in civilian branches.

The process of restructuring

The estimated $30 billion of Russian-owned 'capital hovering abroad' is four times the value of the 500 top first-stage enterprises and ten times the sum (in rubles) which the Russian government hopes to raise from the second stage of privatization in 1995—at least 9 trillion rubles, the equivalent of $2.9 billion.[78] Such funds are thus capable of taking over Russian industry in its entirety. But, as noted in Chapter 2, cash paid for shares in the second round will go to the companies privatized, and thereby reduce the need for outside finance for restructuring.

The microeconomic prospect is well known. Part of the investment required to bring plant and buildings to those standard in a Western market economy is for financial restructuring and environmental repair, but much capital is needed to render obsolete and misdirected projects competitive and efficient in terms of resources used. Many estimates have been made of the value subtracted—instead of value added—by Russian manufacturing when inputs and outputs are repriced to world relativities. Enterprises shown to be deficient in any of these regards may face no alternative but closure; the entry of new firms to employ those redundant involves further investment.

An examination of the problems of restructuring after privatization requires further study. However, brief note may be made of the microeconomic issues being posed. It goes without saying that their solution involves an appropriate macroeconomic strategy.

— *The fostering of competition.* A crucial objective of transition is a more efficient utilization of human, capital and natural resources, the attainment of which would be hindered by the continuance or new establishment of monopoly. Russian policy hitherto has been more anti-monopoly than pro-competition, such as demolishing barriers to new entry.[79]

— *Rebuilding contractual linkage.* The new states require the development not only of a normal market but also of its appropriate legal and financial infrastructure. International and foreign agencies are furnishing advice, and contributions can be expected from the associations of private business which are now emerging.[80]

— *The remolding of labor relations.* The Soviet-period association of the former trade union structure with the Communist Party and the new autonomy of enterprises, many with insider control, have changed the basis of workplace relations.[81]

— *Regulation.* Central European countries were able to revive and adapt legislation from the 1930s, but for the CIS the practice of the Tsarist empire is too remote and irrelevant; each CIS country is introducing legislation and conventions for a changed role of the state with respect to producers and for consumer protection.

— *Mobilization of domestic saving.* The Russian Minister of the Economy, Aleksandr Shokhin, announced in August 1994 a series of six decrees to generate more domestic private investment: he estimated the current stock of private savings at 30 trillion rubles ($6 trillion), but the propensity to save (6 per cent of household income) is low.[82] Positive interest rates and a network of financial intermediation are conditions for raising it. In the first nine months of 1994, 10 trillion rubles were invested from private sources and 20 trillion rubles from mixed private and state resources: together they accounted for half of capital formation (23 trillion from state funds and 6 trillion from municipal money).[83]

— *Facilitation of portfolio investment.* Secondary markets for privatized shares have been established on a formal or informal basis in all CIS states, but Russia has gone furthest, and will of course remain the biggest, in creating an organized market. Foreign investment is beginning to be attracted and a number of Western investment companies are already taking part.

— *The attraction of foreign capital.* CIS countries differ in policy towards foreign investment, notably in any offer of tax concessions during a set-up period. Russia has chosen to offer no specific advantage but, as with all, is seeking to ensure a predictable and familiar framework in which capital and technological transfer can be made. The First Deputy Minister of the Economy, Yakov Urinson, forecast an inflow of $5 to $6 billion a year from 1995 under an envisaged program of encouragement to foreign funds and of 'reasonable protection' for the sale of products on the Russian domestic market.[84] The cumulative value of foreign direct investment by the end of 1993 was $2.6 billion and of foreign portfolio investment $0.3 billion.

— *Debt for equity swap.* Aleksandr Shokhin said that a scheme might be considered after conclusion of foreign debt rescheduling. The supply of shares to a value of about $30 billion (of a total external debt of $80 billion) to creditors was his order of magnitude, and he particularly saw the shares being bought out of flight capital.[85]

If normally operating market economies and the full benefits of privatization are to be achieved appropriate political and economic solutions need to be found.

Notes to Chapter 4

1. On examples of the linkage of the two groups, see Stephen Handelman, *Comrade Criminal: The Theft of the Second Russian Revolution* (London: Michael Joseph, 1994).

2. The term 'privatization' is as relatively novel in Russian as it is in English: it did not appear in the *Oxford English Dictionary* until 1982 and in *Webster's Dictionary* until 1983. In comparison with the term in previous use, 'denationalization' in English, *razgosudarstvlenie* in Russian, it evokes private incentives and the positive value of transfer to the private sector rather than the negation of a previous status or of governmental divestment. The introduction of the newer word was a significant symbol in late *perestroika* days in the former USSR, as Yevgeny Yasin, then a chief adviser to Gorbachev, pointed out in 'Razgosudarstvlenie i privatizatsiya', *Kommunist*, no. 5, 1991, pp. 99-111. Philip Hanson, *From Stagnation to Catastroika* (New York: Praeger, 1992), ch. 13, 'Ownership and Economic Reform', dates the emergence of privatization in open Soviet debate to early 1988, due particularly to Academician Oleg Bogomolov (as mooted to a specialist East-West audience at a conference in Gyòr, Hungary).

3. Cited by Simon Clarke, 'The Politics of Privatization in Russia', in Stephen White (ed.), *New Developments in Soviet Politics* (London: Macmillan, 1994), within a concise history of what he terms 'Russia's managerial revolution'. For a fuller history (to April 1993), see Scott Thomas and Heidi Kroll, 'The Political Economy of Privatization in Russia', *Communist Economies and Economic Transformation*, vol. 5, no. 4, 1993, pp. 445-59.

4. 'The ideology of privatization emerged as a necessary weapon in the fight against the totalitarian socialist state . . . Mythological elements were especially strong in the writings of those authors who were first in espousing privatization' (Vladimir Shlapentoch, 'Privatization Debates in Russia: 1989-1992', *Comparative Economic Studies*, vol. 35, no. 2, summer 1993, pp. 20-21).

5. A public opinion poll in Russia in February 1991 showed almost the same percentages in favor both of private enterprise and of democratic reform—high in the case of Yeltsin supporters and low in the case of Gorbachev supporters (Richard Dobson and Steven Grant, 'Public Opinion and the Transformation of the Soviet Union', *International Journal of Public Opinion Research*, vol. 4, no. 4, winter 1992, p. 315). A Hungarian observer, however, considers that 'the economic programme enjoyed no direct popular legitimation whatsoever until April 1993' (Laszlo Csaba, review of Åslund and Layard, op. cit., in *Acta Oeconomica*, vol. 45, nos 3-4, 1993, p. 439).

6. 'Rural township and village enterprises allowed rural communities to translate control over assets into income despite the absence of asset markets . . . and restrictions on factor mobility. Rural residents were forbidden to migrate to urban areas' (Barry Naughton, 'Chinese Institutional Innovation and Privatization from Below', *American Economic Review*, vol. 84, no. 2, 1994, pp. 268-9).

7. Among many studies on China or on China and Russia, see recently, Jeffrey Sachs and Wing Thye Woo, 'Structural Factors in the Economic Reforms of China, Eastern Europe and the Former Soviet Union', *Economic Policy*, no. 18, April 1994, pp. 101-31. Gerard Roland, 'The Role of Political Constraints in Transition Strategies', *Economics of Transition*, vol. 2, no. 1, 1994, p. 37, argues that the absence of political change was not a cause of Chinese economic success, but that political decentralization allowed the economic institutions to evolve as they did. Richard Pomfret, 'Chinese Economic Reform, 1978-1994', *Moct-Most: Economic Policy in Transitional Economies*, vol. 5, no. 1, 1995, pp. 13-27, concludes that the signal Chinese failure has been the lack of fiscal and financial reforms until 1994 and the soft budgets of effectively bankrupt state enterprises.

8. 'The prior growth of rural industry, the dispersion of large-scale manufacturing facilities [to assure local competition] and the availability of knowledge and resources from overseas Chinese' (Thomas Rawski, 'Chinese Industrial Reform: Accomplishments, Prospects and Implications', *American Economic Review*, vol. 84, no. 2, 1994, p. 274).

9. Philip Hanson, *Regions, Local Power and Economic Change in Russia*, Post-Soviet Business Forum (London: Royal Institute of International Affairs, 1994), chapter 3.

10. Clarke, op. cit., describes 'a progressive weakening of the government's initial principles as it accommodated itself to the demands of the industrial nomenclatura and to popular pressure'.

11. Hanson, op. cit., p. 1.

12. Both references from Roman Solchanyk, 'The Politics of State Building: Centre-Periphery Relations in Post-Soviet Ukraine', *Europe-Asia Studies*, vol. 46, no. 1, 1994, pp. 59, 61.

13. See particularly Pål Kolstø and Andrei Edemsky, 'The Dniester Conflict: Between Irridentism and Separatism', *Europe-Asia Studies*, vol. 45, no. 6, 1993, pp. 973-1000.

14. A Russian poll in the summer of 1994 found that 73 per cent of workers thought unions ineffective at defending workers' rights (David Goodhart and Chrystia Freeland, 'Eastern Comrades Strike Back', *Financial Times*, 7 September 1994).

15. Richard Jackman and Michal Rutkowski, 'Labour Markets: Wages and Employment', in Nicholas Barr (ed.), *Labour Markets and Social Policy in Central and Eastern Europe: The Transition and Beyond* (Oxford: Oxford University Press for the World Bank, 1994), p. 152.

16. Richard Layard and Andrea Richter, 'Why So Few Layoffs?' *Russian Economic Trends*, vol. 3, no. 2, 1994, p. 15.

17. *Sotsial'no-ekonomicheskoe polozhenie Rossii*, January-September 1994, op. cit., p. 73.

18. Lecture by Dr Mary McAuley (St Hilda's College, Oxford) at the University of Birmingham, 14 December 1994.

19. *The World Today*, December 1994, p. 226.

20. Yuri Kochevrin, Igor Filatochev and Roy Bradshaw, 'Institutional Transformation in Russia: A Transaction Costs Approach', *Economics of Transition*, vol. 2, no. 3, 1994, p. 385.

21. On dispersing the oil industry, see Arild Moe and Valeriy Kryukov, 'Observations of the Reorganization of the Russian Oil Industry', *Post-Soviet Geography*, 1994, pp. 89-101.

22. Gazprom has been allocated only about half the country's identified gas reserves (25 out of 48 trillion cubic metres) but operates virtually all the existing wells (98 per cent of production in 1993).

23. Timothy Ash and Paul Hare, 'Privatisation in the Russian Federation: Changing Enterprise Behaviour in the Transition Period', *Cambridge Journal of Economics*, vol. 18, no. 6, December 1994, pp. 627-8.

24. Chrystia Freeland, 'Fears over Share Security Deter Investors in Russia', *Financial Times*, 16 November 1994, citing a London-based holding company whose shares had been struck out by a Krasnoyarsk firm.

25. Case cited by Simon Clarke, Peter Fairbrother, Vadim Borisov and Petr Bizyukov, 'The Privatization of Industrial Enterprises in Russia: Four Case Studies', *Europe-Asia Studies*, vol. 46, no. 2, 1994, p. 205. They do not identify the city, but another enquiry of the same 'Plastmass' Enterprise puts it in Voronezh: to that questioner the director complained of lack of funds for restructuring, pointing out that voucher privatization brought in no money and that clients failed to settle their bills (Lynn Nelson and Irina Kuzes, 'Evaluating the Russian Privatization Program', *Comparative Economic Studies*, vol. 36, no. 1, spring 1994, p. 58).

26. Ibid., pp. 201-8, among other instances, describes a conflict in a chemicals enterprise between the director and the chief economist to buy up employee shares, which involved the latter's dismissal and his pursuance of the matter through the provincial committee for economic reform on which the director was a powerful figure.

27. Nelson and Kuzes, op. cit., p. 59.

28. John Bonin, Derek Jones and Louis Putterman, 'Theoretical and Empirical Studies of Producer Cooperatives: Will Ever the Twain Meet?' *Journal of Economic Literature*, vol. 31, no. 3 (September) 1993, p. 1316. But there are theoretical grounds for the allocation of labor in a labor-managed economy to be identical with that in a competitive capital-managed economy and perhaps superior under imperfect competition (Christophre Georges, 'A Dynamic Macroeconomic

Model of the Labor-Managed Economy', *Journal of Comparative Economics,* vol. 18, no. 1, February 1994, pp. 46-63). Moreover, the Yugoslav experience does not show that rents from holding assets in an imperfect capital market explained actual earnings dispersion (Saul Estrin and Jan Svejnar, 'Wage Determination in Labor-Managed Firms under Market-Oriented Reforms', ibid., vol. 17, no. 3, September 1993, pp. 687-700). Many of these issues are considered in Anthony Atkinson (ed.), *Alternatives to Capitalism: The Economics of Partnership* (London: Macmillan, 1993).

29. Jozef Van Brabant, 'Lessons from the Wholesale Transformations of the East', *Comparative Economic Studies,* vol. 35, no. 4, p. 87, observes that there are cases of insiders decapitalizing their firm for short-term gain, ignoring a longer-term viability.

30. Trevor Buck, Igor Filatochev and Mike Wright, 'Employee Buyouts and the Transformation of Russian Industry', *Comparative Economic Studies,* vol. 36, no. 2, summer 1994, pp. 3-9.

31. An electronics works in Vladimir *oblast* and a bakery in Moscow, cited by Buck et al., op. cit., pp. 11-12.

32. EBRD, *Transition Report 1994,* op. cit., p. 10.

33. Success in this regard depends on sequencing: Barbara Katz and Joel Owen, 'Privatization: Choosing the Optimal Time Path', *Journal of Comparative Economics,* vol. 17, no. 4, December 1993, pp. 715-36.

34. The withholding of bank loans to soft-budget state enterprises is a precondition for banks to assume a strategic insider role, as descibed in the next paragraphs (Charles Goodhart, 'Banks and the Control of Corporations', *Economic Notes: Monte dei Paschi di Siena,* vol. 23, no. 1, 1994, p. 12).

35. Peter Young and Paul Reynolds, *The Amnesia of Reform: A Review of Post-communist Privatization* (London: Adam Smith Institute, 1994), p. 7.

36. Marek Dåbrowski [the Polish adviser to the Russian government mentioned in Chapter 1], 'Two Years of Economic Reform in Russia—Main Results', *Moct-Most: Economic Policy in Transitional Economies,* vol. 4, no. 1, 1994, p. 32.

37. Jozef Van Brabant, 'Privatization, Industrial Policy and Governing the Transitions', ibid., p . 77.

38. Peter Rutland, 'Privatization in Russia. One Step Forward—Two Steps Back?' *Europe-Asia Studies,* vol. 46, no. 7, pp. 1109-31.

39. Monique Meyer, 'Vouchers and the Financing of the Russian Economy', *Moct-Most: Economic Policy in Transitional Economies,* vol. 3, no. 3, 1993, pp. 101-3. By contrast some outsiders bought up small and leasehold enterprises from employees (Leila Webster and Joshua Charap, *A Survey of Private Manufacturers in St Petersburg,* EBRD Working Paper no. 5, July 1993, p. 64).

40. *Business Central Europe,* July/August 1993, p. 57.

41. Daniel Cohen, 'Economic Transformation in Russia', *Economics of Transition,* vol. 2, no. 2, 1994, p. 260.

42. Goldman, op. cit., p. 135.

43. Ibid., p. 135; *Euromoney,* July 1994.

44. Ibid. The group, the creation of Mikhail Harshan, has a bank, First Voucher Bank, and other money market interests.

45. MMMInvest advertisement, *Financial Times,* 27 June 1994.

46. AlfaCapital advertisement for foreign investors, *The Economist,* 26 November 1994.

47. Sutela, op. cit., p. 430.

48. The first advocacy of such a role was in Jenny Corbett and Colin Meyer, 'Financial Reform in Eastern Europe: Progress with the Wrong Model', *Oxford Review of Economic Policy,* vol. 7, no. 4, winter 1991, pp. 57-77. The case for the 'German/Japanese model' for transition economies is further argued, with many literature references, by Goodhart, op. cit., pp. 1-18.

49. *Euromoney*, loc. cit. and Kochevrin, Filatochev and Bradshaw, op. cit., p. 385.

50. Zoltan Acs and Felix FitzRoy, 'A Constitution for Privatizing Large Eastern Enterprises', *Economics of Transition*, vol. 2, no. 1, 1994, p. 88.

51. Michel Albert, *Capitalisme contre capitalisme* (Paris: Editions du Seuil, 1991), trans. *Capitalism against Capitalism* (London: Whurr, 1993); and Colin Crouch and David Marquand (eds), *Ethics and Markets: Co-operation and Competition within Capitalist Economies* (Oxford: Blackwell, 1993).

52. Yuri Kochevrin, Igor Filatochev and Roy Bradshaw, 'Institutional Transformation in Russia: A Transaction Costs Approach', *Economics of Transition*, vol. 2, no. 3, 1994, p. 377.

53. EBRD, *Transition Report 1994*, op. cit., p. 35.

54. Estimate by CS First Boston, the sole licensed investment fund with foreign ownership at the time, *Financial Times*, 10 October 1994.

55. Nasdaq is the acronym for the National Association of Securities Dealers Inc.

56. *Financial Times*, 22 June 1994.

57. Meyer, op. cit., p. 108; she provides much other detail to July 1993; as do Joshua Charap and Leila Webster, 'Constraints on the Development of Private Manufacturing in St Petersburg', *Economics of Transition*, vol. 1, no. 3, 1993, pp. 309-11.

58. The recommendation is by Young and Reynolds, op. cit., p. 26, who throughout the privatization process advocate greater transparency than generally exists.

59. On the Russian companies see particularly *Financial Times*, 27, 30 July, 2 August; *The Times*, 26 July; and *The Economist*, 5 November 1994. On the Georgian, see *Guardian*, 12 August 1994.

60. Chrystia Freeland, 'Tangled Mesh of Corporate Debt Ties Down Russia's Economy', *Financial Times*, 12 August 1994.

61. *Sotsial'no-ekonomicheskoe polozhenie Rossii*, op. cit., p. 106.

62. The argument is from Goldman. op. cit., ch. 1.

63. The value estimates are from Mark Galeotti, 'Perestroika, Perestrelka, Pereborka: Policing Russia in a Time of Change', *Europe-Asia Studies*, vol. 45, no. 5, 1993, p. 783, applied to GDP from EBRD, *Transition Report 1994*, op. cit., p. 167. Other references are *The Economist*, 9 July 1994, *Financial Times*, 30 September and 6 October 1994 and *The Times*, 27 September 1994.

64. *Financial Times*, 23 July 1994.

65. Economist Intelligence Unit, *Georgia, Armenia* [etc.], op. cit.

66. Bank for International Settlements, *The Maturity, Sectoral and Nationality Distribution of International Banking and Financial Market Developments*, Basle, January 1995, pp. 1 and 6.

67. Ibid., p. 31: FSU less the three Baltic states.

68. *Ekonomika i zhizn'*, no. 3, 1993, p. 29.

69. Daniel Yergin and Thane Gustafson, *Russia 2010 and What it Means for the World* (London: Nicholas Brealey, 1994).

70. *Central Asia Newsfile*, no. 17, March 1994.

71. From Marie Lavigne (see above, fn 3, Chapter 2).

72. Young and Reynolds, op. cit., p. 12.

73. *Russian Economic Trends*, vol. 3, no. 1, 1994, p. 117.

74. *500 krupneishikh privatizirovannykh predpriyatii*, Moscow, Rossiisky tsentr privatizatsii, 1994.

75. Calculations by Maxim Boycko and Andrei Shleifer, cited in *The Economist*, 5 November 1994.

76. This is the explanation of *The Economist*, loc. cit.

77. *The Economist*, 16 July 1994, points out that Lukoil's valuation puts its 15.7 billion barrels of oil reserves at five US cents a barrel, whereas Royal Dutch/Shell has a stock market valuation of $5.36 a barrel for its 17.5 billion barrels of proven reserves.

78. At the November 1994 exchange rate when Anatoly Chubais, just then named First Deputy Prime Minister in charge of the economy, made the announcement to a foreign investment conference in Moscow.

79. David Dyker and Michael Barrow, *Monopoly and Competition in Russia*, Post-Soviet Business Forum (London: Royal Institute of International Affairs, 1994); Irina Starodubrovskaya, 'The Nature of Monopoly and Barriers to Entry in Russia', *Communist Economies and Economic Transformation*, vol. 6, no. 1, 1994, pp. 3-18; V. Capelik, 'Should Monopoly be Regulated in Russia?' ibid., pp. 19-32; Andrei Yakovlev, 'Anti-Monopoly Policy in Russia', ibid., pp. 33-44; Jim Leitzel, 'A Note on Monopoly and Russian Economic Reform', ibid., pp. 45-54; and Saul Estrin and Martin Cave, 'Competition Policy in the Transitional Economies', *Moct-Most: Economic Policy in Transitional Economies*, vol. 4, no. 2, 1994, pp. 15-30.

80. The First Congress of Russian Businessmen gathered in Moscow on 19 December 1994 to form a national association to represent their interests (*Financial Times*, 20 December 1994). Three smaller bodies had previously emerged—the Russian Union of Industrialists and Entrepreneurs, the Union of Entrepreneurs and Leaseholders of the Russian Federation and the Russian Professional Union of Medium and Small Business; some transnational corporations are members of the first-named (for details see V. Z. Gushchin, 'Obshchestvennye ob"edineniya i zashchita prav predprinimatelei', *Gosudarstvo i pravo*, no. 11, 1993, pp. 51-60).

81. On industrial relations see, *inter alia*, A. I. Shebanova, 'Soglasheniya i kollektivnye dogovory v usloviyakh formirovaniya rynochnykh otnoshenii', ibid., no. 5, 1993, pp. 69-79.

82. *Financial Times*, 27 August 1994, and *Sotsial'noe-economicheskoe polozhenie Rossii*, op. cit., p. 72.

83. *Sotsial'no-ekonomicheskoe polozhenie Rossii*, op. cit., p. 31.

84. Reported in *Financial Times*, 28 October 1994.

85. Report of ITAR-TASS News Agency of 9 September 1994, in BBC Monitoring Service, op. cit.

Part 4

TRADE AND PAYMENTS BETWEEN THE FORMER SOVIET REPUBLICS

Alan Smith

The collapse of communism in Eastern Europe and the Soviet Union has destroyed one of the largest contiguous trade blocs in the world. The destruction of traditional trade relations and payments mechanisms between the former Soviet republics themselves and between the former Soviet states and their largest external trade partners in Eastern Europe has contributed to a major fall in demand and output in the former Soviet republics. This has greatly increased the costs of the transition to a market economy which threatens popular support for reform. In addition, the non-Russian republics of the former Soviet Union benefited from significant resource transfers from Russia itself during the Soviet era which have been significantly reduced since the dissolution of the Soviet Union. While this will offer long-term advantages to Russia, it has further complicated the transition in the non-Russian republics.

The failure to establish a properly functioning system of interrepublican trade and payments to replace the ruble zone in the former Soviet Union (the collapse of which was unavoidable) has greatly complicated the process of macroeconomic stabilization, has contributed to hyperinflationary pressure and has hampered attempts to create trade links which will be viable in the long term. The process of creating independent central banks, new financial institutions and new currencies in the former Soviet republics is now under way.

The creation of a new set of economic relations which reflect the long-term comparative advantage of the former Soviet economies is essential both for economic recovery and for peace and stability in the region. This will be difficult without external support in the form of finance as well as advice and assistance in the creation of mechanisms that will facilitate rational trade flows between the former Soviet republics, perhaps involving measures to create new payments mechanisms. The development of efficient trade relations will also mean the redirection of trade toward new markets and trade partners. This will have broader implications for existing international trade flows and for producers outside the region, who will face new sources of competition as well as enjoying the opportunities provided by new markets.

CHAPTER ONE

Introduction

The break-up of the Soviet trade bloc

The collapse of communism in Central and Eastern Europe at the end of 1989 and the subsequent break-up of Comecon (the Council for Mutual Economic Assistance or CMEA), followed by the dissolution of the Soviet Union in December 1991, led to the destruction of a contiguous trade preference area which extended over a fifth of the earth's land surface and encompassed 400 million people comprising more than 100 different nationalities. The Russian Federation, which has a population of 148 million people and a territory of 17 million square kilometers, and which contains enormous mineral and energy reserves, is by far the largest single economic and political unit to emerge from the break-up. It should not be forgotten that the Russian economy had extensive trade links both with the other republics inside the Soviet Union and with the independent socialist states of Eastern Europe, whose combined population is approximately equivalent to that of the USA. The economic impact of the destruction of these trade links on both Russia and its trade partners should not be underestimated.

The Soviet bloc as a whole was relatively insignificant in world trade, and accounted for only 2.7 percent of aggregate international trade flows outside the region itself in 1989. This largely reflected Stalin's preference for 'regional autarky', which he encapsulated in the theory of the 'two world economic systems'. This theory posited that the socialist states/republics (inside and outside the Soviet Union) should seek to conduct trade between themselves, even at the expense of the pursuit of trade flows with nonsocialist countries, which would have been more rational from a microeconomic, geographical or even historical perspective. Beyond that, the pattern of industrial development imposed on the Soviet empire resulted in the construction of a capital stock which reflected Stalin's preference for heavy industry, and which was geared toward meeting regional/internal demand rather than the demands of the world market. Finally, the very nature of the planning system and the foreign trade system isolated domestic enterprises from world markets and severely limited their access to international capital and technology.

The former Soviet empire can, therefore, be seen as a trade preference area which diverted trade that would otherwise have taken place with partners outside the bloc to partners inside the bloc. This involved the participating countries in a loss of aggregate economic efficiency and welfare. Although this loss may have been partially offset by trade creation through the removal of trade barriers between the former socialist economies themselves (particularly between the republics that constituted the Soviet Union), Franklyn Holzman (1987) has argued convincingly that the operation of the CMEA did indeed result in the member states' trading in total less than would have been the case under a market-based trading system.

Nevertheless, it is clear that the destruction of the socialist bloc network of trade will involve considerable short-term transitional costs for some or all of the participants, even in cases where new trade relationships can eventually be established. Permanent loss of any of the genuinely mutually advantageous trade that was created by the old system (whatever its other disadvantages and inefficiencies) will result in a long-term loss of economic welfare. The collapse of the Soviet trade bloc will also have major repercussions for world trade flows and international relations and stability, as former members of the bloc are deprived of traditional markets and suppliers, and are either forced or induced to seek new trade partners, new sources of capital and new outlets for their products.

The pattern that emerges from the break-up of the Soviet trading area will be influenced by specific economic and political circumstances that are distinct from (and more complicated than) those that would result from the peaceful disintegration of a market-based customs union or free trade area such as the European Union or EFTA. Trade relations between the former Soviet republics, and between members of the CMEA, were largely determined by 'planners' preferences', which reflected a low degree of market rationality. Soviet planners (or their political masters) specifically displayed a preference for an unusually high level of military expenditure in relation to national income. Any move to replace central planning with market relations in the domestic economies is likely to shift the structure of domestic demand away from the production of military and heavy engineering goods toward the production of consumer-oriented light industrial goods and services. This will inevitably have an effect on trade flows between the former socialist republics themselves and on their trade flows with the outside world.

Historical experience indicates that the structural changes required by the transition to a more consumption-oriented production structure will not be achieved smoothly and painlessly. The exceedingly limited moves to expand the production of consumer goods following the death of Stalin in 1953 created major problems for the more industrialized economies of Eastern Europe which were faced with the loss of markets for engineering products. This resulted in significant disputes within the CMEA itself which were never properly resolved and which contributed to the final collapse of the CMEA. The break-up of the traditional pattern of intra-socialist trade relations has already contributed to a loss of output and employment, resulting in reduced money incomes, greater uncertainty and falling demand for consumer goods in the domestic market in the short term. Central planning had some appeal for the working population (particularly in industry) in that it provided a significant proportion with guaranteed employment, slowly rising money incomes and stable prices for basic items of consumption (at least until the late 1970s, when decelerating growth and micro- and macroeconomic disequilibriums contributed to growing shortages in many areas of the socialist bloc). Although it is to be hoped that the costs of transition will be outweighed by the aggregate benefits of more dynamic and efficient economies in the long term, the costs and benefits will not be equally distributed among all participants, with the probability that some sectors of the population, or in some cases entire nations, will be net losers from the process. It must be expected that politicians will resist changes that are detrimental to the national interests of their countries, even if the aggregate benefits of these changes outweigh the costs. This, in turn, is likely to promote appeals for protectionism and the emergence of forms of economic nationalism.

As a broad generalization, the independent states that have emerged since the collapse of the Soviet empire can be divided in historical terms into four groups:

— Russia, or the Russian Federation, itself, which incorporates sixteen autonomous republics;
— those states that have had long-standing economic relationships with Russia, were part of the Tsarist empire, and became part of the Soviet Union at its foundation. These can be further subdivided in geopolitical terms into:
— the European states of Belarus, Ukraine and Moldova (all of which

acquired additional territories from East European neighbors as part of post-Second World War settlements);
— the Central Asian republics, whose current borders were fixed during the Soviet period; and
— the Transcaucasian republics.
— the Baltic republics, which had fallen under Tsarist rule in the eighteenth century, had gained independence in the interwar period, but were incorporated into the Soviet Union following the Nazi-Soviet Pact of 1939 and which have not become members of the CIS;
— the East European nations that came under Soviet hegemony after the Second World War, but retained their own separate national institutions and identities and became founder members of the CMEA.

This paper will examine the potential new trade relations that may emerge following the collapse of the Soviet empire, and explore the potential for the emergence of new economic groupings and for the redirection of trade from inside the former Soviet bloc toward new trade partners. In keeping with the title of this book, the dominant focus will be on the development of potential Russian trade relations, both with the former Soviet republics (all of which, with the exception of the Baltic states, are now members of the Commonwealth of Independent States) and with the wider world.

CHAPTER TWO

Trade Relations in the Soviet Era

During the Soviet era, financial relations and the flow of resources between institutions inside the Russian Soviet Federated Socialist Republic (RSFSR) and institutions outside its borders were determined by the Soviet authorities. For purposes of analysis it is convenient in the first instance to distinguish between relations with former Soviet republics and those with states outside the former Soviet Union.

The organization of trade relations between the Soviet republics

Although the Soviet Union was nominally a federation of free republics with the right to secede from the Union, it remained in practice, until the late 1980s, a centralized unitary economy with a single currency, a single monetary and financial system, a central budget which played a key role in financing investment throughout the Union, centrally determined prices and wages, and a state monopoly over foreign trade which was responsible for all trade relations outside the Union. Interrepublican trade amounted to no more than internal trade between different regions within a single economy, the pattern and composition of which was largely determined by central planners and industrial ministries located in Moscow.

Soviet thinking on the nature of internal economic organization was dominated (until Gorbachev's second wave of reforms in the late 1980s) by the concept of 'USSR Incorporated', in the context of which the entire economy was seen as a single plant (Sutela 1991, Chapter 6). The state as the 'single owner' of the plant had the right to transfer assets anywhere within its sphere of operations. Consequently flows of goods, services and capital could be (and were) transferred between enterprises in different republics according to central administrative fiat. The nominally independent republics were, in terms of economic organization, little more than administrative regions in a highly centralized nation-state (or economic space). Interrepublican trade relations were essentially determined by a single set of centralized (all-Union) institutions; the most important of these were the USSR Gosplan (State Planning Commission), the industrial ministries (which administered and coordinated the actions of enterprises in a given industrial branch Union-wide), and Gossnab (State Material-Technical Supply Agency), which directly administered interindustry relations between enterprises in different republics and supervised deliveries of finished goods from one republic to another according to central instructions. Republican authorities which mirrored the central all-Union authorities (e.g. Republican Planning and Supply Agencies) were subservient to the appropriate Moscow-based central authority and had little real autonomy.

The model was characterized by the supremacy of physical planning over financial criteria. As a result money and prices played an essentially passive, *ex post* accountancy function, and were shaped to facilitate plan fulfillment. The day-to-day operation of the monetary and financial system was controlled by the State Bank, which performed the functions both of a central bank (control of monetary emission; banker to the central government) and of commercial banks and other financial institutions (supply of credit to production agencies; holder of personal savings deposits; and so on). The bank also played a crucial role in supervising plan fulfillment by checking that revenues and costs were consistent with resource flows established in the plan. Internal wholesale and retail prices in the state sector were established by the State Committee for Prices and remained unchanged for several years. At best, Soviet internal wholesale prices were a rough and ready approximation to historically determined average costs of production, to which producer subsidies were frequently applied. They were not determined by supply and demand, and did not adequately reflect domestic or international scarcity (or in some cases surpluses), rising marginal costs of production, interregional cost variations or the underwriting of enterprise losses.

The Soviet monetary and fiscal system remained highly centralized by the standards of Western market economies until 1988. Republican 'central' banks were little more than subsidiaries of the State Bank responsible for administering the financial affairs of enterprises under their jurisdiction and channeling enterprise profits to the state budget. Monetary and price relations between republics were largely passive. Gosbank awarded an 'exporting' enterprise with a cashless credit for the delivery of goods to another enterprise or retail agency in accordance with the state plan, and similarly debited it for the receipt of inputs irrespective of whether the delivery crossed a republican border. The payment of cash wages (which gave limited command over resources to individuals provided the goods were made available in state stores) was similarly administered by the bank in accordance with the state cash plan and the centrally determined wage plan of the individual enterprise.

The fiscal system incorporated a central all-Union budget with republican and local budgets which were combined into a single balance. Republican and local budgets were not autonomous, and largely functioned as a conduit for centrally determined decisions concerning revenues and expenditures. The bulk of investment decisions which were taken centrally were funded by the state budget, which enabled the central authorities to make interrepublican capital transfers without reference to the populations of donor republics. The breakdown of fiscal relations between the central state budget and the republics in the late 1980s, following partial attempts at decentralization, was a major factor contributing to macroeconomic destabilization and the break-up of the Soviet economy in 1990–91.

The organization of external trade relations

Trade with countries outside the Soviet Union was a state monopoly exercised by the Ministry of Foreign Trade, which conducted all economic relations with countries outside the Soviet Union before administrative reforms were introduced in 1987. The ministry directly controlled the flow of extra-Union exports and imports of the individual republics and acted as a major barrier between republics and the world economy. Enterprises in individual republics which consumed imports or produced exports did not normally deal directly with their counterparts in foreign countries, but effectively 'sold' exports to the Ministry of Foreign Trade in domestic prices and 'bought' imports from the ministry in domestic prices. As a result, domestic relative prices were insulated from world market prices, and domestic enterprises had no direct knowledge of world market prices and were not influenced by changes in such prices. Similarly, they had little or no direct experience of opportunities, conditions or quality specifications on world markets.

Soviet trade with the majority of industrialized market economies (trade with Finland, which was conducted on the basis of bilateral clearing, was a notable exception) and with some developing countries was conducted in convertible currencies at prices that bore a close approximation to world market prices. These prices were then converted into 'valuta' (foreign-exchange) rubles at the official, but largely arbitrary exchange rate for accounting and statistical purposes. The prices of imported goods and exports were equated with domestic prices by a system of subsidies (normally provided to low-priced exports) and taxes (normally on imports which bore high prices in the domestic market). In theory, the Soviet Union imported commodities that were relatively expensive to produce domestically (and consequently had a high domestic price) and exported commodities with a low domestic cost of production (which carried a low domestic price) to pay for them. The difference between the domestic price paid to exporters and the domestic price of imports made a significant contribution to the state budget. In practice many domestic prices bore little or no relation to production costs. This made the evaluation of the profitability of imports and exports highly complicated. Furthermore the exchange rate was substantially overvalued, necessitating the payment of subsidies to exporters of products whose domestic prices were higher than the world market price when converted at the official exchange rate.

Soviet trade with the majority of Third World countries (including just under 60 percent of Soviet arms exports) was conducted on the basis of bilateral clearing accounts denominated in soft currencies. In principle trade deficits incurred by a trade partner in one period should be offset by surpluses of equivalent value in a later period. In practice the Soviet Union permitted Third World countries (and arms importers in particular) to accumulate significant arrears in trade denominated in both hard and soft currencies. This resulted in outstanding Soviet claims estimated by the IMF (IMF, The World Bank, OECD, EBRD (1991), p. 118) to amount to $64.5 bn in October 1989.

The organization of trade relations in the CMEA

Soviet trade relations with members of the CMEA also constituted external trade and were administered by the Ministry of Foreign Trade. In view of the relative importance of the CMEA's trade links with the Soviet economy, it is worth considering the nature of these relations in some detail.

Stalin was either reluctant, or unable, to follow the precedent that had been created in the case of the formerly independent Baltic republics by annexing the East European states and incorporating them into the Soviet Union. As a result, it was necessary to create different institutional structures to administer the internal and external economic relations of the East European states that came to form the outer part of the Soviet empire. These countries retained their own separate national identities and languages and created separate national economic institutions, including state planning agencies, fiscal and monetary systems, domestic price systems, domestic retail and wholesale trade systems, domestic currencies, official exchange rates, foreign trade monopolies and balance-of-payments accounts. Trade relations between CMEA countries were determined by state-to-state negotiations conducted by the foreign trade ministries of the respective states. Direct economic and technical contacts between enterprises in different countries were poorly developed.

National currencies were nonconvertible, and could not be used as a means of international payment. Domestic price systems reflected neither demand nor scarcity, and foreign trade between CMEA partners was conducted according to a predetermined, modified version of world market prices based in principle, from 1975 onwards, on a sliding average of the preceding five years' world market prices. Trade imbalances were (for the most part) cleared in a common 'currency', the transferable ruble, which had no physical existence, and which the 'holder' could not convert into goods, services or assets of deficit countries, or into convertible currencies. The transferable ruble was little more than a unit of account for the conversion of world market prices into clearing accounts held at the International Bank for Economic Cooperation (IBEC), and for statistical purposes. It had no direct linkage with the Soviet ruble used in domestic trade.

As a result, central authorities in Eastern Europe took a distinctly anti-mercantilist view of intra-CMEA trade and tended to regard exports to CMEA partners as a necessary evil, involving the diversion of resources from domestic uses to pay for imports. In principle they were willing to provide exports in exchange for a guaranteed flow of imports of at least equivalent value. But equivalence was difficult to assess because of the irrationality of domestic price systems. As trade partners were provided with no incentive to run a current account surplus, trade flows between CMEA partners tended to be bilaterally balanced in the aggregate. Similarly, the difficulty of identifying the value relationship between imports and exports from diverse products resulted in the phenomenon of commodity bilateralism, the tendency to export goods from one broad product category only in exchange for imports of a similar or comparable specification. At its simplest, this was reflected in the distinction between 'hard goods' and 'soft goods'. CMEA countries were only willing to export the former (normally goods that could be sold on world markets for hard currency) in exchange for imports of hard goods of an equivalent value. Likewise, they attempted to balance imports and exports of soft goods (goods that could not be traded in world markets) with each trade partner, to avoid any possibility of 'claims' for exports of hard goods to balance trade. The key exception to this rule was the delivery by the Soviet Union of energy and raw materials to Eastern Europe in exchange for manufactured goods. The latter frequently did not meet world market standards in terms of quality and technological modernity.

Domestic central economic institutions were responsible for the implementation of foreign trade protocols agreed by the foreign trade ministries of the respective countries. National planning agencies received instructions for exports which were passed down the administrative chain to the appropriate enterprise for fulfillment. Provided export orders did not make undue demands in terms of quality specifications, such as might result in a failure to achieve bonus-forming gross output targets, enterprises were indifferent as to whether production was for export to the CMEA or for the domestic market.

The distinguishing characteristic of trade relations within the CMEA, as opposed to those within the Soviet Union itself, lay in the fact that the CMEA was a multinational organization, while the USSR was a supranational one. The basic logic of centrally planned (or more strictly of unreformed centrally directed) economies is that fundamental decisions concerning resource allocation can be taken only by central planners, though other financial indicators or parameters may be used to guide lower-level decision-makers in the direction of centrally determined objectives. Enterprises or regions can have limited autonomy but only to pursue goals that do not conflict with central objectives. Within the Soviet Union monetary relations were subservient to plan flows, and the republican state banks were responsible for supervising monetary flows in accordance with the state plan under the tutelage of the (all-Union) USSR State Bank.

Logically, the full integration of the East European centrally planned economies with the Soviet economy would have required the submission of the former to decisions taken by a single central planning agency, which would inevitably have been Soviet-dominated. Khrushchev went as far as to propose establishing a common planning organization for the CMEA region in November 1962, but the supranational implications were too much for the East European states to swallow, and the proposal was defeated, with particularly strong opposition from Romania. From that period until the formal dissolution of the CMEA in July 1991, the Soviet authorities were unable, or unwilling, to establish multinational planning organizations for the CMEA region as a whole.

The East European countries were forced to divert their trade away from prewar partners in Western Europe (and Germany in particular), toward the Soviet market, in the period following the imposition of the Soviet political and economic system in Eastern Europe after 1948. This process was accelerated after the outbreak of the Korean war in 1950, as the individual East European countries were also forced to adopt (or to accelerate) Stalinist industrial programs and concentrate investment on the production of heavy industrial goods (particularly engineering goods and metallurgical products). These programs were pursued with little consideration of the individual country's comparative advantage or resource base.

This led to the development of the 'radial pattern of trade', through which trade between CMEA partners came to resemble the spokes of a wheel which radiated out from the Soviet hub toward the peripheral trade partners in Eastern Europe, as each East European country became dependent both on Soviet supplies of energy and raw materials to meet Soviet-imposed industrial priorities, and on the Soviet market for its industrial products. The radial pattern of trade predominated in Soviet–East European economic relations until the collapse of the CMEA itself, as a result of which the East European economies were highly geared toward the Soviet market and to meeting Soviet demands for heavy industrial products and engineering goods. The collapse of this market was one major factor contributing to the fall in industrial output in Eastern Europe after 1989; the ending of Soviet energy deliveries for soft goods was another.

The existence of the large-scale and relatively safe Soviet market for manufactured goods acted as a barrier in Eastern Europe, both to reform and to the development of exports to more demanding Western markets. East European enterprises were presented with guaranteed orders for existing product lines (which were protected from external competition by the state monopoly of foreign trade), and had little or no incentive to introduce new products or processes, or to improve the technical standards and quality of products to make them competitive on world markets. Likewise they had little incentive to involve themselves in small production runs to meet the demands of Western markets. The guaranteed Soviet market also helped to preserve full employment in industrial enterprises, which helped to consolidate worker support for communist governments.

The inability (or more properly, lack of will) to create a properly functioning system of international payments also hindered the development of multilateral trade links between the East European economies. The pattern of intra-CMEA trade which predominated until the demise of communism in Eastern Europe was 'trade creating' (i.e. creating trade that was consistent with Stalinist industrial priorities), 'trade diverting' (i.e. diverting extra-bloc trade into intra-bloc trade) and, most critically, 'trade destroying' (i.e. preventing the development of trade flows between the member countries which corresponded to their comparative advantage). At the same time the ideological (and in the Russian case historical) bias against the development of forms of private (or foreign) ownership and property rights hindered the flow of capital between different CMEA partners, while nonconvertibility of national currencies acted as a major deterrent to spontaneous labor flows between CMEA countries.

The view that the structure of traditional trade relations with Eastern Europe imposed a 'cost' on the Soviet Union (resulting from the export of energy and raw materials to the East European economies on terms that were less favorable than the Soviet Union could have obtained on world markets) had a profound influence on Gorbachev's economic policies toward Eastern Europe in the late 1980s, which contributed to the collapse of traditional forms of communist authority in those countries in 1989. The decision at that time to replace the traditional intra-CMEA system of payments in soft currencies by trade at world market prices paid for in convertible currencies accelerated the collapse of the CMEA itself.

As the majority of Soviet exports of energy and raw materials to Eastern Europe originated in the RSFSR, the Russian republic taken by itself can be considered to have incurred major losses from the structure of intra-CMEA trade. Russia was also the principal supplier of energy and raw materials to non-Russian republics within the FSU and the major source of the Soviet hard currency exports which financed imports for the Soviet Union as a whole. There is therefore a strong argument in support of the view that the traditional structure of trade within the Soviet bloc involved substantial losses for the Russian Federation as a whole.

This does not mean that the East European economies benefited unambiguously from the nature of trade relations with the FSU. For these largely reflected the imposition of the Soviet growth model and the Soviet system of planning, together with the diversion of East European trade flows away from traditional interwar partners in Western Europe, involving the East European economies in both static and dynamic losses. This form of trade diversion could be viewed as a negative-sum game which imposed costs on both Soviet and East European sides. But not all trade between the FSU and Eastern Europe fell into this category. Furthermore the development of an infrastructure (pipelines, transportation links, technological interdependencies and trading networks) has created long-term interdependencies that it would now be uneconomic to change, even where they have their roots in trade diversion.

Equally critically, the pattern of industrial development within the Soviet Union has created large-scale interdependencies between the former Soviet republics. Although these interdependencies are strongly concentrated on the relations between Russia and the non-Russian republics, the impact of the disruption of trade flows between the non-Russian republics themselves should not be ignored. This disruption has already contributed to major losses of output and welfare for the participants.

Russian trade dependence in the Soviet period: problems of measurement

How important were external trade relations for the economies of the former Soviet republics and for the Russian economy in particular? Attempts to measure the importance of external trade relations to the individual Soviet republics during the Soviet era encounter major statistical and conceptual problems. Most critically, as the individual republics (unlike the members of the European Community) did not maintain their own separate customs controls during the Soviet period, statistics relating to each republic's external trade relations with both the non-Soviet world and other Soviet republics were not collected and recorded on a customs basis. Consequently estimates of the trade flows of the individual former Soviet republics (with other former Soviet republics and the outside world) must be derived from data which have been provided by the Soviet authorities, or their successor organizations and which, in turn, were estimated from data that were initially collected for planning purposes.

This makes it difficult to assess the size and importance of trade for the former Soviet republics and to compare it with that of market economies of a similar size. One conventional measure of trade dependence in a market economy is to relate the value of export receipts in prices actually received in the domestic currency (e.g. US dollars in the case of the USA) to the level of GDP, also measured in the domestic currency. The principle underlying this is that domestic prices in a competitive market economy which is open to foreign trade can be sensibly compared with prices which prevail in international trade. Domestic producers of low-cost goods, who are seeking to maximize profits, will seek to export products to world markets when prices on these markets are higher than those prevailing in the domestic market when converted into the domestic currency at the prevailing exchange rate. This will drive domestic prices of exportable goods up toward world market levels.

Similarly, whenever possible both consumers and producers will seek to replace high-cost domestic inputs and products by cheaper imports (after including transport costs), thereby driving domestic prices down toward world market levels at the prevailing exchange rate and forcing uncompetitive domestic producers out of business.

The operation of the state monopoly of foreign trade, and in particular the separation of domestic prices from world market prices, and the insensitivity of Soviet enterprises to price and cost criteria, meant that this process was impeded in the Soviet economy. Furthermore, as shown above, external trade was conducted on the basis of (at least) three different price systems: with market economies it was normally conducted in world market prices; with CMEA partners at intra-CMEA prices; and with other Soviet republics in Soviet internal prices. As a result it is meaningless to compare value data measured in foreign trade prices actually paid with those measured in internal prices (even for a single product such as oil). For the purposes of estimating trade dependence, there are two alternatives: either Russian GNP should be estimated at world market prices and converted into a unit of convertible currency (normally dollars) which is then compared with the dollar value of all exports and imports in world market prices; or Russian exports and imports should be calculated in prices which reflect internal production costs and then a comparison made with Russian GNP in similar internal prices.

Most published figures relating both to interrepublican trade during the Soviet period and to the trade flows of individual republics with countries outside the Soviet Union appear to have been derived from planning data which measured flows of resources into, and out of, republican branches of Soviet industrial ministries, in terms of domestic wholesale prices. The use of such prices means that exports tend to be undervalued (partly, but not entirely, because of the undervaluation of energy in domestic prices), while imports from the nonsocialist world tend to be overvalued since they are largely composed of goods with high internal prices. Although the value of imports from outside the Soviet Union, measured in internal prices, cannot be strictly compared with data for market economies, it does provide a rough and ready indication of the contribution that imports made to the Soviet (and republican) economy. An analogy may be drawn with a market economy. It would be exceedingly costly to grow tropical fruits in glass houses in Vermont. Consequently any estimate of the value of tropical fruits to the Vermont economy measured in Vermont production costs would be a considerable overestimate. However, an estimate based on world market prices would greatly underestimate the contribution of imported tropical fruits to the health and enjoyment of citizens of Vermont in the winter, in the absence of a near substitute.

Conceptually, estimates based on world market prices are normally preferable to those based on internal prices as they indicate the prices that could have been obtained for interrepublican exports, or paid for imports from other republics, if these had been traded in world markets. Consequently they give a more accurate measurement of the opportunity cost of trade diversion to the former Soviet republics. This argument assumes both that the republics would have been able to divert interrepublican exports to the world market and that the increased net supply would not have affected the world market price for the good in question. The use of world market prices to evaluate foreign trade dependence also yields results that are more comparable with those that would be obtained for the study of a market economy and should provide a closer approximation to the prices that may be expected to prevail in interrepublican trade after full price and trade liberalization have taken place. They also provide a preliminary indication of the scale of the adjustments that will be required by 'debtor republics' to bring external trade into balance after independence and full liberalization. It should be noted, however, that the estimation of the dollar value of the GNP of the former Soviet republics also creates methodological and conceptual problems (most notably the choice of exchange rate for converting production in rubles to production in convertible currencies), where an estimate of the exchange rate based on purchasing power parity (ppp) is normally preferable to the official, or market, exchange rate.

Vavilov and Vjugin (1993) have made a comprehensive attempt to estimate the relationship between domestic GNP and trade flows with other Soviet republics and the outside world for all the former Soviet republics in both internal and international (world market) prices for 1987 on the basis of unpublished data provided to them by Goskomstat. These data are summarized in Table 1.

The table shows three striking features for the trade relations of the non-Russian republics. First, each republic exhibits a high degree of openness. Only Kyrgyzstan (18.8 percent) has an export-to-GNP ratio below 20 percent, while Belarus appears extremely open to trade with an export-to-GDP ratio of 42.3 percent. Second, exports are highly concentrated on interrepublican trade, despite the fact that each republic is contiguous to a non-Soviet territory or a sea outlet. Third, Russia is by far the largest destination for exports of all republics, and in the majority of cases accounts for more than half of the individual republics' 'intra-Soviet' trade. For all republics, except Kyrgyzstan and Tajikistan, exports to Russia account for more than 10 percent of republican

Table 1 *Exports of each Soviet republic as a percentage of GNP in world market prices, 1987*

			Recipient		
Exporter	Total	Russia	Non-Russian USSR	USSR	Foreign (extra-USSR)
Russia	22.8	-	12.9	12.9	9.9
Ukraine	26.5	14.3	6.8	21.1	5.4
Belarus	42.3	20.9	14.5	35.4	6.9
Moldova	27.1	14.1	10.7	24.9	2.2
Estonia	29.5	16.6	10.8	27.5	2.0
Latvia	29.1	13.2	14.5	27.6	1.5
Lithuania	33.4	14.1	15.9	30.0	3.4
Georgia	20.7	10.8	7.9	18.7	2.0
Armenia	25.2	13.1	11.0	24.0	1.2
Azerbaijan	36.1	18.6	14.5	33.0	3.1
Kazakhstan	20.8	11.0	6.9	17.9	2.9
Kyrgyzstan	18.8	7.2	10.6	17.9	0.9
Tajikistan	25.1	8.4	10.0	18.5	6.6
Turkmenistan	38.1	11.5	24.6	35.9	2.2
Uzbekistan	20.9	10.4	7.6	17.9	3.0

Sources: Estimated from data in Vavilov and Vjugin (1993), p. 140. Their source; unpublished Goskomstat data.

GNP. Although the Central Asian republics of Tajikistan, Kyrgyzstan and Turkmenistan show some degree of preference for trade among themselves, there are few signs of regional trade concentrations which do not involve a considerable degree of dependence on trade with Russia.

Vavilov and Vjugin estimated that in world market prices total Russian exports composed 22.8 percent of GNP, with extra-Soviet trade accounting for 9.9 percent and exports to other Soviet republics for 12.9 percent of GNP. Measured in internal prices, Vavilov and Vjugin estimate that in 1987 Russian exports constituted 20 percent of GNP, of which extra-Soviet trade accounted for 6.2 percent and exports to other Soviet republics for 13.8 percent. Imports composed 16.1 percent of GNP, with imports from outside the Soviet Union composing only 6.9 percent and those from other Soviet republics for 9.2 percent. When Russian imports were measured in internal prices they rose to 25.6 percent of GNP, of which extra-Soviet imports constituted 12.5 percent and those from Soviet republics 13.1 percent. These figures suggest that while estimates of Russian exports in internal prices do not differ substantially from

Table 2 *Russian trade dependency in 1990 and 1991 (in current internal prices)*

	1990		1991	
	Rb bn	*% GDP*	*Rb bn*	*% GDP*
GDP	644	100	1,300	100
Exports (total)	109.1	16.9	185.6	14.3
to Soviet Republics	75.4	11.7	136.7	10.5
to Rest of World	33.6	5.2	48.8	3.8
Imports	144.9	22.5	181.6	14.0
from Soviet Republics	67.8	10.5	105.0	8.1
from Rest of World	77.1	12.0	76.7	5.9

Sources: 1990: *Narodnoekhozyaistvo SSSR Rossiiskoi Federatsii*, 1992. 1991: *Rossiiskaya Federatsiya v 1992 Godu.*

estimates in world market prices, estimates of imports (particularly from outside the USSR) were significantly higher as a proportion of GNP when measured in world market prices. The latter is consistent with the analysis that Soviet imports from outside the Soviet Union largely consisted of goods that either had a high domestic production cost, or for which a domestic substitute could not be easily produced, and that consequently have a high notional value for Soviet planners.

The State Committee for Statistics of the Russian Federation (Goskomstat Rossii) has published more comprehensive data on Russian trade relations with former Soviet republics and with countries outside the Soviet Union in internal prices from the late 1980s onwards. Estimates of Russian trade flows as a proportion of GDP in 1990 and 1991 are summarized in Table 2. Table 2 indicates that Russian exports constituted 16.9 percent of Russian GDP in internal prices in 1990, with exports to former Soviet Republics accounting for 11.7 percent and extra-Soviet exports for only 5.2 percent. Imports measured in internal prices were equivalent to 22.5 percent of Russian GDP, with imports from outside the Soviet Union accounting for 12 percent. These figures were significantly reduced in 1991, largely as a result of the collapse of intra-CMEA trade, which fell to a third of its level in 1990. Extra-Soviet exports fell to 3.8 percent of GDP while the value of Russian imports from outside the Soviet Union was halved to only 5.9 percent of recorded GDP.

Crude estimates of per capita exports by the non-Russian republics indicate a relatively low level of penetration of markets outside the Soviet Union, and of the markets of the industrial West in particular. The CMEA was still the dominant external market in the late 1980s, accounting for over 40 percent of the exports of the non-Russian republics. This market has virtually collapsed since 1990. While Russian exports to developed market economies approached $200 per capita, only those of Belarus and Latvia exceeded $100 per capita, and Ukraine and Lithuania topped $80 per capita. At the other end of the scale, the exports of the Central Asian republics to developed market economies did not exceed $25 per head, although in part this reflects geographical factors. For purposes of comparison, East European exports to the OECD ranged from $437 per capita in Hungary to $89 per capita in Bulgaria.

These figures indicate that production in the non-Russian republics of the Soviet Union was highly geared to the markets of other socialist economies (Russia, the other Soviet republics and the CMEA) during the Soviet era. The collapse of these markets and the loss of supplies from these markets has had, and will continue to have, profound effects on output, employment and possibly social stability in these regions. It can be argued that participation in the Soviet economic system was a negative-sum game which caused a net loss of welfare for the Soviet republics in the aggregate. This implies that once the transitional costs have been overcome the majority of participants should benefit from the creation of a more innovative and dynamic economic system that is geared toward demands of consumers expressed in the market and that is open to foreign trade. The problem is complicated by the fact that participation in the Soviet planning and financial system required the richer republics (notably Russia) to make substantial economic transfers to the poorer republics. The reluctance, or inability, of the richer republics to continue to make these transfers following the break-up of the Soviet Union will impose additional short-term costs on the poorer republics, while the long-term benefits may not be realized for several years or even decades. This will increase the potential for hysteresis, in which the impact on production, employment and living standards in the long run as well as the short run will be determined not by the underlying long-run potential of the newly emerging economies, but by the short-run reactions to the transitional costs created by the collapse of traditional trade relations.

CHAPTER THREE

Trade Relations between Former Soviet Republics

Special features of interrepublican trade relations in the Soviet Union

Economic relations between the republics which constituted the Soviet Union were largely determined by the economic, social and political priorities of the Communist Party. Economic priorities included the stress on heavy industry and defense production and the desire to raise the level of industrialization of the predominantly agrarian republics and to disperse industrial production throughout the Soviet Union. Social priorities included egalitarian policies to raise wage and income levels in the poorer regions of the Union and to reduce regional inequality in the provision of social welfare facilities, including health and education, by the deliberate redistribution of resources between republics. Political priorities including the removal of national barriers and the spread of the Russian language throughout the Union facilitated labor mobility between republics. Thirty million ethnic Russians now live in non-Russian republics, while a similar number of non-Russians live in the Russian Federation. In three republics the indigenous population composes less than 53 percent of the total population (Kazakhstan 39.7 percent, Kyrgyzstan 52.4 percent, Latvia 52 percent). In only three republics does the indigenous population compose more than 80 percent of the total population (Russian Federation 81.5 percent, Azerbaijan 82.7 percent, Armenia 93.3 percent) (Narodnoekhozyaistvo SSSR, 1989, p. 67). Russification, although resisted in many cases, removed some of the barriers to flows of goods, services and factors of production.

Net flows of income and resources from richer to poorer regions also arise in market economies. In economies which have a centralized budget and a single currency, regional tax revenues do not coincide with regional budget expenditures, since per capita tax revenues on income and expenditure tend to be higher in richer regions, and per capita welfare expenditures are higher in poorer regions. Centralized budgets therefore lead to the redistribution of income from citizens in richer regions to those in poorer regions. However, the scale of the problem in the Soviet Union was far larger than that encountered in the majority of market economies. No other European empire has attempted to incorporate its colonies into a single economic space and to reduce wage inequalities to the extent that occurred in the Russian empire during the Soviet period. Similarly, even within the USA much of the funding and provision of welfare and education facilities is determined at the state, not the federal, level. The formation of the Soviet Union differed substantially from that of other empires in that it involved the unification of vastly different economies into a single fiscal and currency area, thereby opening the way to major interrepublican transfers.

Interrepublican trade flows were also critically affected by the *modus operandi* of the Soviet planning system. Consequently the extent to which net transfers of resources between republics were the deliberate result of strategic goals established by the Soviet leadership or were an unintended (but tolerated) by-product of the Soviet system of planning and price formation cannot be easily determined. Systemic factors included, first, the high degree of subsidization of energy and transport costs in the Soviet Union which obscured the true cost of interrepublican trade and stimulated inefficient trade flows and irrational cross-hauls of goods. The relative underdevelopment of the road network, and the convergence of rail routes (and those major roads that were constructed) on Moscow, increased republican trade dependence on the Moscow region (McAuley, 1991a). These factors were equally important in determining the pattern of trade flows within the Russian Federation itself. Secondly, the desire to reduce the dependence of the socialist bloc on imports (regional autarky) stimulated domestic production and trade at the expense of trade relations with the non-Soviet world. The operation of the foreign trade system, in particular the centralization of foreign trade and the inconvertibility of the ruble, complicated and discouraged external trade links, including cross-border trade, in favor of internal Soviet trade links. Thirdly, the Stalinist belief in the virtues of economies of scale led to the construction of large plants (which also simplified the process of interenterprise and interindustry planning) and resulted in a marked degree of product monopoly, which has created a high level of interrepublican interdependence. Fourth, the centralization of investment (including investment that would normally be undertaken by the private sector and by foreign direct investment in an open market economy), combined with *de facto* interrepublican capital transfers through the state budget, created a different structure and regional composition of investment from what might have emerged out of the free play of market forces.

There were also essential financial differences arising from the nature of resource transfers between Soviet republics and those that would have resulted from trade flows between capitalist economies. In the latter they largely come from interregional and international flows of goods, services and capital responding to price signals. They are (normally) matched by monetary flows (or by titles of ownership) moving in the opposite direction; these increase the claims on wealth of the net transfer of resources and correspondingly reduce the wealth claims (or increase the debts) of net recipients of resources. Normally, no attempt is made within a single-currency area to balance interregional resource flows over a given period. Independent states managing their own currencies, however, are required to finance any deficit caused by a net inflow of goods and services (which contributes to a deficit on current account) by either reducing reserves or generating a surplus on capital account (e.g. foreign credits, foreign investment); this gives a corresponding claim on domestic resources (wealth).

This situation did not prevail in the Soviet Union for three main reasons. First, investment was largely financed by the state budget. Consequently interrepublican capital flows were analogous to state or federal budgetary expenditure in a market economy with a single currency, and did not give rise to claims by citizens of net investing republics against those of recipient republics. Secondly, the 'passive' nature of money in a centrally planned economy meant that changes in money balances did not give automatic command over wealth or resources. Monetary transfers resulting from resource transfers had little or no economic significance. Effectively this meant that even attempts to equalize wage rates or to provide welfare payments to poorer regions were of little direct economic significance unless they were matched by a corresponding transfer of goods and services to citizens of the region.

Thirdly, as Soviet republics were part of a unified economic system with a common currency, individual republics were under no obligation or pressure to equilibrate their trade or current account balances, either with other republics within the Soviet Union, or outside the Union, or even in the aggregate (outside and inside the Union). Similarly, there was no need to develop adjustment mechanisms to restore external equilibrium to a republic that was in chronic external deficit on its current account. An individual republic could consistently consume more than it produced without incurring external debt, as the central authorities were able to impose *de facto* capital transfers from republics that produced more than they consumed. As in the case of interrepublican flows linked to investment, these capital transfers were 'unrequited' in that they did not involve the issue of financial assets, and did not give rise to claims by 'creditor' republics over the assets of 'debtor' republics. If the newly independent republics are required to manage separate currencies and conduct trade on a genuine monetary basis, they will come under increasing pressure to reduce, or eliminate, current account deficits, or will be required to finance such deficits by genuine capital and asset transfers.

As a result, the flows of capital, labor and merchandise between Soviet republics differed substantially from those that would have developed either between independent states with separate monetary and fiscal systems operating within a customs union, or between enterprises which were part of a single market with a common currency. Consequently the break-up of the Soviet Union into separate independent republics and the transition to market-based trade relations would be expected to result in significant changes to the historic trade patterns between the former Soviet republics even if the development of new financial systems and trading methods could be implemented smoothly.

Problems of measuring interrepublican trade flows

Before we can hypothesize about the possible pattern of trade and payments that may emerge between the former Soviet republics themselves and with the outside world, we must examine some basic facts concerning interrepublican trade flows in the Soviet era. The Soviet State Committee for Statistics (Goskomstat SSSR) started to publish selective data concerning the commodity composition of interrepublican trade during the late 1980s. A number of scholars from the West, and from the FSU, have made valuable studies based on these, and on unpublished Goskomstat data for interrepublican trade flows in world market prices. The results of some of these studies (Brown and Belkindas, 1993; McAuley, 1991a, 1991b; Vavilov and Vjugin, 1993; van Selm and Dolle, 1993; and Orlowski, 1993) have been used extensively in this chapter. These have been supplemented by data on Russian trade relations in the Soviet and post-Soviet periods recently published by the State Committee for Statistics of the Russian Federation (Goskomstat Rossii). Unfortunately Soviet and Russian statistical sources provide insufficient detail concerning the methodology used to obtain the data for them to be accepted with complete confidence, and the results must be treated with caution. Some of the more critical statistical problems (particularly those relating to prices) were described in the preceding chapter.

The analysis of the trade of the former Soviet republics since the dissolution of the Soviet Union is more than usually complicated by problems concerning the reliability of the data. Accurate information on recent trade flows between the non-Russian republics themselves remains very difficult to obtain. In most cases the central authorities of the newly independent states have had little prior experience of recording trade flows and have needed to establish entirely new customs procedures and statistical processes for measuring external and interrepublican trade. Private traders, who have a major incentive to underreport trade flows in order to evade government controls over foreign trade and taxes on imports and exports, have exploited the inexperience of the customs authorities. Consequently, foreign trade data published by the customs authorities of the individual countries are frequently revised and tend to differ substantially from foreign trade data taken from balance-of-payments accounts presented by the national banks of the same countries. Foreign trade statistics published by the OECD nations indicate a significantly higher level of trade between the OECD and the former Soviet Union than is indicated by the statistics of the republics themselves, with large and significant discrepancies between exports reported by the OECD and the corresponding imports reported by the former Soviet republics. Although discrepancies of this kind also occur between different data sources provided by economies with more sophisticated procedures for recording trade, the scale of the statistical discrepancies in the trade of the former Soviet republics in the period 1991–4 was far greater than that experienced elsewhere.

Finally, major problems arise when an attempt is made to reduce interrepublican and external trade flows to a meaningful common monetary denominator. These result partly from high rates of inflation *per se*, and more critically from differential price increases (which include substantially different increases for the same good sold in different markets) and from problems concerning the choice of exchange rate (e.g. official, free-market or ppp) for converting the value of goods and services in domestic prices into dollars. This problem is critical in a comparison of data from the Soviet period with post-Soviet data. Consequently all the data presented in the remainder of this chapter must be treated with considerable caution.

Despite these problems a reasonable picture of interrepublican trade relations in the Soviet era and the changes in Russian trade relations with former

Soviet republics since the dissolution of the Soviet Union can be obtained by examining a number of complementary sources. In the final analysis, however, these must remain 'ball-park' estimates.

The commodity structure of interrepublican trade flows in the Soviet period

Goskomstat published comprehensive details on interrepublican trade for 1988 in the journal *Vestnik Statistik* in 1990. These figures have become the starting-point for several Western studies. Table 3.1 summarizes estimates of surpluses and deficits in trade in broad industrial groups, taken from highly aggregated data on the commodity composition of interrepublican trade in internal prices, for some individual republics and groups of republics. Similar figures for subsequent years indicate that the basic commodity structure of interrepublican trade was not significantly altered between 1988 and 1990.

As the majority of calculations to re-estimate interrepublican trade in world market prices start by using these basic data (i.e. both imports and exports for a broad industrial group in internal prices are multiplied by the same coefficient to estimate world market prices), Table 3.1 provides a reasonable guide to the commodity groups in which the republics were either net exporters or net importers in interrepublican trade in the Soviet period. Although the *sign* of the balances will not be affected by the method of pricing used to evaluate trade, the use of internal prices to measure the *size* of the balances means that they should be interpreted with caution. Despite the limitations of the data, however, some clear trade patterns emerge.

Russia was a major net exporter of energy (particularly oil and gas), heavy industrial products (including nonferrous metallurgical products, machine tools and chemicals), and wood and paper products, but was a net importer of foodstuffs and light industrial products. This corresponds to Russia's structure of trade with partners outside the Soviet Union, apart from machine tools and, to a lesser extent, chemicals. In extra-Soviet trade Russia was a substantial net importer of machine tools. This deficit was largely incurred in trade with CMEA partners and the industrialized West, while Russia had a surplus in its exports of machinery and equipment to Third World countries (largely consisting of weapons and defense equipment). Russia was also a net importer of chemicals (including more sophisticated chemical products and fertilizers) from outside the Union. At the very least, the commodity structure of Russia's trade relations with non-Russian republics, measured in internal prices, indicates a degree of trade specialization corresponding to resource endowments

Table 1 *Commodity structure of interrepublican trade balances 1988*
(Internal prices: million rubles)

	Russia	Ukraine	Belarus	Moldova	Baltics	Central Asian	Trans-Caucasus
Total	+260	+3624	+4050	−186	−1257	−8545	+2054
Industry	+3823	+1966	+4079	−388	−1410	−10878	+1915
Energy	+6088	−3613	−814	−652	−1408	−675	−326
Electricity	−36	+2	−110	−2	+115	−51	−23
Oil and gas	+5868	−3574	−644	−514	−1480	−735	−268
Coal	+279	−41	−59	−136	−25	+126	−36
Ferrous metallurgy	−996	+3757	−1131	−259	−770	−1096	−592
Non-ferrous metal	+1459	−983	−337	−157	−375	+492	+87
Chemicals	+2064	−895	+275	−392	−543	−1249	−29
Machine tools	+6266	+2632	+2957	−679	−1166	−7286	−882
Wood and paper	+3381	−1167	+72	−118	+67	−1535	−396
Building materials	+401	+385	−8	−37	−43	−356	+183
Light industry	−5168	−2299	+2351	+347	+1203	+3028	+1872
Food industry	−10537	+4318	+658	+1567	+1640	−1653	+2523
Other industry	+877	−171	+55	+3	−46	−548	−8
Agriculture	−3617	+1432	+52	+219	−13	+1955	+151
Other productive	+45	+226	−81	−18	+164	−409	+18
NMP (billion rubles)	382.5	106.2	26.0	8.0	22.1	69.3	19.0

Sources and notes: *Vestnik Statistik,* 1990, no. 3. Baltic republics = Estonia, Latvia, and Lithuania. Central Asian republics = Kazakhstan, Kyrgyzstan, Tajikistan, Turkmenistan, and Uzbekistan. Transcaucasian republics = Georgia, Armenia, and Azerbaijan. NMP = Net material product.

and perceived comparative advantage. However, a shift away from heavy industrial and military priorities in non-Russian republics, following the collapse of the Soviet Union, will be likely to lead to a significant fall in demand for Russian heavy industrial products. It will be hard, if not impossible, to find alternative markets for these products.

Ukraine, which was in aggregate a major net exporter to other republics at internal prices in 1988, was a major net exporter of foodstuffs and agricultural products, as well as of machine tools and ferrous metal products. It was, however, a major net importer of energy (particularly oil and gas) although it was a net exporter of energy products in foreign (extra-Soviet) trade. Ukraine was also a net importer of light industrial goods, nonferrous metals and chemicals in interrepublican trade, and a net importer of light industrial products, processed foods and agricultural products from outside the Soviet Union. Thus, although Ukraine was a net contributor to Soviet consumption of food and agricultural products in total, it was dependent on Russia for energy, and on other Soviet republics and the outside world for light industrial products. *Belarus* (which was the largest net exporter in interrepublican trade in 1988 in internal prices) was a net exporter of machine tools, light industrial products and food products. But it was dependent on imported energy. *Moldova* was a substantial net exporter of foodstuffs, light industrial products and agricultural products, but was a net importer of all other industrial categories, and particularly of light industrial products from outside the Soviet Union.

The *Baltic republics* show a high degree of regional product specialization. Each of the republics was a net exporter of processed foodstuffs and light industrial products, and a net importer of energy, ferrous and nonferrous metals, chemicals and machine tools. The Baltic republics were also substantial net importers of light industrial products and food and agricultural products from outside the Soviet Union.

The trade structure of the *Central Asian republics* was largely a mirror image of that of Russia. Each republic was a net importer of machine tools. Kazakhstan was the only significant importer of machinery and equipment from outside the Soviet Union, presumably largely composed of specialized equipment for the oil and gas industry. Turkmenistan alone was a net exporter of energy, and all republics were net importers of ferrous metals, chemicals, and wood and paper products. All the Central Asian republics except Tajikistan were net exporters of light industrial products and agricultural goods, including cotton. All the Central Asian republics apart from Kyrgyzstan were also all net importers of processed foods from other republics and from the outside world, partly as a consequence of the concentration on cotton production in the region. Kazakhstan and Kyrgyzstan were, in addition, net importers of light industrial products from outside the Soviet Union.

It is difficult to generalize about the interrepublican trade patterns of the *Transcaucasian republics*. Azerbaijan was the second largest net exporter per capita in interrepublican trade, with substantial net exports of food and light industrial products. Azerbaijan was, however, a net importer in all of these sectors from the outside world. Surpluses in interrepublican trade on consumption items were only partially offset by net imports of heavy industrial products, including machine tools, wood and paper products and ferrous metals. Azerbaijan was also a net exporter of oil and gas in interrepublican trade and extra-Soviet trade. Georgia was a net exporter of food products and light industrial products and a net importer of all other categories of industrial products. Armenia was a net exporter of light industrial products and a net importer of virtually all other goods.

Interrepublican resource transfers: winners and losers

Although the estimation of the size of interrepublican resource transfers is far from precise, it is clear that these made a significant contribution both to the nature of economic life and to the standard of living in several of the former Soviet republics, and that the removal of net resource transfers will have a significant impact on the economies of the recipients in the short term. The continuation of these transfers in the post-Soviet period will depend on the willingness and the ability of political leaders in the richer republics to contribute to development of the poorer republics, as well as on the system of trade relations and international payments that emerges to replace the Soviet system.

CONCEPTUAL PROBLEMS The measurement of 'internal capital transfers' between Soviet republics is hazardous in the absence of published balance-of-payments accounts for the individual republics. We can start with the available data on trade balances, derived from interrepublican trade flows measured in internal (Soviet) prices (e.g. Russian exports to other Soviet republics minus Russian imports from other republics). These figures do not include local cross-border trade and unrecorded shopping by citizens of one republic in another republic. Furthermore the usefulness of these imbalances as an indication of resource transfers is affected by the arbitrary nature of Soviet pricing which meant that internal wholesale prices did not adequately reflect either domestic scarcity or even factor costs.

A second set of conceptual problems arises from the nature of resource transfers themselves. It cannot be assumed that the populations of the recipient countries 'benefited' in a hedonistic sense from the transfers of the Soviet period. While interrepublican transfers of consumer goods bestow some utility on citizens in the recipient republic, this is not necessarily the case for interrepublican transfers of capital goods and defense items. The flows of items that contributed to defense production or expenditure (and which did not contribute to a subsequent recorded outflow from the republic in question) would show up as a net inflow of resources in interrepublican trade data, but would offer no consumption benefit to the population of the republic. (The same argument would also apply to flows of consumer goods dedicated to nonindigenous defense personnel stationed in a specific republic.) Similarly inflows of investment and infrastructural goods (such as machinery and equipment, or pipelines) which were dedicated to producing goods that were ultimately to be consumed outside (or by citizens from outside) the specific republic in a later period will appear as net inflows in any given year, although they may offer little benefit to citizens of that republic.

This is also the case for value-subtracting industries (located on the territories of republics by central decisions over which the local population had no control) when trade flows are measured in world market prices. The value of the industrial products of these industries (republican exports) would have been less, when valued at world prices, than the value of the imported Russian energy and raw materials (republican imports) without any collateral benefit to the local population (who may have been forced to suffer from the effects of environmental pollution). The closure of these industries would result in a loss of domestic employment, but not in any loss of resources for domestic consumption, whatever the balance of trade indicates.

Resource transfers which are not reflected in interrepublican trade flows arise from republican trade deficits with countries outside the Soviet Union, which are financed by surpluses generated in trade outside the Soviet Union by other republics (for example, Russia exported oil and gas to the West which financed imports consumed by, say, Moldova). This problem is greatly exacerbated in the case of republics (e.g. Belarus) that imported crude oil from Russia (which was reflected in interrepublican import data) and exported refined oil products to Eastern Europe or the West (which were not recorded in intrarepublican data) but that did not benefit in the form of either direct claims against East European trade partners or hard-currency receipts, since the latter were centralized by the Soviet Foreign Trade Bank. As in the case of value-subtracting industries the citizens of these republics may have suffered the effects of environmental pollution created by the processing and re-export of raw materials.

It is sometimes argued that as it is impossible to measure the size of the problems outlined above they should be ignored. However it should be remembered that all the problems referred to above are well-known to students of Soviet affairs and that there is no reason to suppose either that they are insignificant, or that they might not nullify results obtained by using relatively sophisticated economic methods of estimation. Although the measurement of these hidden transfers of benefits and costs creates significant problems of conceptualization and measurement, it is possible that they are of greater significance than straightforward internal transfers.

ESTIMATES OF THE SIZE OF INTERREPUBLICAN TRANSFERS A comprehensive study of interrepublican resource transfers has been undertaken by van Selm and Dolle (1993). They estimated the difference between net material product

(NMP) produced (effectively what a republic produces in material terms in internal prices) and NMP utilized (what the republic consumes in material terms) for each republic between 1966 and 1991. They also demonstrated that the difference between these two magnitudes at the republican level could be attributed largely to interrepublican trade flows (measured in internal prices) and foreign trade flows (with net exports converted into domestic rubles at the official exchange rate). Thus the difference between NMP produced and NMP utilized provides an approximation for interrepublican capital transfers in internal prices which also incorporates republican gains from foreign trade operations. Belarus, which produced at least 16 percent more national income than it consumed in each year between 1975 and 1990, and Azerbaijan, which was in surplus throughout the entire period 1966–91 and particularly after 1978, emerge as the largest donor republics in relation to NMP produced, while Kazakhstan, although resource-rich, was the largest net importer throughout the period.

Van Selm and Dolle found that, up to 1978, the predominant pattern of net resource transfers was from the richer (European) republics (Russia, Belarus, Estonia, Latvia and Lithuania) to the poorer (Central Asian) republics (Kyrgyzstan, Tajikistan, Uzbekistan and Turkmenistan). They argue that the pattern of 'equalizing' resource transfers is not so clear after 1978, as Soviet economic priorities moved away from equalizing incomes toward overcoming the slowdown in economic growth. They also found that the disparity in income between the republics widened after 1983 and that the relatively rich Baltic republics changed from being net exporters of resources (donors) to net recipients during the 1980s.

Did this reflect a basic shift in Soviet policy toward domestic income distribution or was it simply the result of a shift in priorities toward investment in the energy sector, following the increases in world energy prices in 1973/4 and 1979? I have argued elsewhere (Smith, 1983) that the Soviet authorities reassessed the costs of their 'outer empire' in the late 1970s, and imposed far stricter terms of trade in their dealings with East European countries from 1978, requiring them to make significant increases in their exports of machinery and equipment to the Soviet Union. It may therefore be reasonable to assume that the Russian authorities conducted a similar reappraisal of the costs of support to the 'inner empire' within the Soviet Union.

However, the reappraisal of the costs of Soviet trade with Eastern Europe required the latter to increase their supply of capital inputs to develop Soviet oil and gas deposits which were largely concentrated in the Russian republic. Thus the increased consumption of resources in the Russian republic after

1979 (which would show up as an increase in NMP utilized) partly reflected the increased supply of East European and Soviet (both Russian and non-Russian) physical capital in the development of Siberian energy sources in the late 1970s and early 1980s. Investment in the energy sector (excluding pipelines) rose to 30.1 percent of Soviet industrial investment in the 1976–80 five-year plan period, and to 36.2 percent in 1981–5, the bulk of it being concentrated in Russia. Van Selm and Dolle also find that net transfers from Azerbaijan, which produced two-thirds of Soviet oil industry equipment, jumped to over 20 percent of NMP produced in 1978, and remained above this level until 1990. The high level of net inflows of resources to Kazakhstan is also consistent with investment in the energy sector. Although energy investment contributed to increased flows of Russian oil and gas to the non-Russian republics in subsequent years, the impact of this on NMP utilized in the non-Russian republics would have been affected by the low domestic wholesale price of Russian energy. Similarly, attempts to measure intra-republican trade flows in domestic prices would have underestimated the impact of deliveries of oil and gas on the net contributions and receipts of exporting republics and importing republics, thereby driving down the apparent Russian contribution to resource transfers.

INTERREPUBLICAN RESOURCE FLOWS IN INTERNAL PRICES Other attempts to measure interrepublican resource flows have started from estimates of the commodity structure of interrepublican trade in internal prices, converting these into world market prices. Goskomstat has published highly aggregated data on interrepublican trade flows in internal prices for 1988–90. Balances derived from these data are summarized in Table 2.

These figures do not include trade in invisibles. The data display a high degree of consistency from year to year, indicating that interrepublican trade flows were highly regulated. Only four republics were net exporters in interrepublican trade in all three years, namely Russia, Belarus, Azerbaijan and Georgia, while Ukraine moved from a substantial surplus in 1988 to a small deficit in 1990. The Central Asian republics were all net importers in all years, with Kazakhstan the largest. Armenia incurred a small deficit in all years, while Moldova moved from deficit in 1988 to surplus in 1990. The Baltic republics all registered small deficits in interrepublican trade in 1988, while Latvia and Lithuania recorded surpluses in 1989, which Latvia maintained in 1990.

Table 2 also reproduces estimates by the United Nations Economic Commission for Europe (UNECE) of the relationship of exports, imports and bal-

Table 2 *Interrepublican trade in 1988 and 1989 in actual internal prices (billion rubles)*

Republic	1988 balance	1989 balance	1990 balance	1990 % NMP	1990 % NMP	1990 % NMP
Russia	+0.27	+4.40	+7.43	16.8	15.1	+1.7
European republics						
Ukraine	+3.63	+0.49	−0.67	32.5	33.0	−0.5
Belarus	+4.05	+3.47	+2.38	58.4	50.3	+8.1
Moldova	−0.20	0	+0.86	62.0	52.9	+9.1
Transcaucasus						
Georgia	+0.28	+0.83	+0.78	52.7	45.5	+7.1
Azerbaijan	+2.10	+2.88	+1.86	57.0	49.6	+17.3
Armenia	−0.34	−0.24	−0.29	49.1	53.2	−4.1
Central Asia						
Kazakhstan	−5.40	−6.37	−5.87	24.3	41.3	−16.9
Kyrgyzstan	−0.50	−0.81	−0.73	40.6	52.8	−12.2
Tajikistan	−1.02	−1.07	−0.98	45.2	63.9	−18.7
Turkmenistan	−0.10	−0.32	−0.45	46.4	54.9	−8.5
Uzbekistan	−1.66	−3.51	−3.70	34.9	50.7	−15.8
Baltic republics						
Estonia	−0.30	−0.33	−0.26	53.2	57.9	−4.7
Latvia	−0.10	+0.52	+0.32	56.8	53.2	+3.6
Lithuania	−0.81	+0.06	−0.67	53.5	60.2	−6.7

Sources: 1988 from *Narodnoekhozyaistvo SSSR v 1989*, p. 634. 1989 from *Narodnoekhozyaistvo SSSR v 1990*, p. 636. 1990 from UNECE, vol. 44, p. 85.

ances to NMP for each republic in 1990. The Central Asian republics were the largest recipients of resources in internal prices, with Tajikistan receiving 18.7 percent of NMP, Kyrgyzstan 12.2 percent, Uzbekistan 15.8 percent, and Turkmenistan 8.5 percent. Resource-rich Kazakhstan was the largest net recipient of transfers, with net imports equivalent to 16.9 percent of NMP in 1990. This can be explained partly by capital inflows for the oil and gas sectors, but is also related to food imports. The largest net exporter of resources was the fourth poorest republic, Azerbaijan, whose net exports accounted for 17.3 percent of NMP (largely explained by exports of equipment to the Russian oil industry). While the richer European republics were also substantial net exporters in interrepublican trade in 1988 and 1989, Russia was shouldering a greater share of the burden by 1990. Belarus registered net exports equivalent to 8.1 percent of NMP in 1990 (down from 14.8 percent of NMP in 1988); Ukraine was in deficit in 1990 compared with a surplus of 3.3 percent in 1988. Russia was the largest exporter by values in 1989 and 1990. Although these surpluses translate into a relatively small proportion of NMP, to a great extent this reflects the Soviet system of internal pricing. Russian net transfers in internal prices are considerably larger when Soviet wholesale prices are adjusted to take account of producer subsidies and taxes which result in a divergence between wholesale prices and factor costs of production or, more critically, when interrepublican trade is measured in world market prices.

ESTIMATES OF TRADE RELATIONS OF THE INDIVIDUAL REPUBLICS IN WORLD MARKET PRICES. Orlowski (1993) estimates that Soviet internal prices undervalued exports of energy (especially oil and gas, the price of which should be multiplied by a factor of 2.7), ferrous metals (by 1.18), nonferrous metals (by 1.66), and machinery and equipment (1.10); and that they overvalued processed foodstuffs (0.38), unprocessed foodstuffs (0.45) and light industrial products (0.33), when compared with relative prices on world markets in 1990. This implies that trade balances in internal prices underestimate the opportunity cost of trade diversion to the Russian republic, which was a major net exporter of underpriced items and a net importer of overpriced items.

The USSR Goskomstat has published estimates of each republic's foreign trade (aggregating interrepublican and extra-Soviet trade) in world market prices for 1987–90 and has provided a more detailed breakdown of the commodity structure of interrepublican trade in both internal and world market prices for 1990. Unfortunately the explanations provided with the tables leave considerable room for interpretation. It appears that the estimates of extra-Soviet trade in world market prices have been obtained by multiplying coefficients to trade data obtained in internal prices, not by converting foreign trade data in actual prices to foreign trade rubles at the official exchange rate. In this case estimated net balances would also include an element of resource transfers resulting from deviations from world market prices in trade with CMEA partners.

Table 3 shows aggregate trade balances in world market prices for each republic in 1987–9, with an estimate of per capita resource transfers by republic and estimates by Vavilov and Vjugin (1993) of interrepublican and foreign trade balances as a percentage of GNP for 1987, based on unpublished Goskomstat data. These figures give an approximate indication of the opportunity cost to the individual republics arising from their participation in the socialist economic system, including interrepublican transfers arising from foreign (extra-Soviet) trade operations. A negative sign indicates that a republic is a net recipient of resources when estimated at world market prices.

The trade balances indicate that when trade is evaluated at world market prices the Russian republic alone was a net exporter in all years, with Azerbaijan in rough balance, while all other republics incurred significant deficits.

Table 3 *Aggregate trade balances by republic in world market prices*

Republic	Foreign and intra-republican trade balances in world market prices (Rb bn)				Trade balance as a percent of GNP (in 1987)		
	1987	1988	1989	Balance per head Rb 1989	Internal	Foreign	Total
Russia	+41.3	+30.8	+32.1	+218	+3.7	+3.0	+6.7
European republics							
Ukraine	−5.4	−2.9	−5.1	−99	−1.7	−0.8	−2.4
Belarus	−2.5	−2.1	−1.5	−146	+0.1	−5.0	−4.9
Moldova	−1.9	−2.6	−3.1	−719	−11.8	−7.1	−18.9
Transcaucasus							
Georgia	−1.8	−1.9	−2.1	−383	−7.0	−12.3	−19.3
Azerbaijan	−	−0.5	+0.6	+78	+9.1	−4.7	+4.4
Armenia	−0.5	−1.4	−1.4	−410	−5.3	−7.9	−13.2
Central Asia							
Kazakhstan	−7.7	−6.6	−7.2	−434	−14.4*	−3.0	−17.4
Kyrgyzstan	−1.4	−1.1	−1.5	−350	−13.5	−9.9	−23.4
Tajikistan	−1.3	−1.1	−1.6	−307	−23.0	−4.5	−27.5
Turkmenistan	−0.5	−	−0.3	−74	+5.9	−5.2	-0.7
Uzbekistan	−4.4	−2.5	−4.5	−228	−14.6	−3.7	−18.3
Baltic republics							
Estonia	−1.4	−1.3	−1.4	−890	−13.9	−8.4	−22.3
Latvia	−1.7	−1.3	−1.3	−470	−14.9	−10.9	−25.8
Lithuania	−3.5	−3.7	−3.3	−900	−15.8	−5.8	−21.7

Sources: 1987: Brown and Belkindas; 1988: *Narodnoekhozyaistvo SSSR v 1989*, p. 639: 1989: *Narodnoekhozyaistvo SSSR v 1990*, p. 642; columns 6-8 Vavilov and Vjugin (1993), p. 143.
* The table in Vavilov and Vjugin has a misprint and gives this as 1.4. I assume that this should read 14.4, which is consistent with the total and other estimates.

Russian net transfers (converted at the official exchange rate) totaled $51 billion in both 1988 and 1989—equivalent to a net transfer of $350 per head of the Russian population or approximately 5–6 percent of Russian GDP. (The size of this net resource transfer is not significantly affected if conversion based on a ppp exchange rate is used.)

All other republics benefited from net transfers when trade is evaluated at world market prices. The Baltic republics were all large net recipients. Lithuania received a per capita transfer of Rb 900 ($1,422) in 1989, Estonia Rb 890 ($1,400) and Latvia Rb 470 ($740). The estimates by Vavilov and Vjugin (Table 3, column 7) indicate that net transfers to the Baltic republics in 1987 were in each case greater than 20 percent of GNP, with Latvia receiving 25.8 percent, Estonia 22.3 percent and Lithuania 21.7 percent. These estimates are all in the same broad region as the per capita estimates, although they appear slightly high in the case of Latvia and low in the case of Estonia and Lithuania.

The Central Asian republics all appear as substantial net recipients of re-sources, with the exception of Turkmenistan. Tajikistan, the poorest republic in the FSU, with an estimated per capita income of $2,000 by the World Bank, received a transfer equivalent to $550 per capita. This is consistent with the estimate by Vavilov and Vjugin of 27.5 percent of GNP. The major part of the transfer originated from interrepublican trade.

These estimates indicate that the break-up of Soviet trade relations and the move toward world market prices in interrepublican trade will involve a sub-stantial improvement in Russian terms of trade *vis-à-vis* the non-Russian re-publics, with many of the poorest republics particularly badly affected.

The collapse in interrepublican trade and output since 1991

Table 4 provides a preliminary attempt to estimate the levels of exports and imports of each individual republic with other former Soviet republics and the outside world in 1993, expressed as a percentage of the level in 1990. The fig-ures are based on estimates of the dollar value of trade levels made by Michaelopoulos and Tarr of the World Bank (1994). Similar estimates of the level of GDP are also shown in column 7. Table 4 indicates that attempts to prevent an excessive collapse in intra-CIS trade announced at the CIS summit in February 1992 were unsuccessful and that a severe contraction in interre-publican trade has taken place. Interrepublican trade (including trade with the Baltic states) fell to just over a third of its 1990 value in 1993, while the dollar values of exports and imports between the former Soviet republics as a whole and the world outside in 1993 were only 40 percent of their level in 1990. Each republic experienced a severe contraction in both interrepublican trade and trade outside the Soviet Union. The total trade turnover of every republic, except the energy-exporting republics of Turkmenistan and Kazakhstan, was at least halved between 1990 and 1993. Only the Baltic states, together with Turkmenistan, Kyrgyzstan and Uzbekistan, succeeded in increasing their ex-ports outside the FSU. The value of total imports for all republics except Turk-menistan halved and in six republics total imports in 1993 were less than 20 percent of their 1990 level. Falls in trade levels were accompanied by substan-tial falls in the levels of reported industrial output and GDP for each republic.

RUSSIAN TRADE RELATIONS WITH THE FSU AND THE REDIRECTION OF TRADE SINCE 1991. The Russian Goskomstat has provided a large volume of data

Table 4 *Republican exports, imports and GDP in 1993 as a percentage of 1990*

| | | Exports | | | Imports | | | |
			extra-FSU	Total	FSU	extra-FSU	Total	GDP
		FSU						
FSU	Total							
Russia		37.9	54.3	43.7	35.6	39.9	37.6	64.9
Ukraine		29.2	47.0	32.4	49.4	29.5	45.6	62.8
Belarus		43.9	21.4	41.4	47.8	14.8	42.6	79.0
Moldova		24.1	42.9	25.5	28.6	14.6	26.6	56.8
Estonia		17.2	232.8	29.5	10.3	104.4	19.8	60.9
Latvia		15.0	151.3	21.1	13.0	20.6	14.3	47.8
Lithuania		21.4	102.5	28.4	15.3	31.4	17.2	45.0
Georgia		11.0	43.1	12.8	17.4	29.8	11.3	27.0
Armenia		16.6	26.6	16.9	18.2	22.0	18.7	36.3
Azerbaijan		18.9	48.5	21.3	20.9	17.1	20.3	66.9
Kazakhstan		56.1	86.0	59.5	47.5	39.0	46.5	66.6
Kyrgyzstan		25.0	125.8	27.7	22.9	8.6	20.0	59.9
Tajikistan		10.5	43.2	16.4	11.3	57.0	16.3	58.8
Turkmenistan	59.3		592.8	81.0	67.2	143.2	75.9	83.0
Uzbekistan		36.2	105.4	43.7	27.9	57.7	31.0	89.0
TOTAL		34.9	55.2	40.0	37.0	37.1	37.0	...

Source: Estimated from data in Michaelopolous and Tarr (1994).

concerning Russian trade relations with the other republics and the outside world. Russian exports accounted for 51 percent of interrepublican exports and 76 percent of the exports of the former Soviet republics outside the FSU. This information provides a valuable insight into the nature of trade flows since the dissolution of the Soviet Union.

Table 5 provides a more detailed breakdown of the branch structure of Russian trade with the FSU and the rest of the world in 1991. The Russian oil and gas industry was still a substantial net exporter both to Soviet republics and to the outside world in the final year of the USSR. The Russian machine tool industry was also a net exporter to both, although it had been a substantial net importer from the world economy in 1990. The reduction in net imports by the machine tool sector from the outside world in 1991 reflects the collapse of imports from the CMEA. Several sectors of the Russian economy related to the provision of consumer goods show a significant degree of dependence on imports both from Soviet republics and from the outside world. Imports by light industry, the food industry and agriculture amounted to 96.6 billion rubles and accounted for 53 percent of all Russian imports. Imports for these sectors were evenly divided between the outside world (48.7 billion rubles)

Table 5 *Inter-branch structure of Russian trade in 1991 in current internal prices (billion rubles)*

	Exports			Imports			Balance		
	Total	FSU	World	Total	FSU	World	Total	FSU	World
Total	185.6	136.7	48.9	181.6	105.0	76.7	+4.0	+31.7	−27.8
Industry	180.3	1322	48.0	165.0	96.2	68.8	+15.3	+36.1	−20.8
Energy									
Electricity	1.6	1.4	0.2	1.2	1.2	–	+0.4	+0.2	+0.2
Oil and gas	32.6	20.4	12.2	3.3	3.2	0.1	+29.3	+17.2	+12.1
Coal	1.4	0.7	0.6	0.8	0.8	–	+0.6	–	+0.6
Ferrous metallurgy	11.5	9.2	2.3	9.6	8.5	1.0	+1.9	+0.7	+1.2
Non-ferrous									
metallurgy	9.2	6.3	2.9	4.6	4.2	0.4	+4.6	+2.1	+2.5
Chemicals	18.8	15.6	3.2	11.6	8.0	3.6	+7.2	+7.6	−3.7
Machine tools	60.8	41.7	19.1	45.4	25.9	19.6	+15.4	+15.8	−0.5
Wood and paper	10.3	7.5	2.8	2.0	1.4	0.7	+8.3	+6.1	+2.2
Building materials	2.3	2.0	0.3	1.9	1.0	0.9	+0.3	+1.0	−0.6
Light industry	20.0	18.7	1.4	38.4	19.3	19.1	−18.4	−0.7	−17.8
Food industry	5.5	3.1	2.4	42.7	20.8	21.8	−37.1	−17.7	−19.4
Other industry	6.3	5.7	0.6	3.5	1.8	1.7	+2.8	+3.9	−1.0
Agriculture	0.7	0.4	0.3	15.5	7.7	7.8	−14.8	−7.3	−7.5
Other productive									
sectors	4.6	4.1	0.6	1.2	1.1	0.1	+3.5	+3.0	+0.5

Source: Rossiiskaya Federatsiya v 1992 Godu, Goskomstat Rossii. pp. 38–9.
Notes: FSU = All former Soviet Union (including the Baltic states). World = All non-Soviet states.

and Soviet republics (47.8 billion rubles) in 1991, accounting for 63.4 percent and 45.5 percent of imports from these sources respectively.

Although Russia was a net exporter of nonfood consumer goods to other Soviet republics in 1991, it was a substantial net importer of foodstuffs and agricultural products from both former Soviet republics and the rest of the world in 1991. Net imports of foodstuffs from other republics accounted for 9 percent of the value of total sales of foodstuffs to the Russian population in 1991 and for 27.3 percent of sales of crop products. Imports from Soviet republics accounted for 43.4 percent of sales of fresh fruit, 23 percent of fresh vegetables, 36.8 percent of sugar, 29 percent of processed tomatoes, 31.3 percent of preserved fruit products and 16.2 percent of canned and frozen vegetables (all figures by weight or physical units). Although their prices may have exceeded world market prices, these imports made a significant contribution to Russian food consumption and helped to alleviate some of the worst areas of shortages and consumer disequilibrium experienced in Russia in 1991.

Table 4 indicates that the dollar value of Russian exports to the former Soviet republics fell by 62 percent between 1990 and 1993, while imports fell by

Table 6 *Russian trade with the CIS and the rest of the world 1990–94 (billion U.S.$)*

	1990	1991	1992	1993	1994 (est)
Total trade					
Exports	199.9	157.2	155.3	112.1	77
Imports	197.8	126.7	90.2	68.9	52
Trade outside the CIS					
Exports	71.1	50.9	42.4	44.3	47
Imports	81.8	44.5	37.0	26.8	29
Balance	−10.7	+6.4	+5.4	+17.5	+18
Trade with the CIS					
Exports	128.8	106.3	112.9	67.7	30
Imports	116.0	82.2	53.2	42.1	23
Balance	+12.0	+24.1	+59.7	+25.6	+7
Dependency rates					
Extra CIS					
Exports as % of GDP	5.7	4.6	4.7	5.6	8.5
Imports as % of GDP	6.6	4.0	4.1	3.4	4.9
Balance	−0.9	+0.6	+0.6	+2.2	+3.6
Trade with CIS					
Exports as % of GDP	10.4	9.5	12.6	8.5	4.0
Imports as % of GDP	9.4	7.4	5.9	5.3	3.1
Balance	+1.0	+2.1	+6.7	+3.2	+0.9
Memorandum items					
GDP ($ bn)	1,238	1,111	894	792	750
ppp rate (Rb:$)	0.52	1.17	20.20	204.9	735

Sources and notes: Trade data are taken from *Russian Economic Trends*, various issues, especially 1994, no. 3. Their source was the Russian Goskomstat. Dollar estimates of GDP and trade with the CIS have been converted from ruble figures at the official Goskomstat ppp exchange rate.

63 percent. UNECE has also estimated that Russian trade turnover with the FSU fell by half between 1991 and 1993 and that the fall in Russian exports was larger than the fall in Russian imports. Table 6 provides final revised Goskomstat estimates of the dollar value of Russian trade with partners in the CIS and the rest of the world (including the Baltic states) from 1990 to 1993. Goskomstat estimated that Russian exports to the CIS fell from 10.5 percent of Russian GDP in 1990 to 8.5 percent in 1993, while Russian GDP itself fell by 35 percent over the same period. Russian imports from the CIS fell from 9.4 percent of Russian GDP in 1991 to 5.9 percent in 1993. Provisional estimates indicate an even sharper fall in 1994, when Russian exports to the CIS dropped to 4 percent of GDP and imports to only 3.1 percent in the first nine months of the year. The figures in Table 6 have been measured in current prices and consequently the increase in the relative price of energy exports to the CIS would have increased the proportion of CIS exports to GDP, while falls in export prices to the rest of the world would have had the opposite ef-

fect. Consequently these estimates understate the degree to which Russia has diverted exports away from the CIS to the rest of the world. The reduction in the volume of Russian exports to the CIS in constant prices would be significantly higher than these figures imply. This also explains the apparent increase in Russian exports to the CIS in 1992 and the smaller fall in exports between 1990 and 1993 (47 percent) shown in Table 6. Estimates in constant prices indicate that the volume of Russian trade with the CIS fell by over 30 percent in 1992.

RUSSIAN ENERGY EXPORTS. Exports of Russian sources of energy, particularly oil and gas (and precious stones and metals to an increasing extent since the fall in world oil prices in 1985), had formed the principal source of Soviet hard-currency earnings and exports to the CMEA since 1974. Similarly energy predominated in Russia's 'exports' to other Soviet republics during that era, despite the artificially low price, and was the major source of unrequited resource transfers. Russian energy exports accounted for 88 percent of the value of Russian exports to the CIS in 1993, compared with 51 percent in 1992. This increase is explained in part by the virtual collapse of nonenergy products in Russian exports to the FSU and in part by the increase in the price charged for energy exports to CIS states, while the volume of energy exports actually declined. The absolute decline in Russian energy exports to the CIS and to other trade partners can be measured in comparable physical units to give an illustration of the switch in the volume of Russian exports from the CIS to the rest of the world. Table 7 shows that despite an overall fall in energy production in the Russian Federation of 15.7 percent (measured in tonnes of standard fuel equivalent) between 1991 and 1993, Russia increased its energy exports to the outside world (for hard currency) by 17.2 percent; this was at the expense of exports to the non-Russian republics, which fell by 38.4 percent. As a result the share of the CIS in Russian energy exports in physical units fell from 60 percent in 1991 to 43 percent in 1993 (despite the collapse of exports to Eastern Europe).

Rough estimates indicate that although Russian oil production fell by 110 million tonnes between 1991 and 1993, Russian exports of crude oil and refined oil products outside the CIS rose by 31 million tonnes, while exports to the CIS fell by 75 million tonnes—a fall of just under 60 percent. Ukraine and Belarus, which were the largest recipients of Russian oil and gas during the Soviet era, suffered from cuts of nearly 66 percent in the volume of Russian crude oil deliveries between 1991 and 1993. Russian exports of natural gas to the CIS were halved to an estimated 77 billion cubic meters over the same period.

Table 7 *Russian energy exports, 1991–3*

	1991	1992	1993
Total energy (mtsfe)			
Production plus imports	1844	1712	1555
Exports	484	452	408
to world	197	210	231
to CIS	384	242	177
Oil (mn tonnes)	1360	1260	1147
Production			
Net exports	462	393	352
Crude	210	173	166
Products	162	131	118
Losses	48	42	48
Consumption	11	10	8
Net exports to world	241	210	178
Crude	84	91	115
Products	57	66	80
Net exports to CIS	27	25	35
Crude oil	126	82	51
Products	105	65	38
Natural gas (bn cu m)	21	17	13
Production	643	641	618
Exports	246	195	175
to world	90	88	96
to CIS	156	107	79
Apparent availability	387	446	443

Sources: *Russian Economic Monitor*,1993, no. 2., *Russian Economic Trends*, 1994, no. 2., *Narodnoye Khozyaistvo*, 1992. *Rossiiskaya Ferderatsiya v 1992 Godu.*
Note: Oil figures from all sources have been adjusted by the author in an attempt to take account of oil imports and refinery losses.

The contraction in Soviet energy exports to the CIS and the diversion of energy exports to the rest of the world continued during 1994. Russian exports of crude oil to the CIS fell by 23 percent in volume during the first nine months of 1994 and exports of refined oil products to the CIS fell by over 60 percent, but exports of natural gas fell by only 3 percent. At the same time Russian exports of crude oil to the rest of the world grew by 11 percent, exports of refined oil products by 16 percent and of natural gas by 17 percent, despite the falls in world market prices for these commodities (*Russian Economic Trends* 1994, no. 3, pp. 76-82).

Falling prices for energy on world markets mean that Russia still experienced a fall in total energy earnings from $26.3bn in 1991 to $22bn in 1993, despite the diversion of Russian oil and gas exports from the FSU to the world market since 1991 (see Table 8). At the same time Russia has experienced a reduction in the real level of imports from the world outside the FSU. Accord-

Table 8 *Russian fuel and energy exports outside the FSU,*
1991–94 (million U.S.$)

	1991	1992	1993	1994
(Jan–Sept)				
Total	26,300	21,711	21,958	15,900
Crude oil	8,673	8,545	8,370	6,601
Oil products	4,739	4,171	3,471	2,556
Natural gas	11,006	7,479	7,443	5,761

Sources: 1991: *Narodnoye Khozyaistvo Rossiiskoi Federatsii 1992;* 1992: *Rossiiskaya Federatsiya v 1992 Godu;* 1993: *Platyezhnii Balanc Rossii za 1993 God;* 1994: *Russian Economic Trends,* 1994, no. 3.

ing to Goskomstat data, the dollar value of imports from outside the FSU fell in each year from 1990 to 1993, while Russia's trade balance with the outside world moved from deficit in 1990 to a surplus estimated as the equivalent of 3.6 percent of GDP in 1994.

RUSSIAN RESOURCE TRANSFERS TO THE FSU SINCE 1991. Table 6 indicates that Russia's exports to the CIS exceeded its imports from the CIS by an amount equivalent to 6.7 percent of GDP in 1992. This was reduced to 3.2 percent of GDP in 1993 and fell further to 0.9 percent of GDP in the first nine months of 1994 (all figures measured in current prices). The Russian Central Bank estimates that Russian bank credits to the FSU as a whole amounted to 8.5 percent of GDP in 1992. If cash advances which were used to finance imports from Russia are added to this sum, Russian credits to the FSU rise to 11.7 percent of Russian GDP in 1992. A substantial tightening of interrepublican credit regulations implemented by the Russian Central Bank at the end of 1992 reduced the flow of new bank credits to other republics to just over 1 percent of Russian GDP in 1993, while cash advances to other republics were reduced to under 2 percent, contributing to the substantial reduction in the ability of non-Russian republics to maintain imports from Russia.

As the chief recipients of Russian oil and gas (Ukraine, Belarus, Kazakhstan and Turkmenistan) faced severe payments problems, Russian trade surpluses have largely resulted in a significant build-up of indebtedness and represented a substantial net outflow of resources to these republics. The energy debts of the former Soviet republics to Russia had reached 5.6 trillion rubles by the end of August 1994, with Ukraine (65 percent) and Belarus (16 percent) the major debtors. Similarly Russian enterprises were, in aggregate, net creditors to enterprises in other CIS states.

Trade figures, however, still understate the opportunity cost of trade relations with the CIS to the Russian economy during this period since the prices Russia charged its CIS partners for energy in 1992 remained substantially lower than those it obtained in world markets. In 1992 the intra-CIS price for crude oil was only 10.3 percent of the price Russia obtained in world markets, while that of natural gas was only 8.1 percent of the extra-CIS export price. Russian export prices to the CIS were gradually increased in real terms during 1993 and 1994, but oil export prices to the CIS were still less than half of the extra-CIS export price in mid-1994, while natural gas prices had risen to 77 percent of the world market price.

The IMF (IMF 1994, p. 11) cites an estimate by the Russian authorities that Russian trade subsidies to the CIS arising from the difference between CIS prices and world market prices for energy came to $12bn in 1992, equivalent to 13 percent of Russian GDP converted at the average exchange rate. The latter estimate is very sensitive to the exchange rate used to evaluate GNP. The World Bank estimated Russian GDP at $6,220 per capita in 1992, using an exchange rate based on purchasing power parity. This is equivalent to total GDP of $924 billion, which would indicate that energy price subsidies were actually only of the order of 1.3–1.5 percent of Russian GDP in 1992.

It is clearly impossible to arrive at anything other than a rough estimate of aggregate Russian net resource transfers to the CIS following the break-up of the Soviet Union. However, it is clear that Russian resource transfers were a significant proportion of Russian GNP in the year after the dissolution of the Soviet Union, while Russian GDP itself was in substantial decline. The lowest estimate would put Russian resource transfers as at least 7.5 percent of GDP in 1992, while it is not unreasonable to suggest they were as high as 10 percent; they could even have reached 13 percent.

Conclusions

The studies cited indicate that although several republics (Belarus, Ukraine, Russia, Azerbaijan and Georgia) made net transfers of resources to other republics in the 1980s when trade flows are measured in domestic prices, Russia alone made a net resource transfer when flows are measured in world market prices.

Russian net transfers arose from three principal sources:

— trade surpluses measured in domestic prices;
— transfers resulting from the undervaluation of exports and overvaluation of imports in interrepublican trade when compared with world market prices;
— Russia's net surplus in foreign (extra-Soviet) trade.

Transfers arising from the difference between world market prices and domestic prices in interrepublican trade were found to be the most significant source of Russian transfers to other republics.

All the republics except Russia (and Azerbaijan in 1989) incurred balance-of-trade deficits in the aggregate, when trade was measured in world market prices. All except Russia incurred trade deficits in extra-Soviet trade, measured in world market prices, while Azerbaijan and Turkmenistan made surpluses in domestic trade when measured in world market prices.

The move to interrepublican trade based on market prices, which is not complete, has resulted in an improvement in Russian terms of trade with the non-Russian republics. The break-up of the 'single Soviet economic space' has reduced pressure on Russia to make unrequited capital transfers to the non-Russian republics, unless these are to be restored for essentially political reasons. All the non-Russian republics are now facing pressures toward substantial current-account deficits in their trade with other republics in the CIS and the rest of the world, which can only be overcome by severe import compression in the absence of alternative sources of finance. The low level of competitiveness and the relatively low quality standards associated with exports from the non-Russian republics suggest that interrepublican trade will continue to contract unless a method can be found to finance the persistent balance-of-payments deficits that the majority of non-Russian republics will incur as trade is increasingly conducted in world market prices. This will either require the Russian republic to continue to make substantial capital transfers (with little prospect of repayment) to the majority of non-Russian republics, or require trade deficits to be financed from loans or grants received from outside the FSU.

The rapid reduction of trade in a highly interdependent economic region will have substantial short-term costs for all participants, including Russia itself, in the form of lost output and employment. In the long term the Russian Federation will stand to derive substantial economic benefits from a reduction in trade with its 'near abroad', and an increase in trade with nations outside the FSU.

All republics, with the possible exception of Azerbaijan, will be adversely affected by a reduction in trade with Russia in the medium to long run; the Central Asian republics will be the worst affected. The smaller republics, which are highly trade-dependent by virtue of their size, have of course been isolated from world markets by the Soviet trade system, and have consequently very little experience of the demands of world markets.

In the long term, it is possible that the non-Russian republics will be able to divert their trade with Russia to nations outside the FSU, and to pursue trade flows with other former Soviet republics which correspond more closely to their comparative advantage. The Baltic republics have already has some success in increasing their trade with European partners, and with the Scandinavian countries in particular. Elsewhere, however, the collapse in interrepublican trade has been accompanied by a collapse in trade with the rest of the world. The prospects for renewed trade links between the Ukraine, Belarus, Moldova and Eastern Europe may become increasingly linked to the question of EU membership for the former CMEA countries of Eastern Europe, which might otherwise be expected to become important trade partners. The Transcaucasian republics might be expected to seek greater trade links with the Black Sea countries. The Central Asian republics, which would be the worst affected by the collapse of trade with Russia, would have to improve their trade links with one another and seek new trade partners in the Middle East.

Of course the estimates based on world market prices cited must be interpreted with extreme caution. It is highly unlikely that Russia would be able to divert to world markets its exports of oil and gas previously directed to Soviet and other socialist markets, without causing a fall in world market prices for these products (assuming that former socialist republics inside and outside the Soviet Union would be unable or unwilling to purchase equivalent amounts of these goods on world markets). The fourfold increase in Russian exports of aluminum between 1989 and 1993 resulted in a major collapse in world aluminum prices. While the impact would probably not be so severe in the case of oil exports, it could well be significant.

Furthermore, there is also little or no evidence to suggest that Russia has been successful in replacing imports from the FSU (which made a major contribution to the Soviet diet) by alternative sources. Russian imports of processed and unprocessed foodstuffs fell from $16.6 bn in 1990 to only $5.3 bn in 1993, partly as a result of changing demand patterns. At the same time domestic production of foodstuffs has fallen in real terms. Although these figures are substantially affected by underreporting of imports, the total supply of foodstuffs to the Russian population has fallen in real terms since 1991.

Prospects for the Creation of Sustainable Trade Relations in the Former Soviet Republics

The absence of active monetary relations and the collapse of Soviet and East European trade

The inability to create and sustain a trading system that could provide Soviet and East European enterprises with an incentive to engage in mutually advantageous trade was a significant factor contributing to the break-up of the CMEA, and the Soviet internal planning system. Without an active monetary unit that gives the holder command over resources (either immediately or in the future), economic agents have no incentive to deliver goods and services to other agents unless they can guarantee that they will receive goods of an equivalent value in exchange. Logically, the complete absence of active monetary relations will result in all transactions' between independent agencies being conducted on a bilateral barter basis. This implies that, in the absence of stable monetary relations, a greater degree of decentralized economic authority *reduces* the possibilities for mutually advantageous trade.

Problems resulting from inactive monetary relations were overcome (albeit imperfectly) under the traditional socialist system through a highly centralized system of decision-making. Within the Soviet economy, central planners instructed producers to deliver goods to end-users, and provided them with the necessary inputs to meet production targets. They rewarded producers with money bonuses that gave some command over consumer goods that planners made available in state stores. Failure to cooperate on the part of enterprises could also result in sanctions. In practice, relations between sub-agencies (e.g. industrial ministries) attempting to meet output targets and to satisfy their own needs under conditions of shortage (or supply constraints) frequently took the form of barter arrangements (Wagener and van Selm, 1993). Successive attempts in Eastern Europe and the Soviet Union to decentralize decision-making to enterprises in a partial manner, by introducing price and profit criteria, had to be abandoned or modified when decentralized decisions came into conflict with central priorities.

Gorbachev attempted (particularly after 1987) to relax central tutelage over enterprises, and to devolve a range of economic decision-taking powers to enterprises, republics and local authorities, but without creating active monetary relations and market-determined prices. He thus created an economic system which by the winter of 1989–90 was effectively neither marketized nor centrally planned, and in which enterprises were increasingly without either the incentive or the compulsion to meet output targets and delivery schedules. The perennial problems of a shortage economy were aggravated by the deterioration in Soviet terms of trade with the West, resulting from the fall in world oil prices, and by ill-advised domestic policies (including the anti-alcohol campaign and new investment priorities) which aggravated internal macroeconomic disequilibrium. As a result, economic relations within the Soviet Union lapsed increasingly into barter relations between enterprises themselves, and between republics or even localities.

The decline in interrepublican trade contributed to the accelerated fall in industrial output and GNP in the former Soviet Union, both by creating supply bottlenecks and by reducing effective demand. Although part of the decline reflected the need to reduce output (and eventually capacity) in the overexpanded heavy industrial and engineering sectors, it is noticeable that output falls have been large even in those economies that have yet to initiate structural change. Major statistical problems notwithstanding, it is apparent that trade flows between the former Soviet republics have declined faster than output. This reflects the failure to find suitable trade partners under a system that is increasingly reliant on barter relations, in the absence of a sound monetary system. It also reflects a tendency to concentrate available output with any value on one's own region, as well as a prevalent penchant for favoring local suppliers to preserve employment.

The minimum internal conditions for creating sustainable trade flows

The immediate goal of trade policy should be to help establish sustainable trade patterns that correspond to the long-term comparative advantages of the states of the region. Given the relative lack of exposure to international competition, and the relative inexperience of world market conditions of the majority of enterprises in the FSU, trade policy should allow for some degree of government intervention to protect industries that may be viable in the long run but that are incapable of withstanding international competition in the short run (the infant-industry argument). The creation of an open economy in which producers and consumers are completely neutral between domestic and foreign markets, and where suppliers and capital flows are determined by market forces, should be the longer-term goal. This may require some degree of protection for the domestic market in the short run (through either price or tariff protection), but the ultimate goal should be to stimulate and promote the gradual build-up of export-oriented sectors on the basis of comparative advantage and relative costs.

What are the minimum conditions for this process? First, a number of internal conditions must be met in order to stimulate internal economic efficiency and investment patterns that are consistent with comparative advantage, and to persuade actual and potential trade partners that the output patterns of the transition economies are determined by genuine market criteria (involving the liberalization of domestic prices and the removal of subsidies). This would make it more difficult for foreign producers who find themselves exposed to new areas of competition to plead for emergency protection through anti-dumping and similar measures.

The creation of a stable (or, at the very least, reasonably stable) domestic currency is a prerequisite for the satisfactory development of internal trade flows. This means that domestic macroeconomic stabilization is essential, and that enterprises must be subjected to hard budget constraints, with at least the expectation of unpleasant consequences for managers and workers if budget constraints are violated. Without hard budget constraints, enterprises will have no incentive to respond to market forces, to utilize the most efficient combination of inputs, to meet cost targets, or to produce goods in demand. Any remaining subsidies provided to enterprises during the transition period (e.g. for temporary employment protection) should be transparent in execution and determined in advance on transparent principles.

It is also essential to end the forced isolation of domestic enterprises and consumers from world markets. It is unlikely that a dynamic competitive edge will be honed if enterprises are allowed to preserve their monopoly position in a captive domestic market. Consequently enterprises should be exposed to either domestic or foreign competition (including competition from other producers in transition economies). In particular they must be exposed to a credible threat of exposure to international competition which will limit the ability of enterprises to increase prices in the domestic market. Finally, the fashioning of export orientation involves not only the removal of existing barriers to trade, but also the creation of incentives to domestic enterprises to enter export markets. This will require, *inter alia*, measures for converting foreign currency earnings into domestic currency on the basis of predetermined rules.

Consequently the introduction of genuine current-account convertibility is required to expose enterprises to international competition in the domestic market and to introduce world market prices directly into the economy (although this can succeed only in conjunction with strict fiscal and monetary policies). The choice of a depreciated rate of exchange (in relation to ppp) offers domestic enterprises a degree of price protection, and makes export markets relatively attractive, thereby stimulating economic growth and employment and providing an inflow of hard currency to protect the chosen rate. On the negative side, a depreciated rate leads to a deterioration in the terms of trade and domestic purchasing power. The impact of this is severe on low-income groups and groups on fixed incomes, as the domestic prices of tradable goods (which include food and energy) are driven up to the world market price at the prevailing exchange rate and cannot be matched by a corresponding increase in wage rates, if the competitive position is to be maintained. This in turn creates pressures for increased government expenditure on social programs, at a time when governments are attempting to reduce expenditure to cut budget deficits (which would normally have to be financed by printing money, in the absence of more sophisticated instruments to finance government debt).

The Central-East European republics were successful in introducing different forms of current account convertibility at a fixed or pegged exchange rate at an early stage in the transition process. Similar schemes based on the creation of a currency board (an independent agency which converts the domestic currency into a reserve currency at a pegged rate on demand) have been introduced in Estonia and Latvia.

Currency areas, and clearing and payments unions

The decline in the volume of trade between the former Soviet republics can be attributed to three major factors:

— the elimination of 'irrational' trade flows linked to obsolete industrial structures;

— changes in the terms of trade in favor of Russia, following the move toward market-determined prices and the reluctance (or inability) of Russia to continue to make substantial resource transfers to the other former Soviet republics which would enable them to sustain imports at a higher level until the required adjustments can be made;

— the collapse of the traditional Soviet system for financing transfers between enterprises in different republics.

The creation of a financial system that will facilitate rational trade flows between republics based on market relations will contribute to a growth in welfare in the region. However, the former Soviet system was essentially based on automatic crediting, without reference to the financial viability of the enterprise to be debited, or the eventual demand for the product. Any system that facilitated the return (or slowed down the replacement) of automatic crediting will increase the wasteful use of resources and impede macroeconomic stabilization.

THE BREAK-UP OF THE RUBLE ZONE. The ruble zone involved the use of a single common currency to finance all transactions within the Soviet Union. Its survival after the dissolution of the Soviet Union would have required the creation of a federal banking system or a single central bank for the whole area, with responsibility for control of the money supply, and invested with powers to regulate the activities of national banks in the newly independent states. Difficulties in devising an effective system of central controls over credit expansion in the individual republics provided the individual national banks of these states with a perverse incentive to expand credit (although by historical accident they could not affect the actual supply of banknotes, the printing of which was concentrated in Russia), as this facilitated an inflow of resources to the republic in question, while the inflationary impact was spread over the entire area.

Sachs has presented powerful arguments for abandoning the ruble zone entirely, and replacing it with separate national currencies that would float against one another. He argues, first, that the former Soviet republics do not meet the conditions for an optimum currency area because labor is insufficiently mobile (particularly after national independence); and, second, that the individual republics have widely differing commodity structures of trade (both inside and outside the Union) and are pursuing different speeds and strategies of transition to the market (see Sachs, 1994, pp. 42–45, and Smith, 1993, pp. 210–14). In the event, the process of monetary disengagement commenced in a largely *ad hoc* fashion in 1992.

During the course of 1992, the Central Bank of Russia (CBR) and the central banks of the newly independent republics created a set of correspondent accounts to monitor trade flows and facilitate payments on a bilateral basis. In July 1992 the CBR ended the system of passively crediting intra-republican bank accounts (whereby a Russian enterprise was in effect automatically credited with rubles for deliveries to non-Russian republics). At the same time an attempt was made to make the system of correspondent accounts held by the republics at the CBR more 'active', by crediting the Russian enterprise only if the central bank of the non-Russian republic had sufficient funds in its deposits with the CBR or had negotiated a credit limit. This system suffered from two principal defects; first it emphasized bilateral rather than multilateral clearing; and, second, debtor states soon reached their credit limits and encountered a payments blockage (IMF, 1994, pp. 34–5). Furthermore the macroeconomic advantages of the new system to Russia were undermined when the CBR granted credits equivalent to 10 percent of Russian GDP in 1992 to the non-Russian central banks, in order to prevent the collapse of Russian exports (Sachs, 1994, pp. 44–5; Fischer, 1994, p. 15).

The new system did at least require the non-Russian republics to reassess the terms on which they received Russian rubles and provided them with an incentive to devise new monetary arrangements. The Baltic states had already initiated moves to establish separate currencies in 1992. In the summer of 1992 Estonia introduced the kroon, which was fixed against the deutsche mark under a currency board system, and it left the ruble zone entirely, while Latvia and Lithuania initially introduced parallel domestic currencies, before phasing out the use of the ruble in the domestic economy and replacing the parallel currency with a new, independent currency (Lainela, 1993). Since the introduction of current-account convertibility, the Baltic currencies have effectively stabilized on the basis of a substantial appreciation against the ruble.

The break-up of the ruble zone was far from orderly in the rest of the FSU. The ruble continued to be used for interenterprise dealings (with the exception of Ukraine, which *de facto* left the ruble zone in November 1992), but these payments could not be directly converted into cash rubles. The remaining former Soviet republics also agreed that cash rubles would continue to circulate on their territories but introduced separate, parallel national currencies or coupons as well, largely as a response to cash shortages. Kyrgyzstan also introduced its own convertible currency, the som, in May 1993.

Soviet banknotes and Russian banknotes printed in 1992 continued to function as legal tender in the ten republics that remained in the ruble zone until July 1993, when the Russian Central Bank withdrew them from circulation. This meant that Russian rubles printed in 1993, which had not been issued outside Russia, became the sole means of cash payment in Russia itself. This led to fears that Soviet and 1992 Russian banknotes (in excess of those that could be legally changed for 1993 notes inside Russia) would be pushed into the other nine republics where they could still be used for cash payment, and accelerated the movement toward the use of separate national currencies as the sole means of payment. Azerbaijan, Georgia, Moldova and Turkmenistan had all left the ruble zone by the end of 1993 and made their national currencies the sole means of payment. Armenia, Belarus, Kazakhstan, Tajikistan and Uzbekistan attempted to renegotiate with the Central Bank of Russia to create a new ruble area, but were unwilling to accept far tighter Russian conditions for the unification of monetary policy and the pooling of gold reserves (Boss and Havlik, 1994, p. 245). Tajikistan was the only republic to continue to use Russian rubles as legal tender in 1994.

Negotiations to resurrect a ruble area in 1994 made little headway, although several theoretical proposals for the re-establishment of a limited-membership ruble zone were made. These have included schemes for the gradual construction of a comprehensive economic union incorporating all members of the CIS; for fast-track reintegration of the Slav republics into a common currency zone or a customs union; and for the creation of looser forms of currency areas involving the participation of some of the Central Asian republics. Political objectives, most notably the desire to re-impose Russian hegemony over its new neighbors, and to re-establish a new form of Russian empire, appear to be uppermost in many of the schemes proposed by Russian specialists and politicians. The principal advantage to the non-Russian participants is that they hope to be able to continue to benefit from resource transfers on concessional terms from Russia.

Since the end of 1992, attempts have been made to establish an Interstate Bank for the members of the CIS republics. Republican central banks would be able to hold accounts in Russian rubles to finance interrepublican trade and to facilitate multilateral clearing with tight credit ceilings and a very limited financing role. Domestic currencies would float against the ruble (see Eichengreen, pp. 315–6 and 342–5). This is historically analogous to the creation of the sterling and franc areas, where the participants introduced separate national currencies for use in internal economic relations, with international settlements between the members of the currency area being made in the denominated currency (namely that of the imperial power). The major difference is that the ruble has not been stabilized, and is not externally convertible. All the (then) CIS members, except Azerbaijan, agreed to establish the Interstate Bank in January 1993. The Bank was still not operational in January 1995, because of continued disagreements about the coordination of monetary policies and the inability to find a satisfactory solution to the problem of structural deficits.

CLEARING OR PAYMENTS UNIONS FOR THE FORMER SOVIET REPUBLICS: PROS AND CONS. Several theoretical proposals for the creation of clearing or payments unions which would embrace some or all of the transition economies have been made by international agencies, politicians and academics. Many of the proposals/discussion documents written before the dissolution of the Soviet Union included the Soviet Union as a single member (e.g. Kenen, 1991). Proposals for payments unions since then have concentrated more on the advantages and disadvantages of creating improved systems of payment between the former Soviet republics (e.g. Bofinger and Gros, 1992; Eichengreen, 1993), and have excluded the Central and East European countries.

Under clearing and payments union arrangements, trade relations between member countries are determined by enterprises responding to market principles, not by central government agencies. This involves the creation of a system whereby payment for goods and services in the currency of the importing member is automatically accepted by the exporting enterprise. The exporter presents the receipt/foreign currency, either to its own national bank or directly to a designated clearing authority, where it is credited to the exporter in the exporter's currency at the current exchange rate. The clearing authority nets off national surpluses and deficits on a multilateral basis at predetermined time intervals. A clearing or payments union helps to multilateralize trade flows by removing the need for bilateral balancing of trade, which reduces trade flows to the export level of the weakest partner.

In principle a clearing union differs from a payments union in that it does not grant credit facilities (Williamson, 1993, pp. 584–7). All outstanding surpluses and deficits after multilateral netting must be cleared in convertible currencies. Under a regime of fixed exchange rates, this requires member governments either to impose domestic macroeconomic discipline, or to operate a system of import licenses, to ensure against pressures for currency depreciation or a run-down of reserves. A payments union allows for the provision of credit, which facilitates dynamic gains from trade, as a country incurring an aggregate deficit in one period can repay it out of surpluses arising in later periods. Creditor countries need to be certain that the accumulation of trade surpluses will provide them with genuine command over resources at a later period. Consequently most proposals for a payments union involve the creation of working capital, including a convertible currency component from either internal or external sources. The European Payments Union, which facilitated multilateral clearing between the West European economies in the period 1950–58 (as a precursor to the introduction of convertibility) allowed creditor countries to receive a proportion of payments in convertible currency, which could be used outside the union. Debtor countries were required to make a partial (but proportionately smaller) payment in convertible currency (Eichengreen, 1993, p. 333).

It was indicated in Chapter 3 that existing volumes of interrepublican trade, measured in world market prices, would result in Russia's running substantial trade surpluses with the non-Russian republics. The scale of the structural transformations required to boost exports from non-Russian republics to Russia, and the expected low price elasticity of demand for energy products (which constitute the major part of Russian exports to other republics), suggest that problems of fundamental trade imbalances will not be alleviated significantly even over the medium term.

Under these circumstances, some combination of the following outcomes is likely, whatever system of pricing and trade and payments is developed:

— Russia will have to continue making transfers to other republics;
— the cost of the transfers will have to be borne by another agent;
— the non-Russian republics will experience a prolonged reduction in living standards;
— Russia, as the structural creditor, will acquires assets of the debtor countries.

Although a clearing union might help to overcome some of the technical problems related to financing interrepublican trade, it would be unable to solve the more serious problem of financing structural deficits. While the Russian government has no economic incentive to participate in a payments union, whereby it would not receive payment in hard currency or acquire assets for structural surpluses arising from exports that could otherwise have been sold on world markets, a payments union would require the provision of external finance.

The IMF accepts that the current system of bilateral correspondent accounts is unsatisfactory as a means for stimulating interrepublican trade and favors moves to facilitate and strengthen the operation of the Interstate Bank as an overseer of a clearing union, participation in which would be voluntary (IMF, 1994, pp. 17–21). The IMF remains strongly opposed to the idea of a payments union for the FSU (particularly one involving external finance). Its principal economic arguments are that the creation of a payments union would result in a new round of bargaining over the distribution of external finance which could actually delay the operation of a supranational clearing union, and that it would stimulate intra-union (interrepublican) trade at the expense of external trade. Guaranteed settlements for trade between Russia and the non-Russian republics (underwritten by an external agency) would provide an artificial stimulus to trade flows which are already abnormally high, and could slow down attempts to increase non-Russian exports outside the Union. Finally, the IMF fears that the creation of a new multi-republican bureaucracy would slow down the implementation of reforms in the member states. There is also the question of funding. Many of the smaller states of the FSU have very low levels of extra-Soviet exports and hard-currency earnings, and would therefore have serious difficulties in repaying debt incurred as a result of their participation in any scheme.

It is clear that a payments union would be effective only if it were subject to strict economic conditions. First, price liberalization would be a necessary condition for the operation of any scheme to multilateralize trade, including that of a clearing union. The experience of intra-CMEA trade demonstrates that governments are unwilling to submit to multilateral clearing arrangements when prices do not reflect genuine costs and scarcities. Secondly, macroeconomic stabilization would be a prerequisite for the operation of the payments union element of the proposal. Eichengreen (1993, pp. 336–40) demonstrates that any attempt to create a payments union based on credits in an environment of shortage and soft budget constraints would stimulate competitive attempts to achieve a debtor position, with the fastest inflating countries obtaining the largest net inflow of resources. This would eventually lead to the collapse of the system as governments attempted to restrict exports. In the end, there would be a return to barter arrangements.

The creation of a payments union need not inhibit, and could even assist, the introduction of current-account convertibility. Williamson, for example (1993, p. 585), argues that the establishment of current-account convertibility for each of the former Soviet republics would require the accumulation of hard-currency reserves approximately five times greater than that required for a payments union involving credits (on the assumption that 80 percent of trade would be conducted within the union). He argues that payments unions can still be useful for financing trade between countries that have established current-account convertibility with the outside world, and that by economizing on the need for foreign-currency reserves the creation of a payments union for the former Soviet republics would facilitate the introduction of current-account convertibility at a less depreciated exchange rate than would otherwise be the case. This argument takes on particular importance when the imperfections of domestic banking systems and currency markets during the transition period are considered.

The provision of external funding offers one possible solution to the problem of structural deficits in trade between Russia and the non-Russian republics. This could be combined with the operation of a clearing union in which participants would be provided with a predetermined ceiling on their multilateral deficits instead of a requirement for strict multilateral balance. Credit limits would be denominated in convertible currency, with the poorer republics receiving proportionally larger shares to enable them to sustain imports from other republics (in particular imports of energy and raw materials from Russia) during the transition period. External funding would have to be reduced progressively to zero, to provide structural debtors with an incentive to make the required structural adjustments on a gradual basis and build up export sectors. The reduction in external funding would have to be strictly enforced to maintain the credibility of the scheme.

Given the low potential for earning hard currency of the majority of the former Soviet republics, this would have to contain a significant grant element. Consequently finance would be provided only by Western governments as an investment in security in the region, and not by the multilateral financial agencies. Furthermore, the low income levels of the states which would be the principal beneficiaries in terms of proportion of GNP, in particular the Central Asian states, would justify the provision of external funding on concessional terms on humanitarian as well as security grounds. This assistance would then indirectly aid the recovery of demand in Russia by stimulating demand for Russian exports to non-Russian republics under conditions that satisfied the needs of the consuming republics, rather than the whims of the Russian government.

Arguments for and against such a scheme are finely balanced. The provision of outside assistance through this (or any other) proposal would have to be linked to the successful implementation of macroeconomic stabilization. The pattern of Russian trade with non-Russian republics when measured in world market prices means that the bulk of the convertible currency provided by the scheme would find its way into the Russian banking system. In theory this could help to establish currency convertibility at an exchange rate which diminishes inflationary pressures, and could be used to finance budgetary programs to reduce poverty. In practice, doubts about the integrity of the Russian banking system mean that much of the currency would merely contribute to the growth of capital flight.

Conclusions

The disintegration of the Soviet Union and the CMEA represents not only the break-up of a trading bloc, but also the collapse of what was effectively the Russian empire. Wars certainly provoke the collapse of empires and traditional patterns of trade. But when empires collapse, leaving people trapped as members of minority groups in countries which have suddenly become independent nations, instability and war can likewise be the result. The probability of war can be reduced by the acceptance of economic interdependence, whereas the disintegration of traditional patterns of trade and economic instability are likely to aggravate nationalist sentiments and tensions. The populations in some of the newly independent states of the FSU may see independence itself as a positive factor which offsets the short-term costs of the transition, and even the long-term costs of a permanent deterioration in their terms of trade with Russia. On the other hand, a significant proportion of the Russian population (inside and outside the Russian Federation), for whom the concept of the Russian empire, the Russian nation, and the Soviet Union were virtually synonymous, has experienced a sense of loss which further complicates the process of transition.

The Russian parliamentary elections of December 1993 gave an indication of the proportion of the Russian population which feels that the disadvantages resulting from the simultaneous collapse of a familiar economic system and of an empire have outweighed the advantages. Feelings of economic uncertainty and apprehension are also shared by large sections of the population of the non-Russian republics of the FSU, a sentiment which may be strongest in those areas where there is a compact Russian ethnic population. The desire to assuage this sense of loss has been reflected in the growing assertiveness of Russian foreign policy, which may in the future be far less amenable to Western influence and policy interests than had once been hoped or expected, particularly as regards former Soviet republics and Eastern Europe. Russia is now likely to evince far stronger opposition to any substantial increase in economic and political links between the outside world and former Soviet republics (particularly those that include a significant Russian population).

The extent to which Russia can afford to pursue a more assertive and interventionist policy toward its former empire against the wishes of the newly independent republics remains in doubt. It has been demonstrated that Russian transfers to non-Russian republics within the FSU may have been as high as $50 billion per annum. A foreign policy which reflects Russia's traditional status as a world power may win popular support in the short term, but the costs of implementing this policy will come into increasing conflict with the need to improve the living standards of the majority of the Russian population over the longer term. The collapse of traditional economic relations has inevitably led to short-term transitional costs, which may or may not be outweighed by long-term advantages once the required adjustments to the new economic circumstances have been completed. Economic disturbances arising from the collapse of the empire will be minimized if transitional arrangements can be made to sustain traditional trade flows, phasing them out only gradually, even if they do not coincide with long-term comparative advantage. The former Soviet republics have experienced a major contraction in their trade with one another and with the outside world. Some of the non-Russian republics (most notably Belarus) may wish to re-enter a form of economic union with Russia precisely in order to continue to benefit from some form of economic transfer. The Baltic republics, like the central and east European states, have embarked on a strategy of reducing their economic ties with the former Soviet Union and redirecting their trade toward the OECD economies and the European Union in particular.

The restoration of rational trade links is an urgent requirement for economic recovery for the remaining former Soviet republics. Further economic development will require a continued expansion of trade. This has wider implications for Western foreign policy, and for international stability. Failure to restore income levels in the FSU carries with it a real threat of widespread poverty combined with substantial widening of income differentials in a group of multi-ethnic states, several of which are already involved in, or are on the verge of, civil war. International efforts to stave off this threat can be justified on both humanitarian and security grounds. However, the choice of strategy to restore trade and output has created major policy dilemmas for the international community (and the West in particular), involving issues of long-term stability as well as economic consideration.

References for Part 4

Åslund, A. (ed.) (1994), *Economic Transformation in Russia*, Pinter, London.

Bakos, G. (1993), 'After Comecon: A Free Trade Area in Central Europe?', *Europe-Asia Studies* 45 (6), pp. 102–544.

Bofinger, P. (1991), 'Options for the Payments and Exchange Rate System in Eastern Europe in European Economy', *The Path of Reform in Central and Eastern Europe*, Special Edition, no. 2, Commission of the European Communities, Brussels.

Bofinger, P., and Gros, D. (1992), 'A Post-Soviet Payments Union: Why and How', in Flemming, J., and Rollo, J.M.C. (eds) (1992), *Trade, Payments and Adjustment in Central and Eastern Europe*, RIIA/EBRD, London.

Boss, H. and Havlik, P. (1994), 'Slavic (Dis)union: Consequences for Russia, Belarus and Ukraine'. *Economics of Transition,* vol. 2, no. 2.

Bradshaw, M. (1993), *The Economic Effects of Soviet Dissolution*, Post-Soviet Business Forum, RIIA.

Brown, S.S., and Belkindas, M.V (1993), 'Who's Feeding Whom? An Analysis of Soviet Interrepublic Trade', in Kaufman, R.F, and Hardt, J.P (eds), *The Former Soviet Union in Transition*, Joint Economic Committee, Congress of the United States. Washington DC.

de Simone, F.N. (1994), 'Ukraine's New Currency and the Unstable Ruble Currency Area', *Communist Economies and Economic Transformation*, 6 (1), pp. 99–112.

Drabek, Z. (1992), 'Convertibility or a Payments Union? Convertibility!', in Flemming, J., and Rollo, J.M.C. (eds) (1992), *Trade, Payments and Adjustment in Central and Eastern Europe*, RIIA/EBRD, London.

Dyker, D.A. (1992), *After the Soviet Union: The International Trading Environment*, Post-Soviet Business Forum, RIIA.

Economic Commission for Europe (1993), *Economic Bulletin for Europe*, vol. 44, United Nations, New York.

Economic Commission for Europe (1994), *Economic Survey of Europe in 1993-1994*, United Nations, New York and Geneva.

Eichengreen B. (1993), 'A Payments Mechanism for the FSU: is the EPU a Relevant Precedent?', *Economic Policy*, 17, pp. 310–45.

European Bank for Reconstruction and Development (1994), *Transition Report*, EBRD, London.

Fischer, S. (1994), 'Prospects for Russian Stabilization in the Summer of 1993', in Åslund, A. (ed.) (1994), *Economic Transformation in Russia*, Pinter, London.

Flemming, J., and Rollo, J.M.C. (eds) (1992), *Trade, Payments and Adjustment in Central and Eastern Europe*, RIIA/EBRD, London.

Holzman, F.D. (1987), *The Economics of Soviet Bloc Trade*, Westview Press, Boulder,
CO, and Oxford.

IMF, The World Bank, OECD, EBRD (1991), *A Study of the Soviet Economy*, three
vols. Paris, OECD.

International Monetary Fund (1994), 'Financial Relations among Countries in the Former Soviet Union', *IMF Economic Reviews*, 1994, no. 1.

Kenen, P.B. (1991), 'Transitional Arrangements for Trade and Payments Among the
CMEA Economies', *IMF Staff Papers*, 38 (2), pp. 235–66.

Koves, A. (1992), *Central and East European Economies in Transition: The International Dimension*, Westview Press, Boulder, CO, and Oxford.

Lainela, S. (1993), 'Currency Reform in the Baltic States', *Communist Economies and
Economic Transformation*, 5 (4), pp. 424–44.

McAuley, A. (1991a), 'Costs and Benefits of De-Integration in the USSR', *Most*, 2, pp.
51–65.

McAuley, A. (1991b), 'The Economic Consequences of Soviet Disintegration', *Soviet
Economy*, 7 (3), pp. 189–214.

Michalopolous, C., and Tarr, D. G. (1994), 'A Program for Trade Recovery in the New
Independent States', *Transition*, The World Bank, Washington, vol. 5, no. 9.

Orlowski, L.T. (1993), 'Indirect Transfers in Trade Among FSU Republics: Sources,
Patterns and Policy Responses in the Post-Soviet Period', *Europe-Asia Studies*, 45
(6), pp. 1001–1024.

Sachs, J.D. (1994), 'Prospects for Monetary Stabilisation in Russia', in Åslund, A.
(ed.) (1994), *Economic Transformation in Russia*, Pinter, London, pp. 34–58.

Sizov, V. (1993), 'Ekonomika Rossii i Drugikh Stran SNG v Nachale 90 godov',
Mirovaya Ekonomika i Mezhdunarodniye Otnosheniya, no. 7.

Smith, A. H. (1983), *The Planned Economies of Eastern Europe*, Croom Helm, London.

Smith, A. H. (1993), *Russia and the World Economy*, Routledge, London.

Sutela, P. (1991), *Economic Thought and Economic Reform in the Soviet Union*, Cambridge University Press, Cambridge.

van Selm, G., and Dolle, M. (1993), 'Soviet Inter-republican Capital Transfers and the
Republics' Level of Development, 196–691', *Most*, 1, pp. 133–49.

Vavilov, A., and Vjugin, O. (1993), 'Trade Patterns after Integration into the World
Economy', in Williamson, J. (ed.) (1993), *Economic Consequences of Soviet Disintegration*, Institute for International Economics, Washington DC, pp. 99–175.

Wagener, H. J., and van Selm, G. (1993), 'Soviet Regional Disintegration and Monetary Problems', *Communist Economies and Economic Transformation*, 5 (4), pp.
41–126.

Williamson, J. (1993), 'Trade and Payments after Soviet Disintegration', in
Williamson, J. (ed.) (1993), *Economic Consequences of Soviet Disintegration*, Institute for International Economics, Washington DC.

Statistical sources and other sources of information

EBRD, *Quarterly Economic Review*, various issues, London.
Economist Intelligence Unit, *Country Reports* (quarterly), various issues, London.
The Financial Times.
Narodnoe Khozyaistvo SSSR, Moscow (annual), Goskomstat USSR, Moscow.
Narodnoe Khozyaistvo RSFSR, Moscow (annual), Goskomstat RSFSR, Moscow.
Narodnoe Khozyaistvo Rossiiskoi Federatsii 1992 (1992), Goskomstat Rossii, Moscow.
OECD, *Monthly Statistics of Foreign Trade*, Series A.
OECD, Short-Term Economic Indicators: Transition Economies (quarterly), various –issues.
Rossiiskaya Federatsiya v 1992 Godu (1993), Goskomstat Rossii, Moscow.
Russian Economic Monitor, 1993, Institute for Economic Forecasting of the Russian Academy of Sciences, Moscow.
Russian Economic Trends, various issues, Government of the Russian Federation and Centre for Economic Performance, London School of Economics, Whurr Publishers, London.
Vestnik Statistik, Moscow (monthly).

Index

Achi, 190

Administrative territories of Russia, 21–22, 130. *See also* Provinces

Advisers, foreign, in CIS, 122, 152, 153, 154, 161, 177, 189

Agriculture: collective farms, 129, 170, 171; monopolistic market, 92–93; private, 43; privatization of related industries, 159, 160, 175; problems, 170–71; reforms, 172–73; Soviet policies, 169–70; subsidies, 26n, 172, 175; trade protection, 65. *See also* Land reform

Akayev, Askar, 162, 178

AKKOR (Association of Peasant Farms and Agricultural Cooperatives of Russia), 172

Alcohol industry, 91–92, 191

Alekperov, Vagit, 184

AlfaBank, 187–88

AlfaCapital, 186, 187–88

Aliyev, Heydar, 157

Almaty Tobacco Combine, 152

Aluminum industry, 88, 110–12, 247; trade agreement, 111–12

Andrle, V., 39

Anti-Monopoly Committees: in CIS, 84; functions, 68, 108, 136; proposal to abolish, 112–13; Russian, 83–84

AO-MMM, 189–90

Armenia: criminal gangs, 191; currency, 254; housing privatization, 163; indigenous population, 223; inflation, 162; land reform, 118, 172–73, 177; privatization, 118, 162–64; trade in Soviet era, 230, 234–35

Arms exports, 212, 228

Åslund, Anders, 7, 8–9, 15

Asset valuation, 127–28, 138, 193–95

Association of Peasant Farms and Agricultural Cooperatives of Russia (AKKOR), 172

Auctions: privatization, 128, 139, 140, 185, 186

Autonomies, 28, 30, 32. *See also* Provinces

Autonomy: in Russian provinces, 33–36

Azderdzis, Andrei, 191

Azerbaijan: criminal gangs, 191; currency, 254; foreign investment, 158; housing privatization, 157; indigenous population, 223; joint ventures, 158; land reform, 177; Nagorno-Karabakh, 130, 164; privatization, 123–24, 157–58, 184; stock exchange legislation, 189; trade in Soviet era, 230, 233, 234–35, 236–37

Azerbaijan National Oil Company, 158

Badzey, Georgy, 153

Bagratian, Grant, 164

Bahry, D., 29

Bailey, E.E., 95

Bakyrchik gold mines, 152